LANGUAGE AND STAGE IN MEDIEVAL AND RENAISSANCE ENGLAND

This is the first major study in recent years to explore the language and staging of medieval and Renaissance English drama. In this book Janette Dillon analyses the relationship between English and other languages, which combined to create new and important kinds of performance in this period. Latin was especially evocative in English-language plays: until the medieval period it was regarded as the sacramental language of authority, but with the Reformation it became a potent symbol of the newly demonised enemy, Rome. Dillon examines why, from 1400 to 1600, other languages increasingly invade English plays and illuminates their significance by attention to developments in church and state within the context of the advancing Reformation and expanding English nationalism. In marked contrast to many related studies, Dillon focuses on drama as performance, employing a wide range of works, from the mystery cycles and morality plays, through early Tudor drama, to the plays of Shakespeare and many of his lesser-known contemporaries.

LANGUAGE AND STAGE IN MEDIEVAL AND RENAISSANCE ENGLAND

JANETTE DILLON

University of Nottingham

CAMBRIDGE
UNIVERSITY PRESS

CAMBRIDGE UNIVERSITY PRESS
Cambridge, New York, Melbourne, Madrid, Cape Town, Singapore, São Paulo

Cambridge University Press
The Edinburgh Building, Cambridge CB2 2RU, UK

Published in the United States of America by Cambridge University Press, New York

www.cambridge.org
Information on this title: www.cambridge.org/9780521593342

© Cambridge University Press 1998

First published 1998
This digitally printed first paperback version 2006

A catalogue record for this publication is available from the British Library

Library of Congress Cataloguing in Publication data
Dillon, Janette, 1953 –
Language and stage in medieval and Renaissance England / Janette Dillon.
p. cm.
Includes bibliographical references and index.
ISBN 0 521 59334 4 (hardback)
1. English drama – Early modern, 1500–1700 – History and criticism.
2. English drama – Middle English, 1100–1500 – History and criticism.
3. Latin language, Medieval and modern – England. 4. Civilization,
Medieval, in literature. 5. Language and culture – England – History.
6. Languages in contact – England – History. 7. Theater – England – History.
8. Renaissance – England. I. Title.
PR646.D55 1998
822'.209–dc21 97–8795 CIP

ISBN-13 978-0-521-59334-2 hardback
ISBN-10 0-521-59334-4 hardback

ISBN-13 978-0-521-03215-5 paperback
ISBN-10 0-521-03215-6 paperback

To my mother

Contents

Preface

This book began with a set of related questions: why are other languages so conspicuous in English plays of the sixteenth century? what does their presence mean? and how do they address a range of different spectators, from those who understand only English to those with a smattering of foreign vernaculars from their travels and those who can understand, even converse in, academic Latin?

In attempting to answer these questions, this study aims to examine individual plays within their cultural context and to look at how changes in English culture from the fourteenth to the sixteenth century produce the need to keep reworking and restaging the interface between English and alien languages. Attitudes to alien language are closely tied up with religious change and developing nationalism, so that these are two dominant concerns of the book. Protestant England defines itself against both Babel and Babylon, the voices of other nations and other faiths, and at the same time seeks to strengthen its own position by collapsing distinctions between the two.

Chapter 1 begins by surveying attitudes to language in the fourteenth century and assessing the impact of the Lollards on linguistic thinking. Latin, until now the sacramental language of authority, becomes the potential enemy in the newly politicised linguistic arena of the late fourteenth century.

In chapter 2 I compare two mystery cycles, N-Town and Wakefield, in terms of how they stage English and Latin. N-Town, possibly monastic in origin, is reverent towards Latin, constructing it as the language of 'holy speakers', while in Wakefield plain English is the language of the virtuous, with Latin and other foreign languages the signs of corruption.

The next chapter turns to morality plays, offering an extended analysis of how English and Latin operate in one play which seems particularly concerned with language use: *Mankind*. Written in late fifteenth-century East Anglia, at a time of renewed prosecutions for heresy in the area, it may be read as a plea for plainer language on the part of the orthodox church.

Chapter 4 moves forward to the early sixteenth century and the beginnings of Protestantism. As church and state become more closely intertwined, and England moves towards Reform, so Latin is increasingly demonised as the language of Catholic Rome. John Bale's drama, written as conscious propaganda for the English Protestant state, is the subject of this chapter's exploration of the urge to remake history in the image of Reformed belief.

The early years of Elizabeth's reign are the focus of chapter 5, which concentrates on the issue of learning, approached from the two directions of Foxe's *Book of Martyrs* and the classical interlude. Using three short plays on the subject of education, together with Wager's *The Longer Thou Livest the More Fool Thou Art*, I explore a peculiarly Protestant dilemma in relation to learning, which is simultaneously prized by Protestants for the access it gives to the written word, above all the bible, yet viewed with suspicion for its potential exclusiveness and elitism.

Chapter 6 examines the close interrelation between Latin and English in different cultural contexts, and especially in performance. In particular it looks at how a range of Elizabethan plays from the 1580s and early 1590s, including *The Spanish Tragedy*, exploit Latin for specific dramaturgical effects which operate in tension with the political framework of language use.

In chapter 7 *The Spanish Tragedy* is approached through its staging of alien vernacular languages rather than Latin. The chapter surveys attitudes towards foreigners first, across a number of plays, from the perspective of Londoners learning to live with alien immigrants, and then from the perspective of England as empire, as mediated through Shakespeare's *Henry V.*

Chapter 8 focuses on outsiders endemic to England: witches, rogues, vagabonds, Catholics and traitors, categories regularly over-lapping with each other. Using *2 Henry VI*, it supplements the previous chapter's focus on race and empire by looking at the making of the nation in terms of the 'internal' discourses of class and domestic politics.

As the conclusion indicates, the book's subject is much bigger than the book. I have chosen to draw the study to a close at the end of the sixteenth century not because the staging of Babel ceases to become an issue then, but because the parameters of the study shift markedly at that point. The babble of other languages continues to make itself heard in English drama until the closing of the theatres, but to cover those cultural shifts properly would take another book.

I would like to thank the friends and colleagues who helped this book along the way: Simon Shepherd willingly read the whole thing in draft and made helpful suggestions at every stage. Thorlac Turville-Petre and Alan Fletcher commented on early chapters, and Andrew Gurr and A. J. Hoenselaars willingly responded to queries. My thanks are due too to Sarah Stanton, Audrey Cotterell and the readers of the manuscript at Cambridge University Press. Errors remaining are of course my own.

Writing the book would have taken much longer had it not been for the support of the Department of English Studies at Nottingham University, which granted me a period of study leave in order to begin work on this subject. The University also supported my work by giving me a travel grant to enable me to make the necessary visits to other libraries.

Versions of material now incorporated into parts of chapters 1, 3, 6 and 7 of this book have appeared in *Medievalia et Humanistica* 1993, in *Research Opportunities in English Drama* 1995 and in *English and the Other Languages*, ed. A. J. Hoenselaars, forthcoming. I am grateful to the editors and publishers concerned for permission to publish revised versions here.

Conventions and abbreviations

Quotations from plays are regularly taken from the collected editions listed in the Bibliography except where otherwise noted. Where no collected edition is cited, quotations are from the individual editions listed. Quotations from the works of Shakespeare are taken from the Riverside edition. Plays are dated according to the third edition of Alfred Harbage's *Annals of English Drama 975–1700*, revised S. Schoenbaum and Sylvia Stoler Wagonheim (London and New York: Routledge, 1989) unless otherwise indicated.

References are in the standard form of act, scene, line where such divisions are available, but for some plays the only available numeration is that of scene and line, or sometimes of line only. In some editions there is no lineation at all, and here I have had to cite page references.

I have retained the spelling of the texts or editions from which I quote, but have modernised typography, substituting modern equivalents for obsolete characters, expanding contractions and rationalising conventions such as u/v spelling. I have also placed all quotations from other languages in italics, regardless of whether they are italicised in the source. In chapters 2 and 3 I have retained a regional spelling which may look especially unfamiliar to modern readers: 'x' for 'sh' (as in 'xall/shall' and 'xuld/shuld'). I have also anglicised American spellings in my quotations from the *Riverside Shakespeare*. Old-style dating has been emended in accordance with modern use.

I have normally translated Latin, except where the focus of the discussion is on what the author does or does not choose to translate. In such contexts, to supply translation would be to undercut the effects under discussion. Inserted translations are mine where not otherwise specified.

The only abbreviations used in the text of the book are OED (for the Oxford English Dictionary, 2nd edition), MED (for the Middle English Dictionary, ed. Hans Kurath et al. (Ann Arbor: University of Michigan Press, 1956–) and *Revels* for *The Revels History of Drama in English*, cited in full in the Bibliography. Abbreviations in use only in the bibliography are MSR, for the Malone Society Reprints, and EETS, OS, ES, SS, for Early English Text Society, Original Series, Extra Series and Supplementary Series. Journal titles are cited in full except for *English Literary History* (*ELH*), *English Literary Renaissance* (*ELR*) and *Publications of the Modern Language Association of America* (*PMLA*).

CHAPTER I

'Verbum Dei' and the rise of English

The Word had potent kinds of meaning beyond the semantic for laypeople during the Middle Ages. While theologians throughout Christendom lectured on the traditional glosses to the Vulgate Bible (all in Latin, lectures and glosses as well as the bible), laypeople received the incarnate Word in the form of the sacred host, accepting that the words of consecration were uttered in a sacred other language which they could not understand. Understanding the words that were spoken was unimportant to participation in the mass. What the congregation needed to grasp was the sacramental power of the Word, its transforming mystery. The Latin liturgy, at once so remote from and so familiar to ordinary people, functioned via this paradox both to comfort the faithful with the repetition of words heard only and always in this sacred context and to underline their awareness of the ineffable mystery of God. A dialogue between the young Mary Tudor, wondering about the role of the congregation, and her almoner emphasises two different senses of 'understanding':

In my God, I cannot see what we shall do at the Mass, if we pray not.
Ye shall think to the mystery of the Mass and shall harken to the words that
    the priest say.
Yea, and what shall they do which understand it not?
They shall behold, and shall hear, and think, and by that they shall
    understand.   (Brigden, *London and the Reformation*, p. 14)

Outside the church, the Latin Word of the bible might continue to cast its quasi-magical spell. It could be used to ward off or exorcise evil spirits, to cast out devils, to protect against sickness or injury (Thomas, *Religion and the Decline of Magic*, pp. 27–57; Duffy, *The Stripping of the Altars*, ch.8). Nor did the precious words even need to be uttered, far less understood. They could be written down and sewn into the clothes or sealed in a little amulet to be worn around the neck. Even learned clerics are to be found confirming popular superstition: 'Sacred words bound to the body are marvellously protective', the writers of the fifteenth-century *Malleus Maleficarum*, approved by the pope, assure their readers (Kramer and Sprenger, *Malleus Maleficarum*, p. 92).[1] The most highly revered text for such purposes was the first verse of St John's gospel. As late as 1603 Samuel Harsnett notes Catholic priests still using this text as a test of witchcraft: 'If S. Johns Gospel being put in a Casket, and applied unto her, she rubbe, or scratch any part of her body, and cry it burnes, it is an evident demonstration, that the enemie dooth lurke in that part' (*A Declaration of Egregious Popish Impostures*, p. 24).

The written text of this verse, when used as a charm in the medieval period, would naturally be in Latin, but in the familiar English of the Authorised Version it reads 'In the Beginning was the Word, and the Word was with God, and the Word was God.'[2] It is easy to see why this text was valued above all others: it is a self-reflexive text, the Word pronouncing on its own value and authority. The Word, it insists, does not simply issue from God, but *is* God, the point of origin, the absolute.

The Word, however, like mankind, experienced a fall from grace. According to Augustine, Adam's knowledge of God had been direct and unmediated, a truth transmitted inwardly without the need for material signs: 'God watered [the soul] by an interior spring, speaking to its intellect, so that it did not receive words from the outside.'[3] Yet Augustine also recognises a spoken language, beginning with Adam's naming of all living creatures (Genesis 2.19–20), and identifies this *Ursprache* as Hebrew, thus creating a continuum between the language of Eden and the language of scripture. Even this language, however, is subject to corruption in the primal myth of Eden, since it is the language shared by Adam, Eve and the serpent, the language used so eloquently first by the serpent to tempt Eve and then by Eve to tempt Adam. For Augustine, himself a teacher of rhetoric before his conversion, the Fall demonstrates the dangers inherent in language: as soon as it becomes a set of material signs, a potential gap opens up between words and truth, and that gap can be exploited by an appeal to the rhetorical pleasure of the signs themselves. It is here, then, that the Christian anxiety about the relationship between words and truth begins, an anxiety which is central to discussions about language, theology or both down to at least the seventeenth century.[4]

If the myth of the Fall was central to the thinking of medieval commentators on language, the myth of Babel entered equally deeply into the thinking of Renaissance writers.[5] Before Babel, according to the biblical account, 'the whole earth was of one language, and of one speech' (Genesis 11.1). But then, as in the Garden of Eden, mankind's *hubris* destroyed the state of nature. God saw his people struggling to build 'a tower, whose top may reach unto heaven' (11.4) and punished their pride by dividing their unitary language into a plurality:

So the Lord scattered them abroad from thence upon the face of all the earth: and they left off to build the city.
Therefore is the name of it called Babel; because the Lord did there confound the language of all the earth: and from thence did the Lord scatter them abroad upon the face of all the earth. (11.8–9)

After the loss of a single language, words became not merely material signs but arbitrary material signs. The single prelapsarian relation between word and thing gave way to a purely nominal, contingent and plural relation. No word could now offer a better claim than any other to denote a particular concept, and the making of language was reduced to a merely human activity. The *Ursprache* that had bound word to meaning was gone. Now the potential corruption in language was even greater than in Eden, and eloquence had become even more suspect. Words had to be understood as able to speak lies as well as truth and to look like truth even as they spoke their lies.

In the terms of the New Testament, however, the Word was redeemed for the faithful through its incarnation in Christ. The sacrifice of the Crucifixion atoned for the Fall, and the mass, with its regular celebration of that sacrifice, offered every believer the chance to receive the redeemed word made flesh. Indeed, it was the utterance of the holy words over the host that transformed it into God's body. Pentecost offered proof that the Holy Spirit could again fill words with a grace that transcended the barriers of individual languages. And such grace occasionally inspired medieval saints: St Vincent Ferrer was famous for the fact that his preaching could be understood in all languages, and the miraculous comprehensibility of Margery Kempe is further discussed below (p. 24). This was a theological, not a rational, view of language, which had faith in the possibility that even though words could not, of their own accord, frame the radically singular truth of God, they could function as vehicles for that truth if it sought them out by grace.

Although there could never again be one language across all the earth, Latin, the language of the Vulgate Bible and the liturgy of the Western church, in use throughout the Christian world, gradually acquired authority by long association through the Middle Ages. Jerome's Latin bible was not in any sense an 'original' text; it was a translation. But it was by the late Middle Ages a translation so ancient, so familiar and so uncontested that it was invested with the aura of the authentic. And while it did not unite all the peoples of the world, it did unite the Christian peoples of the West and became the language not only of the church, but of scholarship, teaching, international relations and the vast majority of European written texts.

The obscurity of Latin to laypeople came to seem part of its power and purpose. St Augustine, writing of the Greek and Hebrew texts at a time when Jerome's Latin translation was still relatively new, argued that obscurities in the original texts were there to combat pride and to prevent readers underestimating the worth of the meaning discovered (*On Christian Doctrine*, p. 37). It is not surprising, then, that when the Latin text was challenged by the desire for vernacular bibles, the Augustinian argument was recycled. Pope Gregory VII's letter, written in 1080 in response to a request from the Duke of the Bohemians to celebrate the divine service in the vernacular, justifies the obscurity of the now established and canonical Latin text along precisely these lines: 'it is clear to thoughtful men that it has quite rightly pleased Almighty God to have sacred Scripture obscure in certain places, lest it be perhaps debased and brought into contempt if it should be openly exposed to all, or lest, wrongly understood by common men, it should lead them into error' (Harrison, *The Description of England*, p. 35, n.33).

William Harrison quotes the text of this letter (in Latin) in his *Description of England* (published in 1587) as part of his own Protestant attack on traditional papal hostility to church services in the vernacular, which England, to Harrison's relief, has finally instated. Conducting the mass in an alien language, then, was clearly perceived by Harrison's time as a matter of papal policy rather than an accident of history. The medieval church, however, encouraged the laity in the belief that a sacred event was appropriately expressed in a language surpassing common understanding:

It was part of the power of the words of consecration that they were hidden, too sacred to be communicated to the 'lewed', and this very element of mystery gave legitimacy to the sacred character of Latin itself, as higher and holier than the vernacular. Moreover, since the words of scripture and the liturgy came from God, they were held to convey power even to those who did not fully comprehend them. One author, writing to help lay men and women participate properly in the Mass, compared the beneficial effect of such uncomprehending hearing at mass to that of a charm upon adders! (Duffy, *The Stripping of the Altars*, pp. 217–18; cf Aston, *Lollards and Reformers*, pp. 131–4)

Mikhail Bakhtin's work has underlined the way Latin shaped the growth and consciousness of vernacular languages in the Middle Ages. Latin, he argues, and the sacred words of scripture in particular, invaded European vernaculars as the controlling authority against which they came to know and assess themselves. 'Under cover of holiday and festival merrymaking', vernacular languages attempted to dislodge Latin from its position of ideological dominance[6] and at the same time came to see themselves more clearly: 'one language can, after all, see itself only in the light of another language' (Bakhtin, *The Dialogic Imagination*, pp. 77, 12). The particularities of different languages became visible, available for representation. Every utterance was underpinned by an awareness of potential otherness, not only the otherness of a different language, but the otherness of different discourses within a single language. Utterance itself, as Bakhtin shows, becomes inherently dialogic, engaging always with other possible forms of utterance that it does not voice.

Medieval manuscripts display this dialogic quality spatially as well as verbally. The text is characteristically framed by glosses, decoration and other marginalia which enter into a potential dialogue with it that may explore, supplement, question or parody it, while never fully dislodging its higher authority (see further Camille, *Image on the Edge*). And not only written culture but performance culture plays across the boundary between authorised material and 'commentary' on it. Vernacular difference irrupts into liturgical space in music and drama: obscene vernacular tenor parts twine with Latin top parts (Camille, *Image on the Edge*, p. 26); Mary Magdalene, Joseph of Arimathea, Pilate and even Mary the mother of Jesus, speak in German within the Latin Benediktbeuern Passion play (Bevington, *Medieval Drama*, pp. 203–23). Robert Weimann, in *Shakespeare and the*

Popular Tradition in the Theater, explores medieval staging practices in similar terms. Relations between *locus* and *platea,* the area of fixed location and the area of unfixed space, offer another realisation of this characteristically dialogic playfulness. As the margin frames the central text of a manuscript page, so the *platea* frames the narrative of the fixed *locus.* Playtexts move back and forward between 'straight' linear narrative or exposition and a freer, more direct and improvisatory mode of address, moving physically closer to the audience as they free themselves from the fiction they enact. The actors playing directly to the audience from the *platea* temporarily unfix the reality of the action within the represented fiction, so that more than one perspective on reality may come into play.

ENGLAND BEFORE 1400

Three languages, Latin, French and English, were in use in England up to about 1400. Each recorded use of a given language makes statements about the speaker or writer, the audience and the context. Individuals competent in all three made choices according to the moment of speech or writing. Jocelin of Brakelond, for example, describes how Abbot Samson in the twelfth century 'was a good speaker, in both French and Latin ... could read books written in English most elegantly, and ... used to preach to the people in English, but in the Norfolk dialect, for that was where he was born and brought up' (*Chronicle,* p. 37). As an abbot and a monk he needed Latin to read theology, to preach to the clergy and to communicate with other monks or with high-ranking or non-English-speaking clerics; as a member of the social elite he needed French to converse with king and court and with other members of the nobility; and as a churchman with a responsibility to teach the laity about God he needed idiomatic English in order to make himself understood. The twelfth-century Canterbury Psalter demonstrates the same hierarchy visually. It presents the Latin text in large and beautiful script, using elaborately ornamented capitals; two further versions of the Latin text in slightly smaller script, still with ornamented capitals; Latin glosses in an even smaller script in the margins and interlined with the main Latin text; and finally, in the same size script as the glosses, but interlined merely with the secondary Latin texts, English and French translations.[7]

At the same time, this hierarchy cannot be imposed as a reductive grid on the written texts of the period. There is, as Elizabeth Salter has demonstrated, 'no simple answer to the question of who read and wrote English poetry during the twelfth and thirteenth centuries' (*Fourteenth-Century Poetry*, p. 22). Salter shows that the choice of English or French cannot be predicted from 'the nature of the patrons, the intended public, or the subject-matter' (p. 23), and discusses the coexistence of the two vernaculars, sometimes even within the same poem, in late thirteenth- and early fourteenth-century manuscripts such as Digby 86 and Harley 2253.

The development of English in the thirteenth and fourteenth centuries is also fuelled by a growing nationalism, which champions the English language as the appropriate language for the English people. Though French had been the language of the court since the arrival of the Normans, hostilities with the French now helped to reinforce the claim of English to be the national language. This anti-French feeling informs the prefaces to some English poems of the late thirteenth and early fourteenth centuries (Salter, *Fourteenth-Century Poetry*, pp. 26–8) and expresses an attempt to speak from a position of national unity which strives to overcome the class divisions associated with different languages. Thorlac Turville-Petre, arguing for the growth of a concept of national identity during the period 1290–1340, considers that language emerges as 'the clearest form of self-definition' for the English nation in this period ('The "Nation" in English Writings of the Early Fourteenth Century', p. 137). As the poem *Of Arthour and Merlin* puts it:

> Right is that Inglische understond
> That was born in Inglond.
> Freynsche use this gentil man
> Ac everich Inglische Inglische can.
> Mani noble ich have yseiye
> That no Freynsche couthe seye.

(It's proper that those born in England should understand English. These well-born people use French, but all the English know English. I've seen many a noble who couldn't speak French).

Statements such as this, Turville-Petre argues, function polemically rather than serving as neutral statements about who speaks what language in England. 'What is strikingly new in this period', he concludes, 'is the conviction that national sentiment is most properly expressed in English, and that the people of England, those who most loyally represent the nation, are the *lewed*, "tho that in this lande wone / that the Latyn no Frankys cone" (those who live in this country who know neither Latin or French) (Mannyng, I, lines 7–8)' ('The "Nation" in English Writings of the Early Fourteenth Century', p. 138–9).

Kings, predictably, understand the political advantages of addressing the nation through this unifying homage to the English language. Edward I claims in 1295 that the French are planning to wipe out the English tongue in England (Prestwich, *English Politics in the Thirteenth Century*, p. 90), and the Chancellor's opening speech to Parliament in 1377 voices the same fear (whether real or strategic) that invasion by enemies may not only destroy king and country, but 'drive out the English language' (Coleman, *English Literature in History 1350–1400*, p. 52). The move towards the adoption of English in high places accelerates during the fourteenth century, and by the end of the century English has become the language in which pleadings are made in the king's court, teaching is conducted in grammar schools and kings take their coronation oaths (see further Coleman, *English Literature in History 1350–1400*, pp. 51–2; Dillon, *Geoffrey Chaucer*, pp. 36–41). It is the normal language of social intercourse at the highest level. Froissart's expression of admiration for Richard II's French reading skills is sufficient indication that fluency in French could no longer be taken for granted even at court. By the reign of Henry V, the currency of the phrase 'the king's English' confirms the ideological usefulness of language conceived as a unifying force that cuts across class barriers and as a right worth fighting for.[8]

Despite the upward mobility of English, however, fourteenth-century language continues to reflect social ranking beneath all the jingoistic talk of unity. While the French/English opposition primarily mirrors the distance between court and nation, the Latin/English polarity particularly highlights the fundamental division between clergy and laity. The overwhelming majority of surviving written texts from the medieval period are in Latin and on theological subjects, which is an indication of the domination of education by the church. Most educated men (and most of the educated *were* men) received their education as the result of an intention to dedicate them to a career in the church, and medieval Latin texts make no clear distinction between the concepts of literacy and clerical status. Not only is there an overlap between the words '*clericus*' and '*litteratus*', since literacy implied clerical status and vice versa, but the concepts of literacy and competence in Latin are inseparable, since Latin was the language of education. Only the self-taught might learn to read English without first learning to read Latin.

There is, not surprisingly, no Latin word denoting a capacity to read in the vernacular, and English equivalents are so heavily influenced by Latin usage that it is usually impossible to be certain whether a word such as 'unlettered' (or '*illiteratus*'), for example, indicates absence of Latin or total illiteracy.[9] The very terminology by which the literate establishment continued to identify its own knowledge of Latin as the only literacy, and refused to share the name of literacy with the vernacular equivalent demonstrates the degree to which language is always politically engaged. Such a refusal to realign the uses of language with the changing pattern of learning expresses a deeper refusal to realign power structures. The thinking is circular and deeply conservative.

Literacy, in whatever language, is a political issue. Nicholas Orme points out that, even as the foundation of free grammar schools expanded in the fourteenth century, education was still largely unavailable to the lowest class by virtue of the fact that a serf needed his lord's permission to send his children to school, and a fee was usually demanded before such permission was forthcoming. Orme goes on to argue, however, that 'this restriction on the education of villeins was not primarily intended to keep them illiterate, since their literacy in itself could have harmed no one. It existed rather because schooling presupposed a career in the church or in some trade or profession, and hence departure from the manor and the acquisition of free status' (*English Schools in the Middle Ages*, p. 50).[10] The second part of this quotation from Orme, however, undermines the assertion that opens it by showing exactly how education of the lower classes did threaten the ruling class. Any route which leads to freedom and power for serfs necessarily threatens the feudal interests of the lord of the manor. Literacy cannot be isolated, and considered as a phenomenon 'in itself'. It is necessarily political, and fourteenth-century lords knew it.

Serfs knew it too. Books and learning were one focus of attack, alongside clerics and secular lords, during the English Rising (Peasants' Revolt) of 1381. The rebels attacked the university archives in Cambridge, and set fire to them in the market square. An old woman called Margery Starre tossed the ashes away, crying 'Away with the learning of the clerks, away with it' (Orme, *English Schools in the Middle Ages*, p. 192). Walsingham reports that the rebels similarly compelled schoolteachers to swear to give up teaching children Latin grammar (*Historia Anglicana*, vol. ii, p. 308).[11]

Latin and the church may well have seemed to the rebels to be a mutually sustaining power structure that functioned by excluding the lower ranks of society from access to its workings. As long as the bible and the literature generated by it remained in Latin, the church's authority was unassailable, since laypeople had no access to the sacred texts other than as mediated by representatives of the church. It was therefore in clerical interests to maintain a linguistic barrier that put some distance between the laity and the Word of God, thus reinforcing their own control. Similarly, as long as the court maintained French and Latin as the languages of government (spoken and written) it effectively insulated itself from most of the population.

Yet before the 1380s the church had worked precisely to break down the barrier of language at strategic points, recognising that any real attempt to expand lay understanding of the faith must address the laity in its own language.[12] Archbishop Pecham's Constitutions of 1281 ruled that parish priests should instruct the laity in English in the basics of the faith at least four times a year, and Archbishop Thoresby had this scheme of instruction adapted into English by John Gaytrick in 1357 in the form that came to be known as the *Lay Folk's Catechism*. The church, in responding to the needs of the laity in this way, also had to recognise the needs of the non-Latinate, and in some cases semi-illiterate, clergy, who needed material in English to help them fulfil their duties. John Mirk's *Festial* explicitly highlighted the problem some clergymen faced of having to deal with overconfident laymen who shamed them with questions concerning the offices of the church which they were not equipped to answer. His text simultaneously addressed the beleaguered clergyman and, more indirectly, the parishioners hungry for instruction. Primers were produced in English, together with rhymed English versions of the most important prayers, so that they could be understood as well as learned more easily. More popular vernacular or macaronic forms, like lyric and drama, also helped to convey the church's message to the people. Richard Morison, a sixteenth-century Protestant writing *c.*1538 or earlier to advocate the need for an anti-papal propaganda campaign, pointed to the medieval church as having mounted just such a campaign in support of its own beliefs and practices. These beliefs, according to Morison, 'were daily by all meanes opened inculked [inculcated] and dryven into the peoples heddes, tought in scoles to children, plaied in playes before the ignoraunt people, songe in mynstrelles songes, and bokes in englisshe purposley to be dyvysed to declare the same at large' (Anglo, 'An Early Tudor Programme', p. 178).

THE LOLLARDS

Towards the end of the fourteenth century, however, two episodes combined at about the same time to halt the steady thrust of English towards a position of greater strength: the translation of the bible and the English Rising. From this point on, issues of language became more explicitly politically charged, and the move towards English was forced, in ecclesiastical contexts at least, to fork along the lines of orthodoxy and heresy. The church, in taking a stand against the legitimacy of an English translation of the bible, could not continue its policy of increasing vernacular provision for the laity, and gradually took on a more confrontational role that demonised English as the language of potential heretics. The choice of English now came to seem a defiantly anticlerical gesture, and one which, increasingly in the fifteenth century, questioned the need for a mediating clergy at all.

Wyclif, whose name is most prominently associated with the first complete English translation of the bible, was himself a highly educated cleric, and many of his earliest followers were men like himself, educated, in holy orders and utterly competent in Latin. The choice of English on the part of such men was a political statement against elitism, evasion and possible ignorance on the part of the orthodox church, perceived by some as wishing to 'kepin the peple in overdon lewydnesse, that hemself in here lewydnesse myghte semyn wyse' (to keep the people in excessive ignorance, so that they themselves in their ignorance might seem wise) (Hudson, 'Old Author, New Work', p. 232). Nicholas Hereford, Philip Repington and John Aston infuriated Archbishop Courtenay during their trial for heresy in 1382 by their insistence on replying in English rather than in Latin, as the Archbishop demanded (*The Acts and Monuments of John Foxe*, vol. III, p. 35; Aston, 'Wyclif and the Vernacular', pp. 297–300). Wyclif himself made it equally clear that his decision to

communicate the *Thirty-three Conclusions* in two languages was based
on a wish to reach laymen as well as clerks,[13] and he was openly
scornful of the stupidity of those 'who wish to damn writings as
heretical on account of the fact that they are written in English and
show clearly the sins which beset that country'.[14]

More conservative clerics hated Wyclif and his supporters with a
venom cultivated by their feeling of having been betrayed by one of
their own. The venom is clearly conveyed in the notebook of the
friar Adam Stocton, where the description of Wyclif as 'venerable
doctor' (*venerabilis doctor*) is crossed out and changed to 'accursed
seducer' (*execrabilis seductor*) (Keen, 'Wyclif, the Bible, and Transubstantiation', p. 5). The sense of a clerical class under threat emerges
very strongly from the earliest stages of the debate over translation of
the bible. The chronicle of Henry Knighton, an Augustinian canon
and himself writing, of course, in Latin, shows clear recognition that
a translated bible would transfer power from the clergy to the laity.
He is insistent on the necessity of clerical mediation. Christ entrusted
the gospel, he writes, 'to clerks and to doctors of the church so that
they might minister it in a wholesome manner to the laity and to less
able people according to the needs of the time and the requirement
of the people in their hunger of mind' (*Chronicon*, vol. II, pp. 151–2).[15]
For him, Wyclif's sin is that of having translated

from Latin into the English [*Anglicam*], not the angelic [*angelicam*], language
so that in this way that which was formerly the province only of learned
clerks and those of good understanding has become common and more
open to the laity, and to those women who know how to read. As a result
the pearl of the gospel is scattered and spread before swine. (*Chronicon*, vol.
II, p. 152)[16]

Walsingham's record of how a certain John Claydon made his son
(or perhaps even his daughter) a priest in order to celebrate mass in
his own home for his wife after her childbirth (Aston, 'Lollardy and
Sedition', p. 13;[17] Cross, ' "Great Reasoners in Scripture" ', p. 360)
similarly displays his fear that a vernacular bible breaks down the
boundary between the laity and the ordained priesthood.

John Trevisa's *Dialogue between a Lord and a Clerk*, originally prefixed
to some copies of his translation of the *Polychronicon* in 1387,[18]
highlights the equation between language and power very clearly.
The object of the translation to which this dialogue is prefixed is not
the bible, but a secular chronicle. It is addressed to a noble patron,

Sir Thomas Berkeley, who asked Trevisa to undertake the work. Yet even here, there is no escape from the political. The attitudes to translation Trevisa depicts in his two speakers suggest an intention to emphasise polarity between lay and clerical attitudes to translation. While the Lord is anxious that Latin chronicles should be translated into English, so that the information in them should be more widely accessible, the Clerk takes the view that there is no need, since both he and the Lord can read Latin. When the Lord argues that those who cannot finance their own education *need* books in English, the Clerk's prejudice emerges quite blatantly: 'hyt neodeth noght that al soche knowe the cronykes' (it is not necessary for all such people to know the chronicles) (Trevisa, *Dialogue between a Lord and a Clerk*, p. 216). The Lord is shocked by such a narrow definition of need on the part of the Clerk, whose wish to control is uppermost: 'hy that understondeth no Latyn', says the Clerk, 'mowe axe and be informed and ytaught of ham that understondeth Latyn' (p. 216). Gradually the dispute moves into the more dangerous area of biblical translation and there is an angry interchange, which rede-fines the traditional meanings of 'lered' (learned) and 'lewed' (ignorant). Ignorance is displayed, according to the Lord, less in the non-Latinity of a so-called 'lewed' audience than in the view held by apparently learned men that Latin is the right medium for such an audience. As the Lord puts it, 'holy wryt in Latyn ys bothe good and fayr, and yet for to make a sermon of holy wryt al yn Latyn to men that konneth Englysch and no Latyn hyt were a lewed dede' (p. 217). When the Clerk continues to argue that theological books should not be translated at all, the Lord is even more direct in his assessment of such an attitude: 'Hyt ys wonder that thou makest so feble argementys and hast ygo so long to scole' (p. 218). The debate ends abruptly with the sudden conversion of the Clerk to the Lord's point of view.

Although the Clerk is obviously a straw man, not to be equated with Trevisa's own point of view, he may well represent a character-istic, if caricatured, clerical attitude towards translation. The Lord, on the other hand, given that Berkeley commissioned and perhaps even actively disseminated the *Dialogue* (Hanna, 'Sir Thomas Berk-eley and his Patronage'), cannot be supposed to represent a view significantly different from Berkeley's own. While it would be naive to see the secular lord as the democratic champion of the English-speaking layman's right to have access to texts that have previously excluded his class, what the dialogue underlines is the clear recognition on the part of both lord and clerk that translation is not simply a literary, but also a political, activity. Access to written texts is also a route of access to power. Clearly it was in the interests of the powerful to continue to restrict such access.

The quarrel over the translation of the bible was at root a quarrel over *who* should have access to the words of scripture. The ecclesiastical authorities did not take exception to translations existing in aristocratic libraries; what they feared was popularisation of an English text amongst the laity, which would tacitly encourage personal interpretation of the words of scripture at a popular level without the mediation of clerical glosses (Deanesly, *The Lollard Bible*). After Archbishop Arundel's Constitutions of 1409, prohibiting the making of any new translation of scripture into English or the owning of a translation made in the time of Wyclif or later, a system of episcopal licences continued to allow privileged individuals to retain possession of pre-Wyclifite translations of scriptural material. The threat to the established church was not really the principle of translation, since the Latin was itself already a translated text from the original Hebrew or Greek, nor the inadequacy of English, although that topic diverted some attention, but the nature of the audience excluded by Latin but included by English.

Those influenced by Wyclif's ideas soon became known as Lollards. The name 'Lollard' probably derives from Dutch *lollen*, to mumble; and Lollards are identified by their contemporaries as 'janglers', abusers of words and the Word.[19] According to Knighton, just as

[their] master John Wyclif was powerful and able above all others in disputation, so they believed themselves second to none in argument; so even if they had been lately attracted to that sect they became exceedingly eloquent, prevailing over others in all craftiness and wordy encounters, strong in words, mighty in prating, outstanding in disputations, outshouting all in litigious strife. So that what they might not achieve by right reasoning they made up for by quarrelsome violence and high-sounding words. (*Chronicon*, vol. II, pp. 187; trans. Myers in *English Historical Documents*, vol. IV, p. 843)[20]

Their emphasis on the word can scarcely be exaggerated. The statute *De Heretico Comburendo* (*2 Henry IV*, *c.15*), passed in 1401 to allow the church to hand over heretics to the state for punishment, so that they could be burned, identifies them as a 'certain new sect

. . . usurping the office of preaching' and condemns them for all the different ways in which they attempt to usurp the power of the word from the orthodox church: 'they make unlawful conventicles and confederacies, they hold and exercise schools, they make and write books, they do wickedly instruct and inform people' (*English Historical Documents*, vol. IV, p. 850). They translated, preached, wrote treatises, and were frequently identified as heretics by the books they owned. Malcolm Lambert identifies a Lollard community as 'above all a reading community, basing its common life on the public and private reading of the Scriptures and of Lollard tracts' (*Medieval Heresy*, p. 270; cf. Aston, *Lollards and Reformers*, pp. 193–217). Such a community obviously placed a very high value on books and the written word, and on teaching basic literacy skills to the illiterate. Lollards also displayed astonishing feats of memory in their concern to spread the word, learning vast excerpts from the bible or from Lollard tracts. This was not, as Anne Hudson underlines, 'a poor alternative to reading', but a specifically evangelising strategy, as well as perhaps, Claire Cross suggests, a way to avoid being found in possession of incriminating books (Hudson, *The Premature Reformation*, p. 191; Cross, '"Great Reasoners in Scripture"', p. 371).

From the very beginning, then, Lollards identified themselves by their focus on the word, and in particular by their focus on the word in English. They valued literacy, but opposed the exclusiveness and elitism of Latin. Knighton characterises them sneeringly as a group 'who have changed the Gospel of Christ into the eternal Gospel, that is, the vernacular and common mother tongue, and thus eternal, because it is reputed among lay people to be better and worthier than the Latin tongue' (*Chronicon*, vol. II, p. 155).[21] They insisted, as at the 1382 trial, on using English in all kinds of traditionally Latin contexts, both spoken and written. A group of Richard II's household knights formulated the 'Twelve Conclusions' of the Lollards in English in 1395 (reprinted in Hudson, *Selections from English Wycliffite Writings*, pp. 24–9; see also p. 150) and, through repeated writing and disputation, the Lollards developed the polemical resources of English. A modernised text of the Prologue to the Wyclifite version may convey something of the flavour of their polemic:

Yet worldly clerks ask much what spirit makes fools so rash as to translate now the Bible into English, since the four great doctors never dared to do this? This argument is so silly that it needs no answer, other than silence or courteous scorn; for the great doctors were not English men . . . but they never ceased until they had holy writ in their mother tongue, of their own people. (*English Historical Documents*, vol. IV, p. 828)[22]

The polemical tone of their special pleading for English is itself the clue to Lollard authorship.

Anne Hudson discusses an English version of Robert of Greatham's *Miroir*, a set of sermons originally written between 1250 and 1300. The translation is thought to be fourteenth-century, and the sermons are, in Hudson's view, superficially very different from Wyclifite sermons, but among other clues to possible Lollard involvement is the confrontational rhetoric of the prologue, which claims that 'hit is ful gret foli to speke Latyn to lewd [lay] folk, and he entermeteth hym of a fol mister [involves himself in a foolish enterprise] that telleth to hym Latyne; for eche man schal be undernome [rebuked] and aresound [called to account] aftur the langage that he hath lered [learned]' (Hudson, *The Premature Reformation*, p. 415, n.107; translations Hudson's). While this kind of rhetoric does not irrefutably identify its writer as a Lollard, it is, as Hudson points out, material likely to have been classified as dangerous after 1400.

The Lollards' insistence on English gave them obvious appeal to the uneducated, and, after the first wave of interest from educated and aristocratic men in the 1380s and 1390s, the movement took root among the artisan and peasant classes.[23] Even before this, Knighton and Walsingham had already made the association between religious dissent and political action. For them, it was no accident that the English Rising occurred when it did. Its horrors were in their eyes only to be expected if the knowledge and power of the sacred scriptures were to be put into the hands of swine. Both of them linked Wyclif's name with that of John Ball, a clerical leader of the Rising (Knighton, *Chronicon*, vol. II, p. 151; Walsingham, *Historia Anglicana*, vol. II, pp. 32–3; *Chronicon Angliae*, pp. 320–2). The *Fasciculi Zizaniorum* (a Carmelite, and therefore hostile, account of the Lollards) goes further, stating that John Ball himself confessed 'that for two years he had been a disciple of Wycliffe and had learned from the latter the heresies which he had taught' (pp. 272–4; trans. Dobson, *The Peasants' Revolt*, p. 378). It is likely, however, that Ball's 'confession' is a fabrication. As R. B. Dobson argues, the *Fasciculi Zizaniorum* fails to deliver its promise to include the text of the confession, and, if it really existed at the time, 'it is inconceivable that it would not have been exploited by contemporary churchmen and chroniclers' (*The Peasants' Revolt*, p. 378). Wyclif himself, moreover, openly condemned the revolt (p. 373).

The 1401 statute, representing agreement between church and state that heretics should be passed to the state for punishment (since the church could not use the death penalty), was symptomatic of a deepening anxiety on the part of both authorities. It seemed to them a short step from religious heterodoxy to political rebellion, and in acting together and with such severity they were attempting to suppress all potential subversiveness before it could spread further. The statute was explicit about its fears concerning the link between heresy and rebellion. After listing the 'sins of the word' of which the Lollards were considered guilty (quoted pp. 14–15 above), it went on to accuse them of attempting to 'stir [people] to sedition and insurrection and make great strife and division among the people' (*English Historical Documents*, vol. IV, p. 850). Questioning the doctrines of the church was seen as the first step on the road to treason. 'Sedition and dissent', to quote Margaret Aston, 'had come of age together' ('Lollardy and Sedition', p. 37).

The prologue to the Wyclifite translation of the bible registers its writer's awareness of this tendency on the part of the establishment to equate heresy with rebellion against the state: 'worldly clerkis crien that holy writ in Englische wole make cristen men at debate, and sugettis [subjects] to rebelle ageyns her sovereyns, and therfor it schal not be suffrid [allowed] among lewed [lay] men' (Hudson, *The Premature Reformation*, p. 276 (first translation mine, second two Hudson's); Aston, *Lollards and Reformers*, p. 11). Lollards tried to resist this equation, arguing that 'ignoraunce of Goddis lawe is cause of alle mevynge and unstabilitie in the comoun pepel . . . redi to rebelle ayens her sovereyns' (Hudson, *Lollards and their Books*, p. 158), but it only continued to harden in official circles.

Lollards also tried to resist the identification between heresy and the English language: 'many men wolen seie that there is moche eresie in Englische bookis, and therfore no man schulde have Goddis lawe in Englische. And I seie be the same skile ther schulde no man have Goddis lawe in bookis of Latyn, for ther is moche heresie in bookis of Latin, more than in Englische bookis' (Hudson, *Lollards and their Books*, p. 158), but with no more success.[24] Vernacular books, especially on theological topics, were suspicious by definition.[25] A statute of convocation in 1416 named the possession of suspect books written in English as one way of identifying a heretic, and house searches for such books were part of the standard procedure for investigation (Thomson, *The Later Lollards*, pp. 223, 227). Lower-class households were particularly vulnerable to this kind of investigation, since literacy itself was suspect below a certain class threshold.[26] The class of the reader and the language of the book were equally liable to be interpreted as danger signs by the investigating authorities. Margaret Aston, offering evidence for 'the development of a general ecclesiastical obsession about the dangers of all works written in English when read by the wrong sort of people', cites ordinances at St Albans in 1426–7 against ' "all false preachers and possessors of books in the vulgar tongue", on the grounds that heresy was largely caused by "the possession and reading of books which are written in our vernacular tongue" ' (Aston, *Lollards and Reformers*, pp. 208–9). Even *The Canterbury Tales* figured in an investigation for heresy in 1464 (Hudson, *The Premature Reformation*, p. 142).

A comparison between the vernacular projects of John Mirk in the late fourteenth century and Bishop Pecock in the mid fifteenth may serve to illustrate the deepening entrenchment of a hostility on the part of the established church towards English in theological works. Both Mirk and Pecock were opponents of the Lollards. It seems likely that Mirk's *Festial*, a collection of vernacular sermons written for clerics who lacked the resources of adequate literacy or access to books to compose their own, was written during the 1380s to counter the emerging Lollard threat (two consecutive sermons explicitly mention heretical opinions held by the Lollards) (Fletcher, 'John Mirk and the Lollards'). The collection was highly successful and presumably seemed in that decade to fit in well with the church's own policy of providing materials in English for the less educated clergy. Mirk's advice on prayer is that 'hit ys moch more spedfull and meritabull to you to say your "Pater Noster" yn Englysche then yn suche Lateyn, as ye dothe. For when ye spekyth yn Englysche, then ye knowen and undyrstondyn wele what ye sayn; and soo, by your undyrstondyng, ye have lykyng and devocyon forto say hit' (*Mirk's Festial*, p. 282). Such advice could have been construed as heretical by the end of the first decade of the fifteenth century.

Pecock, who chose to confront the Lollard errors head-on in theological disputation in English, was prosecuted for heresy in 1457.

Despite his high status in the church, his declared hostility to the Lollards and his recognition of the need to revert to Latin for certain reserved matters not fit to be spoken about in the vernacular, his work proved unacceptable to the climate of his time. V. H. H. Green's view that 'the fact that he wrote in English was probably even more irritating to his accusers than the views which his books contained' (*Bishop Reginald Pecock*, p. 188) is shared by Pecock's contemporary, Thomas Gascoigne, former Chancellor of Oxford University. He expressed the view that Pecock was prosecuted primarily 'because he wrote such profound matters in English, matters more likely to harm those who read or heard them than to benefit them . . . and also he composed a new creed, large and long, in English words' (Hudson's translation).[27]

The kind of English-language text of which the orthodox church did approve is well illustrated by the case of Nicholas Love's *Mirror of the Blessed Life of Jesus Christ*. Love's translation of the Pseudo-Bonaventuran *Meditationes Vitae Christi* addresses itself to the un-learned laity, 'lewde men and women and hem that bene of symple undirstondyng' (Love, *Mirror of the Blessed Life of Jesus Christ*, p. 10) and is a sequence of meditations on the life of Christ designed to enhance devotion. Its primary appeal is to faith, and it works by recreating scenes from Christ's life with an intensity designed to stimulate affective piety. Love suppresses theological material that he considers inappropriate to a lay readership and adds anti-Lollard material, which is highlighted by marginal reference to the fact that the passage in question is written '*contra lollardos*' (against the Lollards). Broadly, however, the strategy is to substitute meditation for disputation and to deflect attention away from social issues and political action by directing the Christian's view inwards.

Love, prior of Mount Grace Charterhouse in Yorkshire, presented the book to Archbishop Arundel around 1410 for his approval in accordance with Arundel's Lambeth Constitutions of 1409, and a 'Memorandum' citing Arundel's approval circulated with some copies of the manuscript. According to the memorandum (written in Latin, naturally, to assert its authoritativeness), the Archbishop 'commended and approved it personally, and further decreed and commanded by his metropolitan authority that it rather be published universally for the edification of the faithful and the confutation of heretics or lollards'.[28]

SPEAKING THE TRUTH

As lay education and vernacular devotion expanded alongside, and partly as a consequence of, the Lollard movement, churchmen became increasingly defensive of their position as 'keepers of the word' (Beckwith, 'Problems of Authority in Late Medieval English Mysticism', p. 185). Just as the Lollards' insistence on English was a conscious attempt to reach and empower a wider and less educated audience, so was the church's insistence on Latin a conscious exclusion of that sector of audience. Translation into English continued to go on, some of it with the church's blessing, but anxiety is often visible. Again, a comparison between two writers of the late fourteenth and early fifteenth centuries illustrates the point. Langland's *Piers Plowman*, versions of which both precede and postdate the rise of the Lollards, moves freely between Latin and English in a way that suggests a clear sense of direction. Reverence for the sacraments, the liturgy and the sacred text of scripture combines easily with the need to expand, develop, and above all teach, in English.[29] The Latin is sometimes translated, sometimes not, depending on the context. A point of lyrical climax, such as the description of the Annunciation, weaves untranslated scriptural Latin easily into the texture of the vernacular. It culminates in a longer Latin citation so familiar to most of Langland's readers from their experience of hearing it in church that it invokes an authority already in place:

> And thanne spak *spiritus sanctus* in Gabrielis mouthe
> To a maide that highte Marie, a meke thyng withalle,
> That oon Jesus, a Justices sone, moste Jouke in hir chambre
> Til *plenitudo temporis* [tyme] comen were
> That Piers fruyt floured and felle to be rype ...
> *Ecce ancilla Domini, fiat michi [secundum verbum tuum].*   (xvi.90–4, 99)[30]

The presence of Latin here is not designed to exclude the non-Latinate reader, but rather to root Langland's work openly in the authority of Holy Church, who is also the first figure of authority to appear to the Dreamer. There is no sense of struggle between the Latin and English in this passage, even though the Latin remains untranslated, but rather a flow between two ways of addressing the reader, one of which invokes the word as incarnate truth, the other of which reaches towards the idea of truth via reason and understanding. The two modes of expression are complementary, not conflicting.

This is not to say, however, that Langland is unaware of the problems of addressing two audiences, the 'lered' and the 'lewed' (learned and unlearned). Other passages make the potential functioning of Latin as a barrier explicit. When Haukyn asks Patience what poverty is, and Patience replies with five lines of Latin, Haukyn is the mouthpiece for a very direct response: ' "I kan noght construe," quod haukyn; "ye moste kenne me this on englissh" ' (xiv.277). This creates the opportunity for a very full exposition of the five lines of Latin over the next forty lines or so, and is clearly a way of motivating some straightforward education of the laity within the context of the poem.

Langland's attitude to Latin has to be seen in the wider context of his attitude to 'clergy', with its two meanings of learning and clerical status. His attitude is complex, including on the one hand a recognition that the ploughman may be saved more easily than the learned cleric, and on the other, a recognition that books, and in particular the bible, are the best guide we have to salvation.[31] A brief extract will illustrate some of the paradoxes:

> 'For oon Piers the Plowman hath impugned us alle,
> And set alle sciences at a sop save love one;
> And no text ne taketh to mayntene his cause
> But *Dilige Deum* and *Domine quis habitabit*;
> And [demeth] that dowel and dobet arn two Infinites,
> Whiche Infinites with a feith fynden out dobest,
> Which shal save mannes soule; thus seith Piers the Plowman.'
> (Conscience speaking at xiii.124–30)

The stated meaning of what is said throws learning ('all sciences') to the winds and sets up love in its place as the supreme value by which men are to be judged; yet Piers Plowman himself nevertheless cites biblical texts in Latin, as he must, to give authority to this commandment, and the poem not only does not translate them at this point, but cites them in abbreviated form, so that the second text in particular ('Lord, who shall dwell [in thy tabernacle]', Psalms 14.1) needs knowledge of the whole text as well as recognition of the Latin for its meaning to be supplied. Similarly, the next few lines, though their sense again exalts simplicity over subtlety in stating that good works are the way to salvation, give expression to that sense with a linguistic subtlety that belies the apparently simple message.

'Infinites' is a word that offers up its full range of meaning only to a
Latinate audience. As well as carrying its present meaning of 'never-
ending', it also plays on the meaning we now express by the word
'infinitive', a meaning available by definition only to those who have
studied grammar, and who recognise the grammatical status of
'dowel' as that of an infinitive (though it can of course also be a
command form) at the same time as understanding its spiritual
status to be infinite in its extent. Even as the text seems to say one
thing its mode of expression says another. Yet, taken as a whole, the
ease with which the poem both moves between English and Latin
and directly addresses its own choice of language speaks of an age
which has not yet developed a fully politicised antagonism between
the two.

   John Lydgate, a monk who chose to translate the *Pilgrimage of the
Life of Man* from French into English in 1426, is much less comfor-
table with the relative status of English and Latin. Despite the fact
that his choice of language suggests a wish to communicate the
teachings of the church to the non-Latinate public, he deliberately
uses Latin to exclude his lay audience on occasion, and labours the
exclusion. He prefaces a Latin poem on the creed, for example,
incorporated into the longer poem, with the explanation that it is
presented

> In latyn only, off entent
> To yive to the entendement,
> And to clerkys that can lettrure,
> And understonde hem in Scrypture,
> That they may, both hih and lowe,
> The maner off thy Skryppe knowe,
> To folwe the ffeyth of crystys secte;
> To hem thys latyn I dyrecte.   (lines 7029–36)

Langland sometimes uses Latin for purposes of exclusion (see, for
example, his mocking of the friars at XIII.70–2), but his most
characteristic use of Latin offers it to laymen as the sacrament is
offered, to be taken on faith rather than subjected to reason. For
Lydgate the divide between laymen and Latin is starker and more
patronising.

   The dismissal of the uneducated populace as incapable of understanding the mysteries of theology surfaces again in the poem, in
English, when a character first labelled simply as the 'Cherl', or
the 'Vyleyn', and subsequently identified as 'Rude Entendement'

(Ignorant Understanding), offers a challenge to Reason. Reason mocks the unlearned peasant by pretending to praise his subtlety in argument, and then explaining condescendingly that

> the gospel
> Ys mor plesynge to the siht –
> To folk that understonde a-ryht –
> Than to swych, wych in ther thouht
> Understonde ther-off ryht nouht.   (lines 10872–6)

The *Judgement* play in the Chester cycle similarly excludes the lay audience at one point: it has the devil quote in Latin the text which states that the saved will be separated from the damned, and explicitly draws attention to the fact that the use of Latin restricts the direction of those words 'to clearkes here present' (*The Chester Mystery Cycle*, 24, line 579).[32]

This insistence on Latin as the language reserved for God's highest mysteries pushed the late medieval church into an irrational position with regard to lay claims to mystic communion with God or the saints. It simply did not seem possible within this framework of thinking about language that God could speak directly to ordinary men and women in the vernacular. As Margaret Aston puts it: 'How could Christ himself have dictated to St. Bridget the rule of the Order of St. Saviour to be followed at Vadstena? Since it was in *Swedish* was this not inherently improbable? Was it not suspicious that when St. Catherine and St. Margaret spoke to Joan of Arc the words they used were *French*?' (*Lollards and Reformers*, p. 132). It is no mere coincidence that this inflexible position towards the vernacular was most hostile to women, who were least likely to have any knowledge of Latin. The divine insistence in St Bridget's *Revelations* that she should learn Latin was one which might in practice authorise her claim to inspiration in the eyes of the sceptical male elite at the centre of the medieval church.

Breaking down this boundary between clerical access to God and lay exclusion from his mysteries, expressed in the linguistic boundary between Latinity and non-Latinity, was difficult. The only route, as the cases of St Bridget and St Joan demonstrate, was via direct authorisation from God. Only the miracle of divine intervention could challenge the institutional authority of the church on earth, and earthly representatives of that authority had to take evidence of such intervention very seriously indeed. St Thomas Aquinas and St

Bonaventure, for example, though both finally rejected female ordination, recognised as strong arguments in favour of women the fact that they had been prophets, and that prophecy is higher than priesthood (Bynum, *Jesus as Mother*, p. 251, n.292).

The Book of Margery Kempe, a fifteenth-century Englishwoman's account of her life and visions, and one very much influenced by the example of St Bridget, has recourse to linguistic miracles on more than one occasion as a way of proving God's authorisation of Kempe's speech. When, on pilgrimage in Rome, Kempe and some English companions find themselves in the company of a German priest who understands no English, she decides, 'in party to comfort hym and in party er ellys meche mor to prevyn the werk of God' (partly to make him feel better and partly, or much more so, to demonstrate the work of God) to tell the assembled company a story from the bible in English: 'Than thei askyd hir confessowr yf he undirstod that sche had seyd, and he a-non in Latyn telde hem the same wordys that sche seyd be-forn in Englisch, for he cowde neyther speke Englysch ne undirstondyn Englisch save only aftyr hir tunge' (*The Book of Margery Kempe*, pp. 97–8). Not only does Kempe's English, through divine grace, become miraculously comprehensible to the German priest, but his retelling confers upon it 'an honorary Latinity'.[33] Similarly Kempe herself, although presented as illiterate even in English, has no trouble glossing a biblical text cited in Latin when invited to do so (*The Book of Margery Kempe*, p. 121). This could be read as another miracle, and one paralleled in the lives of other holy women: St Catherine of Siena, for example, could neither speak Latin nor read her letters, but was given divine power to read in any language after praying for help to read liturgical texts (Raymond of Capua, *The Life of St Catherine of Siena*, pp. 96–7); Lutgard of Aywières, too, was given miraculous power to understand the Latin scriptures, but had to have Latin translated to her under normal circumstances (Bolton, '*Vitae Matrum*', p. 269); and St Umiltà, who dictated her sermons in Latin, also claimed to have gained her powers of literacy miraculously (Petroff, *Medieval Women's Visionary Literature*. p. 235).

Alternatively, we might be encountering in *The Book of Margery Kempe* the simple literary convention of using Latin to cite the bible. The language of medieval written texts has functions which override mere naturalism; recording speech precisely as it occurred is not usually one of its intentions. Records of court proceedings, for example, employ French or Latin as conventional and appropriate to both the readership and the status of the record. The fact that they convey direct speech in the language of record does not mean that ordinary people actually spoke in these languages when they were in court. Similarly, the citation of scripture in Latin within direct speech in *The Book of Margery Kempe* need not suggest that Latin was the language of actual speech, though it may have been. The point is that whatever the language of the actual exchange between Kempe and the cleric, and whatever the language in which Kempe dictated the citation to the scribe, neither of these is as likely to explain the scribe's recording of the citation in Latin as the fact that Latin was the conventional language for written citation of the bible. Given that Kempe was tried for heresy on more than one occasion, it was even more important that the scribe should record such unorthodox exchanges in a language that spoke to the church authorities of orthodoxy. The choice of Latin over English in theological matters is, as we have seen, a political choice in the fifteenth century. The scribe's choice of it here, in documenting a laywoman's glossing of a biblical text, an event that positively invites a charge of heresy,[34] is comparable to St Bridget's attempt to learn Latin, and to the regular translation of holy women's revelations into Latin by their male confessors: all choose a mode of address that targets a reading community united by its shared understanding of Latinity as a guarantee of seriousness and authenticity (see further Lochrie, *Margery Kempe and Translations of the Flesh*, p. 120).[35]

The reason why the struggle between Latin and vernacular language was so bitter is of course that language was the vehicle for far deeper struggles: national, theological and political. The beginning of the fifteenth century in England represents a point in time when language was becoming highly self-conscious concerning the ideologies it encoded, and it was not by chance that so much linguistic confrontation took place within ideologically dominant institutions: parliament, the church, the royal court, the universities, the civil and ecclesiastical courts. 'Every place is a different language', and no language succeeds in taking control over a new place without a fight. The phrase is Susan Sontag's, as quoted by Peter Stallybrass and Allon White, who go on to argue that 'in large part, the history of political struggle has been the history of the attempts made to control significant sites of assembly and spaces of discourse' (*The Politics and Poetics of Transgression*, p. 80).

The medieval struggle between English and Latin was no less than a struggle between opposing claims to truth, and the participants recognised that an attempt to outlaw a given language from a particular arena of discourse was in fact an attempt to outlaw its users' claim to have any access to truth. Wyclifite writings repeatedly appeal to a notion of 'truth' as transcending language:

the trouthe of God stondith not in oo [one] langage more than in another ... therfore the lawe of God writen and taught in Englisch may edifie the commen pepel, as it doith clerkis in Latyn, sithen it is the sustynance to soulis that schulden be saved ... (Hudson, *Selections from English Wycliffite Writings*, p. 107)

Sythen witte stondis not in langage but in groundynge of treuthe, for tho same witte is in Laten that is in Grew [Greek] or Ebrew, and trouthe schuld be openly knowen to alle manere of folke, trowthe moueth mony men to speke sentencis in Yngelysche that thai han gedirid [gathered] in Latyne, and herfore bene men holden heretikis. (Hudson, *Selections from English Wycliffite Writings*, p. 127)

Yet even their appeal to an ideal of transcendent truth is framed in English and hence necessarily takes up a position in the linguistic debate rather than transcends it.

The position that defends English against Latin is in this period also one that defends plain language against elaboration and rejects a sacramental view of language in favour of an emphasis on sense. 'Language, like life, was to be a pilgrimage. Ornate and elaborate images that transfixed the mind were to be put aside' (Kendall, *The Drama of Dissent*, p. 41). Latin, it must be remembered, was the language of the classics as well as the language of the canonical translation of the scriptures, and as such was open to charges of pagan elaboration. Although Augustine had licensed Christians to embellish their teaching with this Egyptian gold, the very letters of the Latin alphabet carried potential dangers. Even in Elizabethan times schoolboys learned their letters from hornbooks which prefixed the Roman letters with the counter spell of the cross (Holloway, 'Crosses and Boxes', p. 62). The problem goes back to the Fall and to the ancient rhetorical dispute between *res* (subject matter, truth) and *verba* (language). Augustine, as we have seen, distrusted the slipperiness of the verbal sign. Though apparently prepared to tolerate rhetorical ornamentation, he elsewhere suggests that action (as in saints' lives) communicates God's truth better than any form of words, and it is this way of thinking about language that informs later Christian tradition (Heffernan, *Sacred Biography*, pp. 4–5).

For the Lollards, this learned tradition, familiar to highly educated clerics, combined with a natural resistance to incomprehensible language on the part of the illiterate or semi-literate to produce a rejection of any kind of language which seemed to behave other than transparently. The obscurity of Latin, according to Lollard polemic, can have no supra-rational function: it is no better for laymen to say '*pater noster qui es in celis*' than to say 'bibull babull' (Hudson, *The Premature Reformation*, p. 31). Interestingly, the phrase 'bibble babble' may well have carried overtones of both 'bible' and 'Babel' for the writer or his audience (or both). The OED, while not deriving the phrase from either, notes the possible influence of 'Babel' on its development, and the context here would certainly suggest it.[36] A poem written *against* the Lollards adds weight to this possibility, in making the charge that it is unnatural for a knight, who should be guarding a king's castle, 'To bable the bibel day and night' (Robbins, *Historical Poems*, p. 153). Similarly, Hoccleve's poem against Sir John Oldcastle, leader of the Lollard rising in 1414, represents the translation of the bible as reproducing the conditions of Babel (though he nowhere uses the word), with ignorant women 'cackling' and disputing, and laymen asking 'Why stant this word heere? and why this word there?' ('The Remonstrance Against Oldcastle', line 156). Babel and the bible, then, were deeply interconnected. The bible had represented Babel as the condition to which a presumptive people were reduced; the conditions of Babel were now an intrinsic part of earthly language, conditions from which only the bible was excepted; and presumptiveness towards the sacred Word could intensify the condition of Babel. But the role of the bible within the world fallen into the condition of Babel was differently perceived by the orthodox church and its Lollard opponents. Bibble babble reduced the bible to the condition of Babel, but exactly how was a focus for opposition. Readers of the bible could be accused, depending on the beliefs of the accuser, of reducing it to Babel/ babble either by parroting it in incomprehensible Latin or by paying an inordinate and inappropriate amount of attention to it in English.

The further association of the issue of bible translation with questions of class (see e.g. Knighton and Trevisa, pp. 12–14 above) made it virtually inevitable that the Babel topos would also become linked with a class polemic, and Hoccleve's specification of those unworthy to 'medle' with doctrine as either working men ('a baillif or reeve/ Or man of craft') or illiterate whores ('Lewed calates') offers proof of this link ('The Remonstrance Against Oldcastle', lines 143–4, 147). Babel, seen from the top of the social hierarchy, expresses the fear of ungoverned speaking. From the perspective of the lower ranks, however, it looks like the exclusive code of a privileged elite. Hence the development of a Lollard rhetoric tying the conviction that truth is best expressed by plain language to an insistence that truth and plain language are both the province of plain men. Lollard texts use the terms 'poor men' and 'true men' more or less interchangeably to describe Lollard believers (see Hudson, *Lollards and their Books*, pp. 165–80 and Hudson, *Selections from English Wycliffite Writings*, p. 181, n.17), and both Knighton and Walsingham note the Lollard tendency to dress in russet clothes (Hudson, *The Premature Reformation*, p. 145). Russet clothes, however, while they may have signalled the actual labouring status of many Lollards, were also expressive of a consciously adopted political strategy which highlighted plain language, plain clothes and plain living as truth effects.[37] 'Poor men', in the Lollard view, are the true images of Christ. The visible image of evangelical poverty is to be read as the guarantee of the truth of their words. 'The apostlis of Crist and othir seintis', they point out, 'weren not graduat men in scolis, but the Holi Goost sodenli enspirid hem, and maden hem plenteuous of hevenli loore'; 'God bothe can and may ... speede symple men out of [outside] the universitee, as myche to kunne hooly writ as maistris in the universitee' (Hudson, *The Premature Reformation*, p. 174).

Langland's *Piers Plowman*, although begun before Wyclif's battles with the established church and not itself a Lollard text, provided a model for the prominence of the ploughman in so many Lollard writings.[38] Stephen Barney ('The Plowshare of the Tongue') shows that the association of preaching with ploughing or general agricultural activity goes back to St Paul and is particularly prominent in Gregory's *Moralia in Job*. For an educated cleric, he argues, the ploughman as preacher would have been a familiar image. Yet Langland does more than take up biblical allegory, and this is where his influence on the Lollards and those without traditional clerical education is so important. His ploughman is to be read literally as well as allegorically; he stands for honest labour as well as preaching. As Elizabeth Kirk ('Langland's Plowman') demonstrates, the ploughman was not before Langland's poem a traditional figure of virtuous labour. Despite the bible's use of agricultural imagery, its narrative tells a different story. The punishment for Adam's sin was that the ground became cursed, demanding labour to make it fruitful, while the opposition between Cain, a tiller of the soil, and Abel, a keeper of sheep, seemed to confirm the link between agricultural labour and sinfulness. It is Langland's work, itself made possible by the context of changing attitudes to manual labour (shaped by the ideals of the Cistercian and Franciscan orders), that links the figure of the ploughman to a clerical tradition of '*sancta rusticitas*', holy rusticity, traceable to the letters of St Jerome (Kirk, 'Langland's Plowman', p. 16). Piers, in Langland's text, serves Truth (God) and attacks churchmen for their failure to serve him properly. His simple life stands as a corrective to their corrupt values, and his holy rusticity is contrasted with their 'sinful eloquence' (Jerome's phrase). As Kirk points out, holy rusticity and sinful eloquence are both, in Jerome's view, failings by contrast with *docta iusticia*, 'learned righteousness', though holy rusticity is preferable to sinful eloquence ('Langland's Plowman', p. 16). But Piers Plowman is not presented in Langland's poem as limited to his rustic nature. His simplicity is combined with learning and inspiration, and he is a figure for Christ as well as for the virtuous labourer.

The complexity of Langland's Piers, however, could not survive popularisation, and the poem was quickly appropriated by both rebels and Lollards. As early as 1381 it is clear from John Ball's famous letter that at least some readers were expected to hear the name of Piers Plowman as a call to rebellion.[39] The Dieulacres Abbey Chronicle goes so far as to list 'Per Plowman' as one of the leaders of the revolt (Hudson, *The Premature Reformation*, p. 399). For Lollards too the ploughman becomes a figure of polemic, and his virtue is expounded without recourse to any superior ideal of learned righteousness. Indeed it is his very unlearnedness which now defines his virtue. He is represented as 'naturally' righteous, entitled to hope for direct, unmediated access to God, uneducated as he is. As the writer of *The Praier and Complaynte of the Ploweman* puts it: 'We lewede men han a belefe . . . oure hope ys that thou wilt as sone yhere a plowmans prayer, and he kepe thyne hestes, as thou wilt do a mans of religion' (Hudson, *The Premature Reformation*, p. 388). At the same time, however, the Lollards wanted the man of religion's books translated into English, and were committed to educating and thereby empowering the simple 'poor man'. 'No man', according to the Lollard *Opus Evangelicum*, is 'so rude a scholar but that he may learn the words of the gospel according to his simplicity' (Lambert, *Medieval Heresy*, p. 239). The ploughman is therefore also used to legitimate the appeal for texts in English as necessary for the salvation of simple men. This is the kind of ploughman who speaks in *Pierce the Ploughmans Crede* of his need for an English version of the Creed:

> A and all myn A.b.c. after have y lerned,
> And [patred] in my *pater-noster* iche poynt after other,
> And after all, myn *Ave-Marie* almost to the ende;
> But all my kare is to comen for y can nohght my Crede (lines 5–8)

English is claimed as the natural entitlement of the plain man, by contrast with the sinfully eloquent Latin which simultaneously excludes him and speaks the pride of those who utter it.

What the ploughman claims as his right is access to God's truth, but what the conflict between English and Latin demonstrates is the Augustinian recognition that there is a gap between words and truth, and that some words may express truth while others obscure, distort or devalue it. 'Language, no longer conceived as a sacrosanct and solitary embodiment of meaning and truth, becomes merely one of many possible ways to hypothesize meaning' (Bakhtin, *The Dialogic Imagination*, p. 370). The gap between an idea of truth and its expression in language opens up a space for negotiation, a space within which different speakers of different languages struggle for priority. It is to the staging of that space that the next chapter turns.

CHAPTER 2

Staging truth

Medieval dramatic tradition used to be conceived within a linear model. Scholars thought in terms of origins and evolution, of a learned, Latin liturgical drama staged inside the church slowly developing into a popular, vernacular religious drama staged in the open air. More recent work has shown that the two kinds of drama and the two modes of staging existed side by side, and intruded into one another's space. There is evidence from as early as the twelfth century of Latin liturgical plays within the church coexisting with both Latin and vernacular plays outside it (Tydeman, *The Theatre in the Middle Ages*, p. 124), and the evidence may well postdate actual conditions. Latin and vernacular plays are not two ends of a spectrum but two sides of a coin, two practices in dialogue with each other, each defined against the known and felt existence of the other. It is not uncommon for either mode to make space for explicit reference to the other, so that its own discourse is perceived against that other possible discourse. Latin playtexts may introduce vernacular speech, while vernacular plays often incorporate sung or spoken Latin. Many plays, such as the N-Town *Mary Play*, the Anglo-Norman *Jeu d'Adam* or the Shrewsbury Fragments, are more truly macaronic than Latin or vernacular. In fact, the evidence of playtexts suggests that a binary division between 'two kinds of drama' is inappropriate. It is perhaps more helpful to think of plays as having access to a plurality of languages and then to explore how particular plays manipulate the boundary between different languages within what we know of their potential audiences.

The simplistic binarism of learned/Latin versus popular/vernacular also produces simplistic notions concerning performers and audience, which do not allow for the wide range of performance contexts we now know to have been available for late medieval and early Tudor drama. No longer is it feasible to line up the authors, actors and audiences for these plays as learned clergy on the one hand and illiterate 'folk' on the other. External evidence as well as the playtexts themselves refute this polarity. Recent work attempting to establish specific conditions of production for individual mystery cycles contests the old notion of all cycle drama as 'popular'.[1] As Gail Gibson argues in proposing monastic auspices for the N-Town cycle, 'we will be misled if we expect the N-Town cycle to look like the civic cycle staged at York' (*The Theater of Devotion*, p. 127; cf. Stevens, *Four Middle English Mystery Cycles*; Meredith, 'Scribes, Texts and Performance'). Gibson suggests the great abbey at Bury as the likely sponsor of the N-Town cycle, a suggestion which invites us to unfix any notion of clerical involvement in drama as restricted to Latin liturgical plays or of cycle drama as exclusively civic. It simultaneously invites us to shed any either/or notions of audience: though East Anglian monks may have been active in the writing and production of the N-Town cycle, it is scarcely possible to imagine that they staged so large an enterprise in the form of closet-drama amongst themselves.[2] The likely setting is a major public event, bringing the religious and secular parts of the community together in a celebration of their interaction and interdependence. It is also worth remembering that John Bale, known in the Tudor period for his active involvement in writing and producing Protestant propagandist interludes, emerged out of a Carmelite monastery, and may well have developed his dramatic skills under Carmelite training (see chapter 4 below).[3]

The work of Richard Beadle and others on the records of East Anglian religious houses suggests that, at a much humbler level too, it is inappropriate to draw a line separating clergy from laity in respect of their relative dramatic activity. Mettingham College in Suffolk, for example, a community of secular canons, resident in Mettingham Castle from 1394, and responsible for the board and education of a small number of boys, was one kind of location where touring lay performers would have played to a mixed audience of clergy and laity (the canons, the boys and their household). The College's accounts from 1404 to 1527 show that the community paid quite regularly for various types of dramatic entertainments, often over Christmas, but also on other occasions (Beadle, 'Dramatic Records of Mettingham College').

Other records showing clergy and parish collaborating to finance dramatic performances suggest further contexts for mixed lay and clerical audiences (e.g. Chambers, *The Medieval Stage*, vol. ii, pp.

121–2). Thetford Priory, for example, made payments towards parish plays in Thetford and village plays round about, as well as to players visiting the monastery (Beadle, 'Plays and Playing at Thetford'), and the Great Dunmow Churchwardens' Book shows a cluster of rural communities regularly staging a play at Corpus Christi with contributions from the Priory as well as the villages (Wright, 'Community Theatre in Late Medieval East Anglia'). References to the origins of the players visiting Mettingham also indicate that plays and players might travel widely, at least within a given region. Those who performed at Mettingham, for example, came from Norwich, Beccles, South Elmham, Dunwich and Great Yarmouth (Beadle, 'Dramatic Records of Mettingham College', p.129). The same performers, then, and probably the same plays, played to a range of audiences, lay, clerical and mixed. Much of the interaction between English and Latin and between different registers of English in morality plays becomes much easier to grasp if we picture it aiming at this range of audiences. The Thetford records also suggest that collaboration between clergy and laity may have gone on not just in terms of financing and attending the plays, but also in terms of performance: several payments are phrased as being to the players '*cum auxilio* (or *cum adiutorio*) *conventus*' (with the help of the monastery) (Beadle, 'Plays and Playing at Thetford', p. 8).

The number of vernacular plays containing some stage directions in Latin suggests widespread clerical involvement in drama outside as well as inside the church,[4] and there is no reason to believe that open-air audiences would have been entirely non-clerical either. An English sermon of *c.*1250 announces a play performed for 'bothe this lewed and this clerkes' (Tydeman, *The Theatre in the Middle Ages*, p. 124)[5] in a natural way that seems to anticipate such mixed attendance as the norm. Just as the lay congregation would have heard the Latin liturgical drama performed inside the church, so many of the clergy must have attended vernacular drama outside, even far outside, the church.

Expectations constructed by the place of performance are crucial. Clerics attending outside performances knew that those plays would be predominantly in the vernacular in the same way as the laity attending the Easter mass expected to hear the dramatic elaborations on the *Quem quaeritis* trope performed in Latin.[6] Tydeman, however, cites the case of a performance of one of Terence's comedies in Latin before a mixed audience of clergy and laity at the episcopal palace in Metz in 1502 which provoked the non-clerical element of the audience to riot when they realised that they were not going to understand the play (*The Theatre in the Middle Ages*, p. 234). Latin was evidently not, in this particular location and on this particular occasion, what all of the audience was expecting. Yet those same rioters, if presented with a sudden attempt to surprise them with a vernacular version of the familiar Easter ritual in church, might well have been equally outraged.

Spectators might register hostility not only to language out of place, but to drama out of place. This is the thrust behind the Lollard *Tretise of Miraclis Pleyinge*. Despite the Lollard conviction of the need for an English bible, this Lollard writer clearly perceives dramatic presentation as an idolatrous way of bringing scripture to the people, a method comparable with the tradition of visual imagery in established churches, and to be linked with Catholic forms of worship. The distinction to be made here is not between the truth-claims of different languages, but between the status of religious truth and dramatic fiction. Dramatising scriptural events is seen as inherently blasphemous:

> whanne we pleyin his myraclis as men don nowe on dayes, God takith more venjaunce on us than a lord, that sodaynly sleeth his servaunt for he pleyide to homely with hym. And, right as that lord thanne in dede seith to his servaunt, 'Pley not with me but pley with thi pere', so whanne we takun in pley and in bourde [jest] the myraclis of God, he, fro us takynge his grace, seith more ernestfully to us than the forseid lord, 'Pley not with me but pley with thi pere'. (Hudson, *Selections from English Wycliffite Writings*, p. 98)

All representation is a form of play; and play is here deemed unacceptable by definition in the arena of sacred truth. This attitude, though not evidently very widely shared even among fifteenth-century Lollards,[7] clearly anticipates the formation of later Puritan responses to the theatre. Theatre itself becomes potentially linked with Catholicism by virtue of its image-making. From a Lollard or Protestant point of view, the very act of theatrical representation stages the gap between itself and the truth it betrays by virtue of its status as mere *re*presentation.

COMPARING MYSTERY CYCLES: N-TOWN

In order to explore relations between drama, language and religious belief, we may compare two cycles, N-Town and Towneley. N-Town, as noted above, has been linked with various East Anglian locations, and in particular with monastic auspices, whereas Towneley, usually linked with Wakefield, has been designated both Lollard and counter-Lollard by different critics. A comparison between these two cycles, focusing on their treatment of language, offers a useful way of looking at relations between English and Latin in this particular type of drama. I will not be concerned here to establish any kind of chronological argument, since there is no evidence that the mystery cycles, all extant in late fifteenth- or early sixteenth-century manuscripts, are to be identified with the performed texts of fourteenth-century Corpus Christi plays, and they continued to be performed well into the reign of Elizabeth I.

The N-Town cycle opens with the creation of heaven, as do the other three extant cycles, and a line of Latin, quoting God's words from Revelations 1.8 and 22.13: *Ego sum alpha et oo, principium et finis* (I am Alpha and Omega, the beginning and the ending). In the manuscript, the speech heading for God (whose words follow) is adjacent to the Latin line, but the most recent editor of the cycle prints the line *above* the speech heading for God, leaving it free of any attribution.[8] While the editor does not supply any note for his practice here, he may be suggesting either a reading of this line that edits it out of performance or a performance that segregates it in some way from the following monologue. Certainly it is visually segregated in the manuscript by being underlined in red and written on a separate line from the first stanza, which is then introduced with a large red capital. Nor is it part of the verse-form of the stanza.

Inferring anything about performance from the layout of the manuscript is a highly dubious activity, since none of the full cycle manuscripts seems to have been at all closely connected with performance (see further Meredith, 'Scribes, Texts and Perform-ance'). Nevertheless, it is important to compare this practice with that of the other cycle manuscripts, all of which open with this same line. In the York manuscript the line is even more set apart visually from the following text than in N-Town: it is indented, in a larger, more elegant, script, with occasional decorated letters. The Chester manuscripts vary, but in every case the line is set apart from the following text in some way. The existence of a number of manu-scripts for this cycle, some beginning with the Drapers' pageant and some with the Tanners', allows the further inference that the line is not perceived as strongly attached to a particular pageant or stanza, but rather to the opening of the cycle. (I postpone comparison with Wakefield to the fuller discussion of that cycle below.) The written texts, then, recognise, in varying degrees, the special status of the opening line.

Martin Stevens argues that these Latin openings celebrate 'beginnings that have to do with the creative act rather than the content of the work' (*Four Middle English Mystery Cycles*, p. 106). But while it is true that both the placing and the highlighting of the Latin here mark its 'writtenness', it is not true that that writtenness is unrelated to the content of the work. On the contrary, the fact that the line is spoken in the authoritative language of the Vulgate Bible combines with its placing at the opening of the creation play, its translated meaning and its biblical origin and context (the Last Judgement) to confirm its positioning before and 'above' everything else. This position is no mere scribal matter, related only to the act of beginning to write, but a doctrinal truth embracing the entire content of the cycle. Its status is that of a discourse above and beyond the vernacular material of the cycle and its images of lived human experience, but without which those images cannot be properly understood.

Yet its centrality to the content of the cycles still does not tell us whether it was performed. The highlighting of the phrase in the N-Town manuscript may suggest a number of possibilities: it may have been understood as too sacred to be performed; it may have been presented as written text in performance (as an open bible? or a banner raised in or framing the performance space?); or it may have been performed. If it was performed, the marking of it in the written text may indicate a difference in the nature of its performance from that of subsequent vernacular speech. The frequent insertion of sung Latin at climactic moments in this cycle may suggest that it was chanted or sung, perhaps by a voice or voices other than that of the performer who then speaks the lines of God. Catherine Dunn's discussion of the performance of English and Latin in the Wakefield *Play of the Prophets* ('The Literary Style of the Towneley Plays', esp. pp. 487–96) is potentially illuminating for N-Town, which has a much more extended interplay between English and Latin than Wakefield. Latin, she notes, 'has a long tradition of heightened and sonorous rhetoric behind it', while English has a relatively low literary status. What she calls 'a difference in elevation' is discernible in the interplay between the two.[9] Her view is that the Latin would most probably have been chanted, 'as it had been chanted for centuries in the liturgical Matins *lectio* and in the Latin prophet plays'. A difference in the pitch of delivery of the two languages would, as she further comments, 'have sharpened the difference in style levels' (p. 489).

Dunn's discussion of delivery here is part of a wider discussion of what she calls, adapting Marius Sepet, 'the voice of the Church', which she considers to be 'the basic voice' in any mystery cycle (p. 483).[10] The phrase, 'voice of the Church', is problematic to a certain extent, since it implies absolute coherence within the church, something that the comparison of N-Town and Wakefield in this chapter seeks to break down, yet the concept of an authoritative voice overarching and framing the voices of individual characters is a useful one. For Dunn, this voice is not confined to Latin, although, as she points out, Sepet 'discovered it in the Latin choral speeches intruding upon the vernacular dialogue of Adam, Eve, and the serpent' in the *Jeu d'Adam* (p. 483). It is, she argues, identical with the voice of the Expositor in most cycles, but in the Wakefield cycle, which has no such character, it can be taken on temporarily by numerous characters. This argument is misleading to a certain extent, since even cycles which have expositors allow other characters (God is an obviously necessary one) to speak in this voice (see below). And although the voice of the church, as Dunn defines it, is not a purely Latin one, it is heavily influenced by Latin and looks back towards Latin as its legitimating source.

Dunn's comments on the voice of the church help to illuminate the function of Latin, which conveys, more fully than the vernacular voice of the expositor, I would argue, the qualities that Dunn identifies for the latter: collective wisdom, philosophical awareness and 'a detachment from the immediate dramatic event, that serves to distance the turmoil or conflict or even comic action and envelop these things in a luminous veil' (p. 483). The veil of Latin, to borrow Dunn's metaphor, is quite simply more intensely luminous than that of the expository voice. The expository voice may participate in the brighter light of God's presence, but Latin directly represents it.

The character of God, when he appears speaking English, is made in a different image from the voice of God that speaks, sings or perhaps only silently 'utters' the Latin line that opens the cycle. The importance of the line lies in its capacity to remind the reader, and perhaps the audience, before the English-speaking God begins his

utterance, that the true God is greater and more mysterious than he
is made to appear in the image of a man speaking English. He is also
the voice of the bible, the unseen presence, the framing authority
behind all human experience, even when he is not made visible. The
Latin opening, then, crucially produces the audience's sense of itself
as humble and enclosed, as human beings living out lives that are
given true shape and meaning only with reference to the scheme of
salvation that will judge them. The precedence of Latin over English
gives precedence to God over man, to the moral universe over life
on earth, to the enormity and authority of biblical discourse over the
mere contingency of vernacular experience.

This pattern of precedence is one often re-enacted in the cycle.
Frequently, when the speaker is God or a figure of virtue, the first
line of a stanza, sometimes the first line of a play, is spoken in Latin
before the discourse moves into English. The Latin usually quotes
the bible and is often composed of phrases that would be familiar to
the audience from the liturgy. It normally occurs at climactic points
in the drama, ends as well as beginnings, and especially sacred
moments for the Christian faith. These are often moments that
portray the intersection of divine and earthly worlds, God directly
intervening or speaking through his prophets or incarnate in his Son
on earth (the saved offering thanks to God after the flood (4: line
253), Isaiah's prophecy of the birth of Christ (7: lines 9–10, 17–18),
Christ's words on the cross (32: lines 214, 221), his command to
Satan to open the gates of Hell (33: line 24) and so on). Latin
mediates the double function of this drama, its status as both
representation and ritual enactment. Scriptural citation both represents biblical incidents truthfully and invites audiences to participate
more directly in the higher truth such incidents purvey through the
heightened intensity of the Latin words. The Latin simultaneously
brings the truth of the Word nearer to the audience while main-
taining its sacred distance from their everyday lives. Its strangeness
allows audiences a sensuous and intense engagement with speech as
truth, but one which bypasses the need to make meanings for each
word.

Latin often has an explicitly didactic function, as well as this
double dramatic function. Quotation of significant Latin phrases
from Christian worship, followed by English translation and explanation, offers to teach the laity the elements of the faith and to
familiarise them with the significance of certain parts of the liturgy.

It is a method long familiar from non-dramatic texts, and the influence of Love's *Mirror*, for example (p. 19 above), on the N-Town cycle is well-established. The ten commandments (6) are given one at a time, first in Latin, followed by one or two stanzas of English which make the meaning quite clear by saying the same thing at more length. Similarly, the *Magnificat* is recited and explained in a section of dialogue between Mary and Elizabeth, where Mary has the first two lines of each stanza to recite the Latin of the psalm, while Elizabeth responds with two lines of English, rhyming with Mary's Latin and translating it (13). The familiar prayer, *Ave Maria*, is not only rooted in its sacred moment of origin (11: line 216), but translated and then explained in English by Gabriel in the lines following. It is then picked up again at the end of a later play by Contemplacio, whose function is that of expositor, and who takes the Latin step by step, explaining how the familiar *Ave Maria* emerged out of a combination of scripture and the church:

> Lystenyth, sovereynys, here is a conclusyon.
> How the Ave was mad here is lernyd us:
> The aungel seyd, '*Ave, gracia plena. Dominus tecum,*
> *Benedicta tu in mulieribus.*'
> Elyzabeth seyd, '*Et benedictus*
> *Fructus ventris tui.*' Thus the Chirch addyd '*Maria*' and '*Jesus*' her.
> Who seyth oure Ladyes Sawtere dayly for a yer thus,
> He hath pardon ten thowsand and eyte hundryd yer.
>
> (13: lines 150A-157A)

Contemplacio functions as an intermediary between the Latin world of the holy mysteries and the English everyday world of the audience. It is not surprising, then, to find him not only quoting and explaining Latin, but himself using a register that amalgamates the two languages. His speech is typically macaronic, since he consciously mediates between the Latin at the heart of the dramatic content and the non-Latinate lay members of the audience. His English must be plain enough to carry out its teaching project successfully, but also sprinkled with a Latinate English vocabulary ('conclusyon' above; cf., for example, his use of Latinate rhymes at 9: lines 294–310: 'presentacyon'/'ocupacyon', 'pacyens'/'prevydens', 'dissponsacyon'/'pawsacyon') that, like his Latin name, reassures the audience of his authority to speak, of his status at a remove from erring humanity.[11]

It is not only Contemplacio that speaks this Latinate English, but any figure whom the audience is required to recognise as removed from human frailty: God, Jesus, Mary, the prophets, patriarchs and saints. This highly artificial and intensely focused discourse allows their words to participate in the Word and underpins their English utterances with the authority of Latin, the fixed word out of time. It maintains the difference of these speakers, investing their speech with a sensuous aesthetic that emphasises sound over meaning, while at the same time making some concessions to the explanation of meaning that allow the audience to feel that their distance does not imply an uncaring remoteness. Their speech is tied into a reality that goes beyond the everyday world. They communicate a level of the real beyond what can (or should, in the church's terms) be made perceptible in a realist vernacular.[12]

The play of this drama across vernacular and heightened modes of speech is well seen in play 16, *The Adoration of the Shepherds*. Elizabeth Salter's work on the topos of the annunciation to the shepherds (*English and International*, pp. 272–92) concentrates on the way their representation in late medieval drama and manuscript illumination reveals a collision between a tradition arising out of exegetical texts and continuing into Latin liturgical drama and a new direction developed under the influence of Cistercian and Franciscan spirituality. Whereas the older tradition portrays the shepherds as types of the clergy, the developing tradition emphasises their humanity, which then comes into opposition with the 'learned strain' deriving from their typological history. The collision between these two modes is developed linguistically, so that the shepherds may be associated with vernacular speech even in the context of a non-vernacular work.[13] Hence, for example, the Holkham Bible Picture Book deviates briefly from its usual Anglo-Norman to make reference to the shepherds in English:

> Songen alle wid one stevene
> Also the angel song that cam fro hevene:
> *Te Deum et Gloria.*
>
> (Salter, *English and International*, p. 287)

Though the sacred song remains in Latin, the use of the vernacular to write about shepherds is a mark of the developing humanist tradition.

Salter comments on the serious tone of the N-Town shepherds' play, noting the familiarity of one shepherd with biblical material and traditional imagery for Christ and Mary (p. 276). But even in this play, a more strongly vernacular strain contests that learning. When '*Gloria in Excelsis Deo*' is sung, either off-stage or by angels, the first shepherd responds:

> Ey! Ey! This was a wondyr note
> That was now songyn above the sky.
> I have that voys ful wele I wote,
> Thei songe, 'Gle, glo, glory'. (16: lines 62–5)

This is a strange moment, since it consciously explores the sound of clerical Latin to an uneducated ear. The materiality of the sacred words is taken up and played upon in a sequence of sounds that mesh nonsense with the 'accidental' discovery of a truth ('gle, glo' with 'glory'). The second shepherd's reply to the first takes the materiality of the words closer to the edge of the grotesque:

> Nay, so moty the [as I hope to thrive], so was it nowth.
> I have that songe ful wele inum [understood].
> In my wyt weyl it is wrought,
> It was 'Gle, glo, glas, glum'. (lines 66–9)[14]

This comic mishearing of Latin momentarily highlights the gap between the uneducated shepherd and the sacred mystery to which he is witness; yet the gap itself becomes dramatically functional, illustrating God's purpose in allowing the Christ-child to be born in a stable and his glory to be made visible first to humble men. The divine purpose is then pointedly revealed by the response of the third shepherd. His miraculous understanding demonstrates the power of this moment to transform earthbound lives through the gift of the incarnate Christ:[15]

> The songe methought it was 'Glory'.
> And aftyrwarde he seyd us to,
> Ther is a chylde born xal be a prynce myghty.
> For to seke that chylde I rede we go. (lines 70–3)

Not only do the three shepherds immediately agree on this course of action, thus uniting them all in recognition of the divine mystery, but they then together sing a Latin song, '*Stella celi extirpavit*', as they go to seek Christ. This is a Pentecostal moment, a celebratory recognition of divine grace intervening in human affairs (see pp. 2, 23–4 above). The playful encounter between Latin sound and vernacular illiteracy intervenes between the two Latin songs in a way that gives intense presence to the return of Latin sound. If the '*Gloria*' song conveys the transcendent nature of the event, the 'Stella' song celebrates the revelation of sacred mystery to poor shepherds. The brief permission of laughter at the sound of the sacred Word is not mocking so much as shocking. It allows the shock of vernacular misunderstanding to frame the Latin momentarily, but it does not question the status of Latin as expressive of holy truth.

Elsewhere, however, this status is much more open to question. The play of *Christ and the Doctors* (21), for example, opens with the doctors speaking a macaronic and highly technical language which clearly mocks both the earthbound inadequacy of their learning and their absurd pride in it:

> PRIMUS DOCTOR. *Scripture sacre esse dinoscimur doctos,*
> We to bere the belle of all maner clergyse.
>
> SECUNDUS DOCTOR. *Velud rosa omnium florum flos.*
> Lyke onto us was nevyr clerke so wyse.
>
> PRIMUS DOCTOR. Loke what scyens ye kan devyse
> Of redynge, wrytynge, and trewe ortografye,
> Amongys all clerkys we bere the prysse
> Of gramer, cadens, and of prosodye.   (lines 1–8)

The highly technical vocabulary and the self-satisfied tone presumably combine with a specific manner of delivery to identify this discourse here as that of non-holy speakers. In context, Jesus' response is relatively plain, though still bound into the Latin/English form: '*Omnis sciencia a Domino Deo est:*/All wytt and wysdam, of God it is lent' (lines 33–4).[16]

The devil too knows how to mimic this holy discourse. Though he opens play 26 speaking a short four-line stanza that announces his own wickedness in relatively plain English, he moves into a longer stanza and more elaborate and Latinate vocabulary when he begins to speak of Christ (lines 25ff.). The rhymes are reminiscent of Contemplacio's and function as a warning to the audience to be on their guard. Satan is after all the great deceiver, and sin comes in many guises. His capacity to adopt the mask of holy discourse is a warning against hypocrites and a brief, if subversive, reminder that holy discourse is not inevitably linked with truth. Like any discourse, it is available for parody and masquerade as well as earnest use. Its meanings are as context-bound as any others.

WAKEFIELD

The Wakefield cycle displays a rather different dialectic between English and Latin. Language has been noted as an explicit theme in this cycle, but there is disagreement as to whether its particular linguistic bias should be identified as Lollard or counter-Lollard.[17] Clearly the uses of English and Latin in the cycle need to be examined to see whether either claim is supportable. The cycle opens, unlike any of the others, with a Latin prayer, written in a large and ornate script clearly differentiated from the script of God's first speech, which follows. On the other hand, the Latin words, '*Ego sum Alpha et O*', are not set apart from the opening speech, as they are in the N-Town manuscript, but clearly incorporated within it. Not only is the phrase visually undifferentiated from the surrounding text and written on the same line as what follows, but it also rhymes with the English phrase that follows and translates it: 'I am the first, the last also.' This visual presentation suggests, first, that the phrase is part of the performed text of the Wakefield cycle, and second, that it is not vocally differentiated from the vernacular text in performance.

The English speech of God that follows is less elevated than that of N-Town, which rhymes on words like 'plesawns'/'substawns', 'Trenyté'/'Powsté'/'magesté'. Though a couple of these words do appear in the course of the Wakefield God's speech, it is much more conspicuous for its strongly vernacular shading, as in its reference to 'The water to norish the fysh swymand;/The erth to norish bestys crepeand '(1: lines 55–6). Martin Stevens has argued for this strongly vernacular slant as specific to the plays of the Wakefield Master.[18] He claims that 'in all the Wakefield Author's plays God makes but one speech, in the *Noah* play, and it is straightforward and distinctly colloquial' ('Language as Theme in the Wakefield Plays', p. 101). This is not strictly true, since God also speaks to Cain with the same directness in the *Killing of Abel*. But the more important point to be made is that the directness of this voice in the plays of the Wakefield Master is not particularly innovative in the context of the rest of the cycle, where God commonly speaks in this plain manner.[19] Indeed, there is no Latinate register identifying holy speakers in the Wakefield cycle. If there is a register identifying such speakers it is plain speaking, free of the swearing, jangling harshness and 'vayn carpyng' (2: line 97; cf. Stevens, 'Language as Theme in the Wakefield Plays', p. 101) that characterise the speech of the rebels against God's law

(Cain, Pharaoh, Herod, Pilate, Christ's tormentors). The holy rarely use Latin or Latinate English in this cycle, and if they do, it is brief and almost homely, as when God offers to translate his Latin for Moses:

> I say the thus: *Ego sum qui sum* –
> 'I am he that is the same.'
> If thou can nother muf nor mom [If you cannot speak at all],
> I shall sheld the from shame. (8: lines 185–8)

A significant exception to this general linking of holy speakers with vernacular plainness in the Wakefield cycle occurs in the *Play of the Prophets*, which is, as discussed above, the subject of Catherine Dunn's study. This play is distinguished from any other play in the cycle by its allocation of extensive Latin lines to moments commanding high reverence. As in N-Town, these lines are often at the beginning of a speech, and in this case also separate from the stanza-form. It may be that the lack of narrative shaping this play, together with the influence of a long-established liturgical Prophets' play, combined to give it this rather different form. It is, furthermore, this play, rather than those of the Wakefield Master, that differs most significantly in terms of linguistic practice from the rest of the cycle. The sneering of the Doctors, for example, is expressed entirely in plain English, and the Annunciation too is presented in a relatively unembellished way. The *Annunciation* play opens with a plain speech from God that ends in the straightforward address to Gabriel: 'Grayth the, Gabriell, and weynd [Get ready, Gabriel, and go]' (10: line 76), which is immediately followed by Gabriel's wholly English rendering of the classic greeting to Mary, 'Hayll, Mary, gracyouse!' (line 77). This is then elaborated with some repetition and patterning, but no Latin. The *Magnificat*, which is given with such formal fullness in N-Town, is presented in Wakefield in a form which cites the opening line in Latin, *Magnificat anima mea dominum*, followed by a complete English translation, with no more Latin (11: lines 49–78).

The Wakefield shepherds are interesting to compare with the N-Town shepherds.[20] Their speech is almost wholly colloquial, so that when any remark deviates from this vernacular norm the other shepherds call attention to it. When, in talking about the food before them, one shepherd in the *First Shepherds' Play* speaks in a self-consciously elevated French/Latinate register:

> Good sawse,
> This is a restorité
> To make a good appeté.   (12: lines 343–5)

another mocks his discourse:

> Yee speke alle by clergé,
> I here by youre clause.
>
> Cowth ye by youre gramery
> Reche us a drynk,
> I shuld be more mery –
> Ye wote what I thynk.   (lines 346–51)

This kind of intervention is at the furthest possible remove from Latin. It privileges the everyday over the elevated in terms of both action and sound.

The same pretentious shepherd drops into a crude macaronic prayer in attempting to protect them all from danger via the sign of the cross:

> For ferde we be fryght,
> A crosse lett us kest –
> Cryst-crosse, benedyght
> Eest and west –
> For drede.
> *Iesus onazorus*
> Crucyefixus,
> Morcus, Andreus
> God be oure spede.   (lines 417–25)

Ironically, the prayer, with its garbled Latin, blurs the voice of the church by overlaying it with popular superstition; yet it also looks forward to the central event of the Christian church, here anachronistically out of place at the moment of Christ's birth.

The same shepherd repeats in Latin the prophecy concerning the root of Jesse (lines 502–3), and although this more conventional use of Latin to quote scriptural prophecy more closely resembles the functioning of the N-Town shepherds, it remains confined within a vernacular framework by virtue of its failure to transform the earthbound response of the other shepherds. There is only the one shepherd, already identified by the others as literate to a degree, who ever participates in this sacred speech; and any reverence the Latin might induce is almost immediately undercut. When this

shepherd cites Virgil a few lines later, he elicits a stream of abuse
from his fellow:

> Weme! tord [turd]! what speke ye
> Here in myn eeres?[21]
> Tell us no clergé!
> I hold you of the freres [Don't speak to us of learning, I think you
>   must be a friar];
> Ye preche.
> It semys by youre Laton
> Ye have lerd youre Caton [Cato (a standard school Latin text)].
>
> (lines 560–6)

Salter suggests that 'what we may have here is the playwright's own
admission that there is some element of incongruity in the spectacle
of rough Yorkshire countrymen expounding Latin as if they were
clerks or priests' (*English and International*, pp. 276–7), though she
rightly warns against a simplistic reading of such a moment as mere
realism. The contrast with the representation of the N-Town
shepherds is striking. Whereas their collective move from English to
Latin authorises Latin as the language in which recognition of
higher truth is properly expressed, the merriment and scorn elicited
by the Wakefield third shepherd's Latin speech marks out his
discourse as the deviant mode, determined as such by the framing
vernacular norm.

This precisely reverses the dramatic method of the N-Town
shepherds' play, where Latin was allowed to colonise the shepherds'
discourse; and the reversal finds a parallel in the functioning of holy
dialect in the two cycles. Whereas Latin and Latinate English are
normally part of the language of holy speakers in N-Town, so that
any deviant use of these dialects is seen as a parody or appropriation
of that norm, in Wakefield a more vernacular norm turns Latin into
a frequent marker of blasphemous speech. This inversion is, as
Stevens has argued, a particular hallmark of the Wakefield Master's
plays (though one which fits in well with the general plain-speaking
of the virtuous throughout the cycle). Both Latin and French, as
Stevens notes, 'appear consistently in the ranting of tyrants for the
purpose of intimidating their listeners' (*Four Middle English Mystery
Cycles*, p. 162), and Herod even self-consciously ends his ranting with
the phrase, 'I can no more Franch' (16: line 740). Pilate's prolonged
macaronic Latin/English rant (24: lines 1–65), with its refusal to
translate any of the Latin into English, seems designed to dominate

rather than enlighten an audience. Notably, when English and Latin are mixed in the discourse of a single speaker in N-Town, the English usually translates or interprets the Latin; here the mixture of the two languages is parallel with the traditionally macaronic speech of the devil, common to both cycles as well as beyond. This kind of speech foregrounds sound not as truthful presence, but as playful obstruction. It immerses the auditors in the materiality of words in order to put a barrier between them and the Word rather than to enact its significance for them.

The Wakefield Master's pageants seem knowingly to court anti-clericalism in the hostility they direct against Latin. Annas and Cayphas, probably costumed as bishops,[22] and certainly as clerics (Cayphas expresses regret at his clerical status because it prevents him from striking Christ – 21: lines 443–6), align themselves with Pilate and confirm their own wickedness through their anger, scheming and evasiveness. Anger is primarily given expression through a vicious vernacular, while plotting and secretiveness are expressed through inserted Latin. Even Cayphas' abusive vernacular rant, however, like Pilate's, incorporates Latin phrases, thus ironically appropriating Latin, cherished by clerics as guardians of holy truth to exclude the laity, as an anticlerical device.

The play encourages the audience to respond negatively to the chaotic jumble of this discourse by setting it against the silence of Christ. In this way, the powerful silence of one who refuses to engage with corruption is highlighted dramatically by the very speech of the corrupt. Cayphas is driven to ever greater heights of rage by Christ's silence: 'Harstow [do you hear], harlott' (line 187); 'Thou shall onys or to-morne / To speke be fulle fayne [you will be glad to speak once before tomorrow]' (lines 198–9); 'Speke on oone word, / Right in the dwyllys name' (lines 209–10); 'Speke on in a torde [turd]' (line 215); 'Though thi lyppis be stokyn [shut] / Yit myght thou say "mom"' (lines 248–9).

When he drops into Latin, his exclusion of the lay audience mimics an on-stage exclusion of Christ. (As in the dramatisation of the N-Town shepherds, realistic continuity of discourse is not a consideration in this drama; Christ, elsewhere the voice of the church, is for the purposes of this moment a layman rather than a cleric, and hence excluded from the understanding of priestly Latin.[23]) The device encourages the audience to align themselves with Christ in mutual exclusion and to be suspicious of Cayphas, whose Latin does in fact indicate, when translated, a plan to exploit the law in an attempt to condemn Christ for silence: '*Et omnis qui tacet/ Hic consentire videtur*' (whoever keeps silent seems to consent) (lines 207–8). Annas, though less violent in speech than Cayphas, similarly employs Latin to exclude Christ, bystanders and audience from his sly manoeuvring when he advises Cayphas to be more moderate:

> Youre wordes ar bustus [fierce];
> *Et hoc nos volumus*
> *Quod de iure possumus* [What we want we can have by law],
> Ye wote what I meyn –
>
> It is best that we trete hym
> With farenes . . .
> And so myght we gett hym
> Som word for to say.   (lines 309–16)

This demonisation of tyrants and hypocritical clerics through macaronic speech is given clarity by the literal manifestation of that demonisation in the mouths of devils. The *Judgement Play*, as Stevens comments, is basically borrowed from York, but significantly altered by the introduction of the devil Tutivillus ('Language as Theme in the Wakefield Plays', pp. 106–7). Tutivillus is notable both for his own language (which mixes Latin, nonsense-language and colloquially abusive English) and for his particular interest in those who have committed sins of the word, 'carpars and cryars', 'lurdans and lyars', 'flytars', 'bakbytars', 'fals swerers' and 'kyrkchaterars'.[24] Tutivillus, as Margaret Jennings ('Tutivillus: The Literary Career of the Recording Demon') has shown, is in fact a conflation of two devils, both devoted to sins of the word. One was said to record slothful speech in church on the part of either priest or congregation, such as the careless recitation of prayers or idle chatter. The other collected in a sack syllables missed or cut short in church. He was thus traditionally associated with the words of men in so far as they betrayed the Word of God. He introduces himself in traditional macaronic mode:

> Mi name is Tutivillus,
> My horne is blawen.
> *Fragmina verborum,*
> *Tutivillus colligit horum;*
> *Belzabub algorum,*
> *Belial belium doliorum*
>   (30: lines following 363, unnumbered)[25]

and, as with the Latin-speaking shepherd, his educated speech is not allowed to pass unnoticed. The Second Demon exclaims: 'What, I se thou can of gramory / And somwhat of arte' (lines 365–6), so that for the audience a distrust of Latin speech is again foregrounded. This distrust is given an even more pointed focus in Tutivillus' use of Latin to make the assertion that *'Diabolus est mendax / Et pater eius* [The devil is a liar, and his father too]' (lines following 415, unnumbered).

At the same time, of course, this kind of attack on a language traditionally associated with the authority of the church produces a transgressive thrill for the audience. Hearing a devil utter words in the language of the bible and the liturgy breaks a taboo and redirects a stock response that would revere priestly authority by introducing risky and transgressive pleasures. It opens up a space for thinking about the naturalised tie between holy speakers and the Latin language, allowing an audience to ask questions about its necessity by encouraging them to take pleasure in its disruption. It is the opening up of this space for questioning, together with an emphatic admiration for plain English in the Wakefield cycle, that leads to the view that these plays may be Wyclifite in intention.[26] And there is one probable reference to the Lollards in the mouth of Tutivillus (which, of course, is precisely where it cannot be trusted). Tutivillus describes himself as 'master Lollar' (line 311) and boasts of the number of souls he has brought to Hell. It is possible, as Margaret Jennings suggests, that the reference is not specifically to Lollards, but to mumbling 'idlers', the spiritually careless who can't be bothered to utter all the syllables of their prayers or liturgical responses ('Tutivillus: The Literary Career of the Recording Demon', p. 60), but highly unlikely, given the date, that an audience would fail to see a reference to Lollardy. Lepow, who reads the cycle as anti-Lollard, reads this remark as highlighting Lollards among the abusers of language (*Enacting the Sacrament*, p. 140); yet the fact that the speaker is Tutivillus may mean, as Stevens argues, that we should decode this as high praise ('Language as Theme in the Wakefield Plays', p. 106). Elsewhere, however, the sinners identified by devilish speakers are truly sinners, and the convention whereby speakers, even deceptive speakers, give straightforward expression to their own moral characters, is widely shared across different dramatic modes at this time. It seems more likely, then, that the reference is intended as a genuine attack on a heretical group.

Hearing an attack on the Lollards here, however, does not mean that we need to accept the cycle as a piece of counter-Lollard propaganda. It is quite possible that the makers of this cycle, realising the political dangers of the potentially pro-Lollard direction of its anticlericalism and linguistic preferences, were protecting themselves from charges against heresy by this overt attack. The cycle may be influenced by Lollard thinking about language and a corrupt clergy, but anxious to pull back from any association with heretical doctrine concerning, for example, the sacraments. It may be seeking to privilege English over Latin, while wishing to dissociate itself from the heretical group most strongly identified with such a linguistic bias. Though the Lollards worked to raise the status of English, their politicisation of it also impeded its wider appeal. What we see in the fifteenth century is a collision between the Lollard struggle to empower English and the simultaneous drive towards English from a wider base that refuses alignment with Lollard thinking beyond issues of language. Despite this drive towards English, however, the positive connotations of Latin are too deeply embedded simply to disappear. The use of Latin, as in N-Town, to produce a sudden fullness of presence and to engage the audience at a level of focus more intense and concentrated than they can bring in response to everyday vernacular language remains part of a continuing dramatic tradition down to the end of the sixteenth century.

CHAPTER 3

The voice of God

Most medieval morality plays tend, like the N-Town cycle and unlike the Wakefield cycle, to set up a dialectic between a relatively formal, Latinate dialect for God and other holy speakers and a colloquial, sometimes obscene or nonsensical, vernacular dialect for the figure of the Vice and his counterparts. Latin, whether quoted directly, or visible through a highly elevated English derived from Latin roots,[1] usually gives holy sanction to the words of those who speak it. The final section of *The Castle of Perseverance* is a clear case in point. The speech of the four daughters of God is sprinkled with Latin, increasingly located at the end of the stanza as the action moves towards its climax. The speech of God the Father, though plain in its English, also highlights the beginnings and endings of some stanzas with Latin, and ends with the final exhortation, '*Te Deum laudamus*' (line 3649). Latin becomes more insistent and more dominant as good triumphs over evil and salvation is affirmed.

Latin, in these plays as elsewhere, is also the language of the clergy, God's representatives on earth. Despite the strong presence of anticlerical satire in fourteenth-century non-dramatic literature, morality plays as a genre tend not to show unworthy clerics until the Reformation creates two churches and two contesting clergies, by which time the genre has arguably been hijacked into something different anyway. Earlier moralities may attack clerical corruption in the abstract, via the speeches of the play, but the clerical figures who actually appear on stage present a simple emblematic identification to the audience: clerical costume and Latinate dialect are the badges of the forces of good.[2] Where characters within these plays mock the clergy or their speech, that mockery identifies its agents as depraved, and casts no shadow over the virtue of its target (though it may unpick some of the trappings of that virtue, as this chapter goes on to argue).[3] When Charity quotes the bible in Latin to Youth in the play of that name, Youth's response both equates that discourse with clerical status and scorns it as ridiculous and incomprehensible: 'What! methink ye be clerkish, / For ye speak good gibb'rish' (lines 113–14). Riot further refers to Charity's speech in the same play as 'crooked language' (line 299). Free Will mocks Perseverance in *Hick Scorner* when he recognises him as some kind of cleric, calling him 'master doctor dottypoll' (line 697; see further chapter 5, n.22 below). Both Youth and Free Will further mock Charity and Perseverance respectively with almost the same foolish question: why do men eat mustard with salt fish/beef? In both cases the corrective response of the virtuous figure identifies the other speaker's discourse for the audience as vain or ignorant: 'This question is but a vanity' (*Youth*, line 123); 'Peace, man! Thou talkest lewdly' (*Hick Scorner*, line 703). Similarly, in Skelton's *Magnificence*, Fansy interrupts the virtuous Felicity with an attack on his discourse: 'Tusche, holde your pece, your langage is vayne' and an offer to show Magnificence the truth 'playnly' himself (lines 251–3). Felicity in turn classifies Fansy's speech as 'jangelynge': 'Nowe leve this jangelynge and to us expounde / Why that ye sayd our langage was in vayne' (lines 263–4). These exchanges between clerical, virtuous characters and non-clerical sinners thus create the context for explicit discussion of language choices and make clear that the expression of moral opposition between the church and its enemies through an opposition of linguistic registers is a deliberate project. Characters identify one another's moral status via their dialects, and in doing so teach the audience the linguistic equation the plays seek to endorse: Latin or elevated English is the discourse of holiness, while aggressively vernacular speech is a rival discourse which wickedly (if also delightfully) seeks to challenge the discourse of Christian truth. As Catherine Belsey argues, 'the play of meaning in the world after Babel permits evil to challenge the knowledge which is guaranteed by God and ensures salvation' (*The Subject of Tragedy*, p. 64). The dramatic project of representing a plurality of discourses is not a morally neutral one, but one that seeks to align one kind of language with truth and another with deceit, and this opposition is sometimes exaggerated by giving the Vice a kind of nonsense-language which performs its own futility.

Occasional bits of foreign vernaculars also begin to insert themselves in the drama of this period, usually as part of the fragmented, playful and uninhibited dialect of untrustworthy speakers. Free Will in *Hick Scorner* makes the familiar plea for space and quiet (part of the tradition of popular mumming plays), and follows it with a variation in French: 'Make you room for a gentleman, sirs, and peace! / *Dieu garde, seigneurs, tout le presse!*' (lines 646–7). An exchange in *Magnificence* presents Cloked Colusyon answering Courtly Abusyon's nonsense-language in French, thus suggesting the parallel functioning of these two modes of speech:

COURTLY ABUSYON. Huffa, huffa taunderum, taunderum tayne,
                huffa, huffa!

CLOKED COLUSYON. This was properly prated, syrs. What sayd a?

COURTLY ABUSYON. Rutty bully joly rutterkyn, heyda!

CLOKED COLUSYON. *De que pays este vous?*   (lines 745–8 and ff.)

Foreign language, then, in these examples at least, becomes part of the ragbag of linguistic abuses that characterise speakers who seek to oppose the authoritative singularity and consistency of holy discourse.[4]

The attractiveness of nonsense-language, foreign borrowings, unrestrained colloquialism, or even obscenity in performance may seem to undermine the didactic matrix that seeks to position them as the devil's instruments. Blake's famous complaint about Milton's Satan pinpoints a problem also central to Christian drama, in that vice is by definition more spectacular and engaging on stage than the necessary fixity of virtue. Robert Weimann's work on staging (*Shakespeare and the Popular Tradition*; cf. chapter 1 above) demonstrates how the different discourses of characters in morality plays position them literally either in a fixed location (usually towards the rear of the playing space, if the play is viewed end-on), firmly attached to the fictional space of the drama, or in the more open space in front or around, which allows movement in and out of fictionality and lets the performer make a freer and more intimate relationship with the audience. As Weimann and others have noted, the vernacular is linked with the popular, the subversive, the carnivalesque, and thus functions to question the dominant ideology encoded in the more formal discourses of Latin or Latinate English. Yet this kind of usage may challenge, without overturning, the conservative position which aligns the vernacular and the popular with Lollardy, heresy, rebellion and, ultimately, damnation. In the end a drama which names its most engaging characters as vices and warns both audience and mankind-figure that they lead to hell speaks for the orthodoxies of church and state. The pleasures and attractions of sin are part of the project to teach the audience to recognise temptation; the risky pleasures remain thrilling partly *because* the audience is encouraged to identify them as transgressive.

MANKIND

A play which invites a fuller investigation of its linguistic allegiances is *Mankind* (1465–70). It seems to share the concern of the Wakefield cycle to make a space for plain English in areas of discourse currently dominated by Latin, while at the same time seeking to prevent identification of its linguistic project with a heretical bias. No other extant play of the period mounts such an extended attack on Latin and Latinate English. While in other plays such attacks are brief and clearly indicators of the impiety of the attackers, here something more complicated is going on. The overall aim of this attack in *Mankind*, I will argue, is to address the question of what kind of discourse is appropriate to use in calling a predominantly non-Latinate audience to repentance.

The play opens with a speech from the character Mercy in a heavily Latinate English:

> The very fownder and begynner of owr fyrst creacyon
> Amonge us synfull wrechys he oweth to be magnyfyede,
> That for owr dysobedyenc he hade non indygnacyon
> To sende hys own son to be torn and crucyfyede.
> Owr obsequyouse servyce to hym xulde be aplyede,
> Where he was lorde of all and made all thynge of nought,
> For the synnfull synnere to hade hym revyvyde
> And for hys redempcyon sett hys own son at nought.   (lines 1–8)

Since the publication in 1947 of Sister Mary Philippa Coogan's study of the play most critics have accepted her argument that internal evidence points to the probability that Mercy is either a priest or a friar, and would have been immediately recognisable as such to a contemporary audience by his long clothes (Coogan, *An Interpretation of the Moral Play, Mankind*, pp. 1–7). The heavy use of Latin quotation and Latinate diction similarly seems to point to clerical authorship (Smart, 'Some Notes on *Mankind*', pp. 116–17; Coogan, *An Interpretation of the Moral Play, Mankind*, Appendix ii; Wenzel, *Acedia in Medieval Thought and Literature*, p. 154; ed. Bevington, *The Macro Plays*, p. xiii).

Mercy's opening speech probably initially struck a fifteenth-century audience in two ways: as the characteristic voice of ecclesiastical authority and, simultaneously, as well-nigh incomprehensible. If the play were to develop differently, this Latinate discourse might remain the naturalised and unquestioned sign of Mercy's clerical status and acknowledged authority, and the audience might allow their reverence for such authority to overshadow their incomprehension. As it does develop, however, Myscheffe is allowed to interrupt Mercy with a wicked parody of this discourse, later described by New Gyse as 'Englysch Laten' (line 123). Myscheffe's parody clearly takes issue with the manner rather than the matter of Mercy's speech by aping its Latinate elements:

> I beseche yow hertyly, leve yowr calcacyon.
> Leve yowr chaffe, leve yowr corn, leve yowr dalyacyon.
> Yowr wytt ys lytyll, yowr hede ys mekyll, ye are full of predycacyon.
>
> (lines 45–7)

The audience is thus encouraged to focus its discomfort with an incomprehensible language and to allow such discomfort to contest the more automatic response of reverence. Attention is directed towards language, and the necessity of the link between the church and such a manner of delivery challenged.

Such parody follows Mercy's words whenever he opens his mouth in the company of Myscheffe or the three N's (New Gyse, Nowadays and Nought). When he gives his name in the same exaggerated Latin register a little further on in the scene: 'Mercy ys my name by denomynacyon. / I conseyve ye have but a lytyll favour in my communycacyon' (lines 121–2), New Gyse shrieks: 'Ey, ey! yowr body ys full of Englysch Laten. / I am aferde yt wyll brest' (lines 124–5), and Nowadays mocks him with obscenity:

> I prey yow hertyly, worschyppull clerke,
> To have this Englysch mad in Laten:
>
> 'I have etun a dyschfull of curdys,
> Ande I have schetun yowr mowth full of turdys.'
> Now opyn yowr sachell wyth Laten wordys
> And sey me this in clerycall manere! (lines 129–34)

Throughout the play it is this aspect of Mercy's speech which the comic characters single out for ridicule, perceiving it as the 'clerycall manere'.

Most critics have argued that if we wish to try to hear Mercy's 'Englysch Laten' (line 124) as a fifteenth-century audience might have heard it, we should try to lose our animosity to it and hear it as the voice of authority, 'the author's version of the high style of the period' (Coogan, *An Interpretation of the Moral Play, Mankind*, p. 98; cf. Ashley, 'Titivullus and the Battle of Words', p. 130; Lester (ed.), *Morality Plays*, p. xxiv; Tydeman, *English Medieval Theatre*, p. 39). While it is true that Mercy's diction does represent the 'high style' and identifies him as the voice of the orthodox church as surely as the scurrilous language of the comic characters identifies them as the voices of sin, this obvious explanation of polarity does not fully account for the foregrounding of language itself in the play. We may expect the vicious to mock the virtuous in a morality play, but when the butt of the mockery is Latin, or Latinate English, and the play itself is in English rather than Latin, a simple lining up of Latin or pseudo-Latin with virtue and English with vice becomes unworkable. If Latinate diction is to be straightforwardly associated with all that is morally desirable, why is it specifically that diction which attracts extended ridicule in the play?

The fifteenth century opened, as we have seen (chapter 1 above), with the strongest possible legislation against the Lollards. What, then, was the situation regarding the Lollards in the later fifteenth century, and specifically in East Anglia in the 1460s, the context for the writing of *Mankind*? Lollard heresy trials continued throughout the fifteenth century, and persecution of the Lollards in East Anglia was especially severe during the second quarter of the century (Thomson, *The Later Lollards*; Hudson, *The Premature Revolution*, ch.10). In his chapter on East Anglia, John Thomson notes that William Sawtry, the first Lollard martyr, was from East Anglia, and that East Anglian Lollards 'seem to have adhered on the whole to the extremer forms of heretical belief' (*The Later Lollards*, p. 125).

Anthony Gash has drawn attention to two heresy trials led by Bishop Chedworth of Lincoln and Bishop Gray of Ely in 1457, close to the probable date of *Mankind* ('Carnival against Lent', p. 95; see further Thomson, *The Later Lollards*, ch.5). The victims of the first trial, on 27 May, were from Somersham in Huntingdonshire; those accused at the second trial, three days later, were from Swaffham, Cambridge and Chesterton. The second group had to perform public penance in the marketplaces of Ely and Cambridge, as well as in their respective parish churches, so their cases would have been familiar over the same geographical area indicated by the topical references in *Mankind* as likely venues for its performance (lines

503–15; see Eccles' note, *The Macro Plays*, p. 222). As Gash points out, Mankind's belief that a prayer made in the field is as good as one offered in a church (line 553) is exactly the belief of which one of the men on trial was accused ('Carnival against Lent', p. 95).[5]

Thomson describes these two trials as isolated in time and place, but notes the general tendency of Lollardy, after the period of intense persecution following the Oldcastle Rising of 1414, to become more secret, displaying a concern 'to avoid detection rather than spreading bills against the Establishment' (*The Later Lollards*, p. 19). Even closer in time to the probable date of the play, however, another, more extreme event highlighted continuing heresy in East Anglia: William Barrow of Walden in Essex was executed for his Lollard beliefs in 1467. The author (or authors) of the play may have been aware of either or both of the 1457 trial proceedings and Barrow's execution. But with or without such awareness of specific events, the play may represent an attempt to tread a dangerous line between sympathy for some Lollard positions and endorsement of the orthodox church. In particular, the author may have found himself in sympathy with the Lollard insistence on the need to use English in order to reach the widest audience, while wishing himself to preach a doctrine that was broadly orthodox (as suggested in relation to the Wakefield cycle at the end of chapter 2). The fact that Mankind makes his remark about a prayer in a field after he has begun to succumb to the devil's temptations may indicate a deliberate attempt to incorporate safeguards in the event of an investigation for heresy. At a time of polarised responses to English and Latin in theological contexts, the play might be seen as striving to moderate such polarity on the part of its audience.

This returns us, then, to the question of audience. What more do we know of the original audience for *Mankind* beyond its date and location? What can we say about its social make-up? Should we picture a group of unlearned churls, such as Lydgate patronises (pp. 22–3 above), or an elite sufficiently literate to understand and recognise the Latin texts which the play cites untranslated? Paula Neuss, for example, observes in a footnote to the learned Latin joke against the friars at lines 325–6 that 'there must have been some quite literate people among the audience, if they were meant to understand this joke' ('Active and Idle Language', p. 54). In making this point, Neuss is implicitly questioning the older view that the audience for *Mankind* was a predominantly popular one. Elements derived from the mumming plays (for example, the reference to Beelzebub's huge head (line 461); calls within the play to an ostler and a tapster (lines 732, 729); communal singing with the audience (lines 333–43); the demand for a collection, together with a suggestion that 'the goodeman of this house' (line 467) make the first contribution to the collection) were first pointed out by Walter K. Smart ('*Mankind* and the Mumming Plays', pp. 21–5). Critics since then have almost universally emphasised the implied 'popular' or 'rural' audience of the play. According to David Bevington, it is 'the most indisputably popular play of the fifteenth century', and Mark Eccles concludes the introduction to his edition by quoting this assertion (Bevington, *From Mankind to Marlowe*, p. 48; Eccles, *The Macro Plays*, p. xlv; cf. Weimann, *Shakespeare and the Popular Tradition*, p. 113 and note 18). The fact that the play invents a 'popular' role for its audience, however, must not be taken as evidence of its actual audiences.

The only critic to dispute the notion of a popular audience at any length is Lawrence Clopper ('*Mankind* and Its Audience'), although Richard Beadle's work on the Macro scribe ('The Scribal Problem in the Macro Manuscript') also begins to suggest a different kind of audience. Clopper takes up precisely the question of the role of Latin in the play. Ridicule of Latinate speech, as he points out, demands no knowledge of Latin, but most of the Latin citations require an understanding of Latin for comprehension of both the religious message and the humour (since some are puns or involve witty mistranslation). His conclusion, based on his recognition of the Latin as 'not merely rhetorical but essential', is that the audience was primarily 'literate or even aristocratic' ('*Mankind* and Its Audience', pp. 350, 353).

Yet the first and most direct reference the play makes to its audience divides them into two groups, or a community with an elite group: 'Ye soverens that sytt and ye brothern that stonde ryght uppe' (line 29). Even without this reference the distance between making scatological jokes in Latin and inviting audience participation in an obscene vernacular song might suggest mixed audiences. Clopper affirms that 'no one ... would dispute the view that the ridiculing of Mercy and his style of speech is intended to force an alignment of the audience with the Three N's, Mischief, and a fallen Mankynd' ('*Mankind* and Its Audience', p. 352), but it seems to me that this alignment is only part of the response the play invites. Those who

understand its learned Latin are further invited to put themselves in
Mercy's shoes and think about their own discourse. And surely the
audience group most likely to be directly targeted by this aspect of
the play's comedy is not the aristocracy, but the clergy?

Beadle's work on the manuscript leads him to suggest the monk,
Hyngham, whose signature claims ownership of both *Wisdom* and
Mankind in the Macro manuscript, as the scribe. Whether or not he
was the scribe, and whether or not both plays are written in the
same hand is of less importance here than the fact that Hyngham
was 'undoubtedly the earliest owner of the manuscript' ('The Scribal
Problem in the Macro Manuscript', p. 9). This gives us a direct link
between the playtext and a potential clerical audience, a link
corroborated at a more general level by the records of performance
discussed in chapter 2 (pp. 32–3 above).

The opening lines of *Mankind* make clear that the discourse of
Mercy, although technically in English, defines itself against its Latin
other in such a way as to try to cross the boundary and to impel
English to take on the authoritative singularity of the sacred Latin
word.[6] Mercy's voice is the voice of the church and is heard, as it
were, in intonational quotation marks, borrowing the discourse of
the other language, and borrowing at the same time the direct link
for the audience between that language and an idea of unassailable,
singular truth. The singular truth that Mercy preaches can be
summed up in the last two lines: 'The corn xall be savyde, the chaff
xall be brente. / I besech yow hertyly, have this premedytacyon'
(lines 43–4). Myscheffe's reply imitates the vocabulary and syntax of
Mercy's last line: 'I beseche yow hertyly, leve yowr calcacyon' (line
45), but does so in order to make his protest more pointed. He is not
simply dismissing Mercy's message of salvation; he is dismissing the
mode of discourse, the Latin model Mercy emulates. His next line:
'Leve yowr chaffe, leve yowr corn, leve yowr dalyacyon' (line 46) not
only repeats the words of Mercy's theme in its command to dismiss
them, but also makes a theme of language itself, by referring to
Mercy's speech via the ambiguous term 'dalyacyon', which can
mean either chatter or solemn utterance.[7] The word punctures the
capacity of Latinate English to command automatic reverence and
insists that the audience consider it as one possible mode of
discourse, rather than as the necessary, or natural, discourse of the
church. The play remains safe by putting the subversive words into
the mouth of a vicious speaker, but the audience responds not, as in

a sermon, to a singular discourse, but to the interaction between oppositional discourses. The audience must make its own meanings in an open, playful space.

Myscheffe's mock-serious appeal to Mercy's authority:

> But, ser, I prey this questyon to claryfye:
> Mysse-masche, dryff-draff,
> Sume was corn and sume was chaffe   (lines 48–50)

turns the image of corn and chaff, crucial to Mercy's message of salvation and to the play as a whole in its representation of good and evil souls, into an image representing types of language.[8] The nonsense words that precede it, 'Mysse-masche, dryff-draff', indicate that the task for the audience, in assessing the words of a speaker, is necessarily a linguistic as well as a moral one. The congregation cannot respond to the message of salvation unless they can first respond to the words which embody it. Myscheffe's mimicry of Mercy's language, his swift reduction of it to nonsense, distances the content of Mercy's message from his method of delivery. Parody punctures the claims of this discourse to be the sole mediator of truth.

As Bakhtin points out, any parody, by orienting itself towards another's language as well as the object (the real world), engages with language itself as an object, but this orientation towards language, as several critics have noted (e.g. Neuss, 'Active and Idle Language'; Ashley, 'Titivullus and the Battle of Words') is particularly explicit in *Mankind*. Mercy condemns Myscheffe for interrupting his 'talkyng delectable' (line 65), and threatens the other Vices that they will repent their 'ydyll language' (line 147), which they themselves rename 'eloquence' (line 150). Mankind finds Mercy's 'lovely words' sweeter than honey to his soul (line 225). Mercy and the Vices openly cast their opposition in terms of style. Nowadays greets Mercy, as he himself says, 'curtly' (line 101) and receives an ironic response from Mercy ('Few wordys, few and well sett' (line 102)) to which New Gyse in turn replies:

> Ser, yt ys the new gyse and the new jett:
> Many wordys, and schortely sett,
> Thys ys the new gyse, every-dele.   (lines 103–5)

The biblical text at the heart of the play's preaching is Matthew 12.36–7: 'But I say unto you that every idle word that men shall speak, they shall give account thereof in the day of judgment. For by thy words thou shalt be justified, and by thy words thou shalt be condemned', and the text is paraphrased and expanded on by Mercy at lines 170–80: 'How may yt be excusyde befor the Justyce of all / When for every ydyll worde we must yelde a reson?' (lines 172–3). Myscheffe's second stanza of response to Mercy's opening speech specifies Mercy's discourse very clearly as the clerical one by parodying sermon-form, making a new mock-Latin verse based on the corn and chaff reference and analysing the new pseudo-text word by word:

> Ande ye sayde the corn xulde be savyde and the chaff xulde be feryde.
> Ande he provyth nay as yt shewth be this verse:
> 'Corn servit bredibus, chaffe horsibus, straw fyrybusque.'
> Thys ys as moche to say, to yowr leude undyrstondynge,
> As the corn xall serve to brede at the nexte bakynge.
> 'Chaff horsybus *et reliqua*,'
> The chaff to horse xall be goode provente,
> When a man ys forcolde the straw may be brent.
> And so forth, *et cetera*. (lines 55–63)

This careful parody of preaching style is clearly written by someone familiar with the method of dividing a theme, and calls attention to its own institutional place not only by the parade of mock-Latin and imaginary learning, but by the patronising phrase that emphasises the distance between the seeming Latin of the speaker and the 'leude undyrstondynge' of the congregation. In performance the parody might well have been further highlighted by dressing Myscheffe in clerical costume, like Mercy.[9]

For the uneducated members of the audience this send-up of the clerical manner as both distant and patronising disentangles religion from its alienating mediations; for the clerical element in the audience it poses the question of mediation as a direct challenge. It may of course have provoked anger, but at the same time it exposed the naturalised link between Latinity and truth as ideologically constructed, and identified the typical clerical discourse as precisely that, a 'priestly dialect'. It confronts this dialect with a radical scepticism, showing that clerics, through their mode of speech, involuntarily convey meanings about themselves and their relations with the laity over and above the direct meanings of the words they choose. 'When we seek to understand a word', as Bakhtin argues, 'what matters is not the direct meaning the word gives to objects and emotions – this is the false front of the word; what matters is rather the actual and always self-interested *use* to which this meaning is put and the way it is expressed by the speaker, a use determined by the speaker's position (profession, social class, etc.) and by the concrete situation' (*The Dialogic Imagination*, p. 401).

The play does not dramatise the linguistic struggle by simply aligning Mercy with Latin and the sinful characters with the vernacular, and this is further evidence for the argument that the play invited its audience to rethink the basis of their usage. The vicious characters use Latin on occasion and Mercy is capable of speaking without excessive elaboration. When, for example, Mercy ignores Nowadays' mocking suggestion that he translate scatological nonsense into Latin (lines 129–34, p. 55 above), Nowadays himself immediately demonstrates that it is possible. He turns on Nought, who has interrupted him, and tells him to '*osculare fundamentum*' (line 142). For the illiterate or non-Latinate members of the audience, the shock is primarily that of hearing Latin in the mouth of a conspicuously disreputable character, although an accompanying gesture could make the meaning of the phrase evident. Ironically, the full force of the joke is aimed at those who understand Latin, those who, like Mercy, are in the habit of using Latin as a way of commanding respect both for their personal authority and for the sacred authority of scripture. Mercy's chastisement, on the other hand, is notably unadorned at this point: 'Thys ydyll language ye shall repent. / Out of this place I wolde ye went' (lines 147–8). Mercy has authority here, but demonstrates it not through inflated language but through control of the playing space and in plain English: he dismisses the Vices and they obey his command.

The audience, then, is asked to unfix its stereotypes, to consider the effects of obscene Latin used to mock virtue and of plain English used to rebuke vice. The 'idle language' which Mercy rebukes actually denotes a scurrilous macaronic discourse which deploys Latin alongside English, and New Gyse's parting speech further highlights this Latinate element in his own discourse against Mercy's vernacular register at this point:

> Goo we hens all thre wyth on assent.
> My fadyr ys yrke of owr eloquence.
> Therfor, I wyll no lenger tary.
> Gode brynge yow, master, and blyssyde Mary,
> To the number of the demonycall frayry!   (lines 149–53)

The word 'eloquence', which New Gyse chooses here to identify his own speech, is itself a Latin derivative, acknowledging the Latinity of its referent, and the speech ends with more open abuse of the clergy in its mock-prayer repeating the joke about friars, which operates only for those in the audience with enough Latin to know that the word 'friar' is a derivative of Latin '*frater*', meaning 'brother', and possibly also to recognise a rather sophisticated wordplay on demonical/Dominican. The audience's engagement is complicated by this reversal of stereotyping which allows the base characters such expertise in Latin: the automatic association between Latin and authority is defamiliarised, and the definition of the vernacular against its Latin other becomes correspondingly problematic.

Crucial, of course, to audience response, is the nature of Mankind's own speech. His entrance is postponed until line 186, by which time the audience may already be wondering how his speech will identify him within this site of slippage between discourses. It is important to take note of Mercy's last words before Mankind's entrance, which are directed towards the audience:

> The goode new gyse nowadays I wyll not dysalow.
> I dyscomende the vycyouse gyse; I prey have me excusyde,
> I nede not to speke of yt, yowr reson wyll tell it yow.
> Take that ys to be takyn and leve that ys to be refusyde. (lines 182–5)

There is some Latinate vocabulary in this ('dysalow', 'dyscomende', 'excusyde', 'refusyde') but the syntax is extremely plain, and whole phrases, such as 'I nede not to speke of yt' and 'Take that is to be takyn', are almost colloquially direct. Against Mercy's discourse at this point, Mankind's first words are heard as excessively Latinate:

> Of the erth and of the cley we have owr propagacyon.
> By the provydens of Gode thus be we deryvatt,
> To whos mercy I recomende this holl congrygacyon:
> I hope onto hys blysse ye be all predestynatt. (lines 186–9)

This is bewildering for an audience. They cannot respond as though the lines between Mercy's opening speech and Mankind's had not been spoken. On the one hand they may make the assumption, correctly, that Mankind is in a state of grace pleasing to Mercy at this point of entry, since this is the discourse so strongly enunciated in Mercy's opening speech; on the other hand, they have seen this discourse cruelly mocked, and Mercy is at this point of the play speaking much more plainly.

The imbalance continues. Mercy welcomes Mankind and introduces himself in the plainest possible terms:

> Cryst sende yow goode comforte! Ye be welcum, my frende.
> Stond uppe on yowr fete, I prey yow aryse.
> My name is Mercy; ye be to me full hende.
> To eschew vyce I wyll yow avyse   (lines 217–20)

and it is instructive to compare this with his earlier introduction of
himself when New Gyse asks for his name at lines 120–1 (p. 55
above). It is that earlier introduction which provokes New Gyse's
outburst about 'Englysch Laten'. Here, however, it is Mankind's
response which is the more Latinate:

> O Mercy, of all grace and vertu ye are the well,
> I have herde tell of ryght worschyppfull clerkys.
> Ye be aproxymatt to Gode and nere of hys consell.
> He hat instytut you above all hys werkys.
>
> O, yowr lovely wordys to my soull are swetere then hony.
>   (lines 221–5)

This is clear in one respect: it underlines the orthodox doctrine that
the clergy have a necessary role to play as mediators between
mankind and God at a time when the Lollards were advocating the
priesthood of all believers. What is less clear is which words we
should understand to be the lovely words which are sweeter than
honey to the soul of Mankind. Are they those Latinate terms which
dominated Mercy's first speeches and now dominate Mankind's, the
elevated and decorative vocabulary to which the adjective 'sweet'
was so regularly attached during the fifteenth century? Or are they
those words which Mankind has actually *heard* Mercy use on stage,
notably plainer and more direct? Or does the play invite the collapse
of polarities at this point, a willingness to hear both the magic of the
sacramental language of traditional clerical discourse and the appeal
of plain speaking in the vernacular? However the audience responds,
or responded, the foregrounding of language as an issue again is
clear.

Mercy's long speech in reply to Mankind's praise is carefully
balanced between extremes. He quotes the bible in Latin (line 228),
but he translates the Latin *before* he pronounces it. The syntax is very
simple: the speech is a sequence of one-line commands, easy for
Mankind and audience alike to understand. Mercy uses familiar
phrases (this life 'ys but a chery tyme') and memorable vernacular

rhyme ('Mesure ys tresure'), and ends with the homely, proverbial warning that a horse treated too lavishly will throw its master in the mire. As he prepares to leave Mankind to face temptation alone, his advice again concerns language. 'Lerne wyll I am here, sett my wordys in herte' (line 259), he advises, and beware the 'large' language of New Gyse, Nowadays and Nought and the whispering of Titivillus (lines 301–3).

Mankind, briefly left alone before the entrance of his tempters, speaks in the same Latinate English and writes down for himself, in Latin, the instruction which he believes will protect him against temptation: ' "*Memento, homo, quod cinis es et in cinerem reverteris*" ' (Remember, man, that thou art dust, and to dust thou shalt return) (line 321),[10] possibly even adopting it as a badge, although the meaning of the next line is not entirely clear. This suggests an almost magical belief (of the kind discussed in chapter 1) in the power of the words themselves, the idea that the Latin text of the bible has power to ward off evil. Immediately, however, New Gyse enters and subverts the sacramental quality of the Word in Latin by displaying his own capacity to quote the sacred Word: ' "*Cum sancto sanctus eris, et cum perverso perverteris*" ' (With the holy thou shalt be holy and with the perverse thou shalt be perverted) (line 324). The quotation, again untranslated, is adapted from the Psalms, and serves as an ironical forecast of Mankind's instability, since he, having been holy with the holy, will now be perverted with the perverse.

The scurrilous song that follows demonstrates even more explicitly that holy words cannot be fixed or protected from the assault of sin: the refrain of the song is a gross perversion of the word 'holy' itself into 'holyke' (line 343). Since the audience are encouraged to join in, they are trapped at a very personal level into acknowledging the complete fickleness of the word by enacting the process of desacralisation themselves. No word, whether Latin or English, is incorruptible.

On the other hand, the corruptibility of mere words is not evidence that such words necessarily corrupt the spirit. Words are emphatically material in this play, subject to fragmentation and transformation in ways that the Christian spirit can learn to resist. Individual members of the audience may choose not to participate in the obscene song, may refuse to enact its blasphemies. Mankind may be corrupted, but the corruption is temporary, suggesting that Mercy's words, or perhaps the Word itself (made material in the '*Memento, homo*' emblem cited above), is more powerful than corruptions of it. Thus, while the surface play of words enacts subversive manoeuvres, the structure of the action recuperates the authority of the sacred Word. Words are corruptible, but spirits may be paradoxically strengthened by them to resist their corruptions.

The materiality of words, and the need to distinguish them from the spirit, is further emphasised in two important ways in the play: by the selection of Titivillus (or Tutivillus) as 'the Fend of helle' (line 886) and by the introduction of the 'neck-verse' into the action. Titivillus, as discussed in chapter 2 above, is characterised by the Latin formula (cited p. 48 above) that underlines his function: to collect the dropped fragments of words that represent failings on the part of their speakers. Words could scarcely be rendered more material than they are by this image. His first line in *Mankind* illustrates his characteristic macaronic speech-pattern: '*Ego sum dominancium dominus* and my name is Titivillus' (line 475).

Titivillus' role in the play is to 'yrke' Mankind, to lead him away from the manual labour of digging, which he pursues, he says, to 'eschew ydullnes' (line 329), and to lead him into the sin of sloth, a sin frequently illustrated in medieval sermons and other religious writing by examples of laziness of speech (see e.g. Wenzel, *Acedia in Medieval Thought and Literature*, pp. 153–4; Jennings, 'Tutivillus', pp. 19, 60; Neuss, 'Active and Idle Language', pp. 45, 52). His net, though thoroughly material in the play, where it appears as a prop at lines 530–1, is apparently a material manifestation of the verbal, since it traditionally represents the lying words by which he tempts Mankind to sin.

The sequence of references to the 'neck-verse' constitute the second major instance of the play's concern with the materiality of words. Traditionally the beginning of the fiftieth psalm ('Have mercy upon me, O God, according to thy loving-kindness; according unto the multitude of thy tender mercies blot out my transgressions'; psalm 51 according to the Authorised Version), the 'neck-verse' was so called because it could save a criminal from hanging. The ability to read aloud this text was used as a test of clerical status by which a cleric might claim the right to be tried in the ecclesiastical courts, thereby escaping the death penalty, which the church could not impose. Its operations in *Mankind* demonstrate the author's scepticism about the capacity of words reduced to pure matter in this way to act as a touchstone of either clerical status or spiritual authority.

New Gyse first recommends as a precaution that the three of them

(Nowadays, Nought and New Gyse himself) should learn their neck-verse well (line 520) and runs in later in the play telling of Myscheffe's escape from hanging for knowing his (line 599) and his own more ignominious escape. (New Gyse himself has a broken halter round his neck at this point, and so presumably did not take his own advice, or was incapable of remembering the phrase at the crucial moment.) The fact that vicious characters can escape their punishment by being able to read a simple Latin tag makes nonsense of the meaning of the verse and exposes the fallacy of linking Latinity either with clerical status or with notions of virtue or authority.

Significantly, however, the last scene of the play shows Mercy trying to reinvest the very same phrase with meaning outside the context of a cynical attempt to escape the gallows. When he finds Mankind so ashamed of his sin that he doubts his own worthiness to ask mercy yet again, Mercy tells him: 'Yet for my lofe ope thy lyppys and sey "*Miserere mei, Deus!*"' (line 830). The strategy, as with the scurrilous song, is to deconstruct words into material signs detachable from the truth they seem to embody, but then to show that the point of such deconstruction is not to prove the word's inherent emptiness, but rather the spiritual state of the speaker or hearer. The right speaker, or the right hearer, has power to reconstitute the word as sacred.

The ability of the vicious characters to use Latin is not merely occasional, but pervades the whole text and functions in very varied ways. Not only do they mock Mercy with Latinate English, translate obscenities into Latin and mingle Latin with English in a kind of macaronic carnival; they also make up pseudo-Latin words from English roots, utter mock prayers and blessings, trivialise some of the most sacred moments of Christian history in the Latin of the Gospels,[11] construct a prolonged pseudo-trial (suggesting the Last Judgement) in a mixture of English, Latin and pseudo-Latin and play with the sheer sound of Latin until it is reduced to nonsense. When, for example, Myscheffe hears Mercy calling for Mankind in Latin, 'My predylecte son, where be ye? Mankynde, *ubi es?*' (line 771), he replies with a mixture of heavy mimicry and open abuse: 'My prepotent fader, when ye sowpe [sup], sowpe owt yowr messe. / Ye are all to-gloryede in yowr termys; ye make many a lesse [falsehood, lie]' '(lines 772–3). New Gyse takes up Myscheffe's mockery of Mercy's unnecessary and superfluous use of Latin in his pretence of answering Mercy's call: '*Hic hyc, hic hic, hic hic, hic hic!* / That ys to sey, here, here, here!' (lines 775–6). The absurdity of translating the Latin in this context, together with the reduction of the words to pure sound, calls attention to the nonsensicality of using clerical Latin for such mundane purposes.

Mercy's words, if they are to save Mankind, must demonstrate their power to overcome the verbal trickery of Myscheffe, the three worldly tempters and the devil, Titivillus; and Mercy, as we have seen, speaks in different voices. After the extreme Latinity of his opening speech, he finds a plainer speech in the middle of the play, and returns in his final speech to a more Latinate mode, but one still much less exaggerated than that of his opening speech. The syntax is straightforward, there are some very brief and direct instructions, and the sense of the Latin quotation is mostly duplicated by the surrounding English text. This return to Latinity (however simplified) may reflect the self-censorship of dangerous times, but is perhaps more likely to represent a plea for a middle way among preachers which would avoid the exclusive excesses of Latinity and admit the necessity of some plain English without incurring the suspicion of heresy. An author (or authors) with strong views on the subject of preaching would seem most likely to be in orders himself, perhaps, as Bevington suggests (*The Macro Plays*, p. xiii), a priest in a rural parish, anxious to reach the least literate members of his flock and aware of how distant, even ridiculous, the extremities of the Latinate discourse associated with the orthodox church must sound to such a congregation.

The difficulty of directing criticism against the language of churchmen at a time when language was itself central to accusations of heresy is evident. If part of the play's purpose is to point the lay audience firmly in the direction of the orthodox church, then Mercy must speak with a voice easily recognisable as the voice of the church in fifteenth-century England. At the same time, if a further part of its purpose is to point clerics in the audience towards a different kind of voice, then the play must also incorporate the possibility that the familiar voice of orthodoxy is open to usurpation by enemies of the church, and cannot automatically be trusted; it must demonstrate that Mercy might speak with a different voice and still speak truth. All discourses, as Bakhtin says, are 'masks'; no one discourse can claim to be 'an authentic, incontestable face' (*The Dialogic Imagination*, p. 273).

Renaming the Latinate English in *Mankind* 'aureation', and

pointing to the popularity of aureation in the fifteenth century, does not solve any problems. Such a description of language in purely stylistic terms is not sufficient explanation of its meaning, because it does not address the political dimension of choice. It seems clear that the changes in Mercy's tone of voice, together with the range of responses to his voice within the play, bear witness to a stylistic dilemma which is not only aesthetic, but also political. The type of language which *Mankind* parodies is the more extreme discourse of orthodox preaching, an extreme developed in opposition to the emphasis on plainness and the vernacular in Lollard preaching. By caricaturing and then subverting the stereotypes of Latin and vernacular discourses the play makes visible the danger, as well as the absurdity, of aligning a single discourse with salvation or damnation. The vicious may utter their blasphemies in Latin, just as the voice of God may be heard speaking in plain English.

CHAPTER 4

The controlling state

Mankind, in attempting to free language from its entrapment in the antagonism between heresy and religious orthodoxy, did not point towards the shape of things to come. Instead, the formulation of linguistic thinking in terms of fixed theological and political positions increasingly hardened into a simplistic polemic that cast English as the language of radicalism and Latin as the language of a conservative establishment. Symbiotic relations between the two languages remained as crucial as in the medieval period, but changing conceptions of each were developing. Whereas most medieval writers had perceived English as the barbarian other defining the authoritative, unitary discourse of Latin, Tudor Reformers were refining the Lollard position that produced English as the plain language for plain truth. Against this conception of English, Latin appeared less a barbarian than a demon. As English, in Reformed discourse, strove to usurp the place of Latin as the language of truth, it had to wrestle with an enemy whose claim to power rested on centuries of dominance. English had had the status of a poor language, hitherto thought unsuitable for truth because inadequate to its complexities; but Latin, smooth, eloquent and highly sophisticated, now seemed to threaten truth by virtue of the very assurance of its rhetoric and the glitter of its surface. Its danger lay not in the possibility of its inadequacy but in its capacity for deliberate deception.

AN ENGLISH BIBLE

As in the late fourteenth century, the focal issue in this hardening of a new polarisation was the question of an English bible.[1] Since the prohibition of English bibles by Archbishop Arundel in 1409 there had been no vernacular bible generally available in England, contrary to the practice of several other European countries (France,

Germany and Italy, for example), where vernacular bibles became increasingly available with the advent of printing in the late fifteenth century. The activity of the Lollards in England was instrumental in constructing a special degree of continuing hostility towards the notion of a vernacular bible within English culture, but developments in Northern Europe could not be ignored. The publication in 1516 of Erasmus' first edition of the New Testament in Greek (which implicitly undermined the authority of the Vulgate by indicating the derivative position of its Latin text in relation to the original Greek) and of Luther's German bible in 1522 and 1524 (the New Testament was published separately before the complete bible) further fuelled the demand for a vernacular bible in England. William Tyndale sought the support of Cuthbert Tunstall, the Bishop of London, in order to work on an English translation of the New Testament, but 'understode at the laste not only that there was no rowme in my lorde of londons palace to translate the new testament, but also that there was no place to do it in all englonde' (Bruce, *History of the Bible in English*, p. 30). He was forced to move to Germany in 1524 to continue his work.

Copies of the first edition of Tyndale's New Testament (published in Worms in 1526) were burned by the same Bishop Tunstall when they arrived in England, and the Bishop further instructed a London merchant, Augustine Packington, to buy up and destroy copies before they left Germany. Though this gesture had symbolic power, its practical futility within a print culture had to be humiliatingly pointed out to Tunstall by Packington, who told him too late that he should have been buying up the standing type. A further irony, according to Hall's *Chronicle*, was that Packington bought the books directly from Tyndale, thereby allowing Tyndale to use Tunstall's money to revise and reissue his translation (Bruce, *History of the Bible in English*, pp. 37–9).

Not all authorities in England were hostile to a vernacular bible, however, and Thomas Cromwell's support for the project was a crucial factor in making a translation available. A. G. Dickens (*The English Reformation*, p. 129) draws attention to correspondence between Cromwell and Miles Coverdale in 1527 which suggests that they were already discussing such a project before Cromwell's appointment first as Henry VIII's principal secretary in 1534, and, the following year, as vicegerent of the English church, acting for Henry as Supreme Head. Henry summoned a group of powerful and learned clergy to discuss the matter in 1530, but they condemned Tyndale's translation as heretical, thus leading the king to issue a proclamation which continued to prohibit ownership of any vernacular bible 'in the English tongue, or in the French or Dutch [German] tongue', while attempting to soften the refusal with the promise of an English bible translated by 'great, learned, and Catholic persons' following the eradication of heresy (Hughes and Larkin, *Tudor Royal Proclamations*, vol. 1, p. 196). Proceedings against heresy were moving increasingly into the armoury of the state. Although the king on this occasion invited the church to rule on the question of whether Tyndale's translation was heretical, their decision was presumably even then constrained by such directions as Henry gave them. Within four years the Act of Supremacy was to make the monarch explicitly responsible for determining and correcting heresy, thus appropriating the position previously belonging to the church, and ultimately to the pope. And heresy laws continued to function as an indicator of changing government regimes: Edward VI's first parliament (1547) repealed the medieval heresy laws, which allowed the death penalty for heresy, while the restoration of these same laws under Queen Mary in 1554 was what paved the way for the burning of Protestants.

By 1534 even the bishops who had vetoed Tyndale's translation in 1530 were pressing for an English bible to be translated by 'certain upright and learned men to be named by the said most illustrious king' (*The Works of William Tindale*, p. 18; Bruce, *History of the Bible in English*, p. 55). Meanwhile Coverdale, like Tyndale (to whom his translation was heavily indebted), had been working on his translation in exile and this he published in 1535, probably at Zürich, without waiting for authorisation from the King of England. He provided his translation nevertheless with an unauthorised dedication to Henry (Bruce, *History of the Bible in English*, pp. 54–7). Cromwell's support enabled an English printer to gain the king's permission to print it later the same year.

Two strands in the narrative of the English bible unwound separately and with cruel irony in the next year. In July 1536 Cromwell devised injunctions ordering parish clergy to provide copies of the bible in both Latin and English in every church 'for every man that will to look and read thereon' (*English Historical Documents*, vol. v, p. 807). Three months later Tyndale was executed at Vilvorde, near Brussels, within the territory of the Holy Roman

Emperor, on a charge of heresy, crying out at the stake his now famous plea: 'Lord, open the King of England's eyes.' Meanwhile Coverdale's bible circulated freely in England. Although Cromwell erased the article above from the injunctions, the timing of its first formulation is critical nonetheless, and sheds a particularly harsh light on Tyndale's death.

Less than a year after Tyndale's execution a new version of the English bible was issued by royal licence. This 'Matthew Bible', so called after its translator, who used the pseudonym of Thomas Matthew, was substantially Tyndale's bible, containing Tyndale's Pentateuch and New Testament, together with his manuscript version of Joshua to II Chronicles. In 1538, the erased injunction of 1536 was published in a form that instructed clerics not only to provide bibles for their parishioners to consult, but actively to encourage such reading:

Item, that ye shall discourage no man privily or apertly from the reading or hearing of the said Bible, but shall expressly provoke, stir, and exhort every person to read the same, as that which is the very lively word of God, that every Christian man is bound to embrace, believe and follow, if he look to be saved. (*English Historical Documents*, vol. v, p. 811)

It was in this year, too, that Cromwell first began planning an English prayer book, for hand in hand with the need to change the Latin bible for an English one went the insistence that the service too needed to be in the language of the people.

It would be easy to misread this sequence of dates and events teleologically, as a steady progress towards a popular, as well as populist, end. In fact, as several recent historians have been at pains to stress, there was no unanimity at popular level about the desirability of a vernacular bible and liturgy (see e.g. Haigh, *English Reformations* and Collinson's review of Haigh, *TLS*, 22 October 1993). Here, as at the highest levels of secular and ecclesiastical authority, there were simply opposing views. Eamon Duffy documents the unwillingness of many parish clergy to teach the creed, the commandments and the Lord's prayer in English, and the unwillingness of the people to learn them. According to one George Constantine in 1539, 'Yea, they jest at it, calling it the New Pater Noster and New Learning' (Duffy, *The Stripping of the Altars*, pp. 420–1; cf. John Bale, p. 88 below). Margaret Aston, citing several tales of difficulty in learning the English *paternoster*, notes that the subject 'seems to have become something of a literary topos' (*England's Iconoclasts*, pp. 356–7 and 357, n.43).

Henry VIII also had reservations about access to the English bible once he had made it available, and his government retreated to markedly more conservative positions after 1538 (Haigh, *English Reformations*, ch.9; see also pp. 84–6 below). It was in this year that the Pope excommunicated Henry and began attempting to organise a crusade against England. The Act of Six Articles (1539), with its return to an endorsement of Catholic theology, marked the beginning of the end for Cromwell, who was executed for treason and heresy in 1540. A statute of 1543 introduced class-based restrictions on bible-reading, which allowed noblemen and gentry to read it to their households, and merchants to read it in private, but prohibited 'woomen ... artificers prentises journeymen serving men of the degrees of yeomen or undre, husbandemen [and] laborers' from reading it at all, on penalty of a month's imprisonment (*35 Henry VIII, c.5*; *Statutes of the Realm*, vol. III, p. 896). Henry VIII's last speech to parliament in 1545 is strongly reminiscent of Henry Knighton's position (p. 12 above) in its suggestion that scripture is somehow sullied by being too widely available: Henry complains about 'how unreverently that most precious jewel, the Word of God, is disputed, rhymed, sung and jangled in every alehouse and tavern' (*Letters and Papers*, vol. xx, part 2, no. 1031). The recantation of Robert Ward, found in possession of 'unlawful bokes', demonstrates by its vocabulary that the words he speaks are put into his mouth by his accusers: he has, he confesses, 'dyverse tymes in alehouses and uncomelie and unmete places taken upon me to bable talke and rangle of the Scripture whiche I understode not, yea, and to expounde it after my folyshe fantasie' (Martin, *Religious Radicals*, p. 72)[2] The very terms again suggest continuity with the Lollard past: Henry's 'jangling' and Ward's 'bable' express fear and derision on the part of the fifteenth-century church, while the alehouse location confirms the class whose ungoverned speaking is to be feared and derided (see chapter 1, pp.14, 27–8 above). There is evidence to suggest too that oppressed as well as oppressors saw the bible as a weapon. Miles Hogarde, a Catholic artisan, claims that London apprentices carried their New Testaments about with them in order to use their knowledge to mock priests (Martin, *Religious Radicals*, p. 72).

A continuous line of polemic from Knighton (pp. 12–14 above) to

Henry VIII and beyond, then, argues for retaining the lesser-known language specifically to exclude the lower classes. But the argument that would prohibit a vernacular bible to the laity because of their relative illiteracy and unworthiness stimulates the counter-accusation that the Catholic church has deliberately withheld truth from large numbers of erring humanity, who need to know it for the salvation of their souls, by disguising it in a foreign language. This was certainly the view of Tyndale. Responding to the Catholic claim that the bible cannot be translated into a language as rude and barbaric as English, he states his view with characteristic bluntness: 'It is not so rude as they are false liars.' 'How shall I know who lieth, and who sayeth truth', he demands, '... when thou wilt not let me see scripture?' He then takes on the argument that scripture is too difficult to be understood without the help of the glosses, exposing what he sees as its faulty logic: 'If I must first believe the doctor, then is the doctor first true, and the truth of the scripture dependeth of his truth; and so the truth of God springeth of the truth of man. Thus antichrist turneth the roots of the trees upward' (*The Works of William Tindale*, pp. 89–90).[3] His parody of the Latinate establishment at work demonstrates his view of scholastic Latin as a pretentious smokescreen to keep the vast majority in ignorance of the word of God. It needs to be quoted at some length to convey the flavour of its scorn:

ye drive them from God's word, and will let no man come therto, until he have been two years master of art. First, they nosel them in sophistry, and in *benefundatum*. And there corrupt they their judgments with apparent arguments, and with alleging unto them texts of logic, of natural *philautia*, of metaphysic, and moral philosophy, and of all manner books of Aristotle, and of all manner doctors which they yet never saw. Moreover, one holdeth this, another that; one is a Real, another a Nominal. What wonderful dreams have they of their predicaments, universals, second intentions, *quiddities, haecceities*, and relatives; and whether *species fundata in chimera* be *vera species*; and whether this proposition be true, *Non ens est aliquid*; whether *ens* be *equivocum*, or *univocum*. *Ens* is a voice only, say some. *Ens* is *univocum*, saith another, and descendeth into *ens creatum*, and into *ens increatum, per modos intrinsecos*. When they have thiswise brawled eight, ten, or twelve or more years, and after that their judgments are utterly corrupt, then they begin their divinity; not at the scripture, but every man taketh a sundry doctor; which doctors are as sundry and as divers, the one contrary unto the other, as there are divers fashions and monstrous shapes, none like another, among our sects of religion. Every religion, every university, and almost every man, hath a sundry divinity. (*The Works of William Tindale*, p. 91)

Bishop Gardiner's attempt to insist later, once an English bible became inevitable, that it should include such phrases as 'This is my dilect son in whom complacui' (Dickens, *The English Reformation*, p. 136) would seem to lend weight to Tyndale's accusation of obfuscation.

On the other hand, Tyndale's dispute with Thomas More elicits a specimen translation of the sixth chapter of St John from More, which indicates the false simplicity of reducing the debate to the extremes demonstrated above. More's translation is, as G. D. Bone points out (in his prefatory essay to Greenslade's edition of Tyndale), slightly less colloquial than Tyndale's, but his willingness to produce a translation shows a genuine attempt to meet Tyndale on his own ground. Furthermore, the medieval church, as shown in chapter 1, had led the way in moving towards the vernacular, and had only been frightened off that course of action by the growth of a heterodox Lollard literature in English. Even Bishop Bonner, in Mary's reign, allowed *An Honest Godly Instruction*, an English explanation of the Latin liturgy, to circulate, ostensibly for the instruction of children (Martin, *Religious Radicals*, p. 5).

The struggle was not simply between a religion couched in language open only to the exclusive few as opposed to a religion in the language of the people, but between a religion of ceremonial practice as opposed to a religion of the word. This is a point which has been made by many scholars, most importantly in recent years by Keith Thomas (*Religion and the Decline of Magic*) and Eamon Duffy (*The Stripping of the Altars*), but it is crucial to understanding the real issues behind the written polemic. When Tyndale denounces Catholics for 'a false kind of praying, wherein the tongue and lips labour ... but the heart talketh not ... nor hath any confidence in the promises of God; but trusteth in the multitude of words, and in the pain and tediousness of the length of the prayer; as a conjuror doth in his circles, characters, and superstitious words of his conjuration' (Thomas, *Religion and the Decline of Magic*, p. 70), he is, perhaps deliberately, ignoring the extent to which a religion of the word depends on both a print culture to maintain it and a semi-literate audience to respond to it, conditions which had only just begun to obtain in Tyndale's lifetime. Though the Lollards first focused on the written word and the importance of understanding, Reformed religion could not have become dominant before the invention of printing and the increase in literacy.[4] As Christina

Larner writes, 'in more senses than one, Protestantism was the "religion of the Book"' (Larner, *Witchcraft and Religion*, p. 120). The attempts of the medieval church to suppress heresy centred, as chapter 1 showed, on rooting out the right books (or the wrong ones, as the church would have it). The religion of a pre-literate age had emerged out of that culture, and centred on doing (going to mass, crossing oneself, saying prayers, giving money to the church) rather than reading. The medieval Catholic church, serving a largely illiterate population without access to books of any kind, had reached out to its congregation through a ceremonial practice that offered a comfort and reassurance which may indeed have been analogous to magic, but which was not for many centuries widely contested by any other way of experiencing the Word of God. What was shared amongst the community was a time-honoured practice, and the definition of the community was in turn dependent on that practice. It not only gave a shape to working lives in the smallest parish, where the rhythms of work were known and measured against the rhythms of the Christian calendar and Sunday rest; it also theoretically linked the tiny parish to the expanse of the Christian community as a whole, all working and worshipping according to the same rhythm.

For Lollards and Reformers, however, the shared literacy of reading groups and conventicles focused on the special activity of the small group consciously at odds with the surrounding community. Though Lollards may have felt a kinship with Hussites or other heretical groups, and Protestants certainly felt themselves to be part of a wider European Reform movement, the determination of their communal identity by its antagonism to the wider community inevitably produced a very different sense of what worship and 'community' meant. For them, redefining the shared understanding of biblical text that drove them into separatism was predictably paramount. The other kind of 'understanding', the kind that emerges *out of* shared practice, as opposed to producing it, could not be available. The advice of Princess Mary's almoner (p.1 above) could not make sense for a religion that had defined itself by insisting on a personal response to the words of scripture. Where for medieval congregations, and for some individual English congregations until at least the early seventeenth century, the Latin words had exerted their power through a sacred aura acquired from their shared and continuous modes of embodiment over centuries and across geographical boundaries, they now became capable of carrying a different charge: a charge of elitism, exclusion and disdain. But it is important to remember that both responses were available throughout the sixteenth century, and for some the experience of Latin must always have been a fragmented and unresolved experience hung between these two poles. The advent of an English bible and prayer book did not and could not completely sever the sense of origins attaching to Latin.

At the same time, the relationship between English and Latin was now so thoroughly politicised that no one could be deaf to those reverberations either, particularly since many of the great Reformers specifically targeted their efforts at 'the plain man', who is in turn a derivative of Lollard writing (pp.28–30 above). Constructed though he is by writers who need him, the plain man is nevertheless a powerful mode of address, and one that seems to speak for a democratising religion that wants to break down traditional oligarchies. The ploughman becomes the symbol of the enlightenment conferred by a vernacular bible across traditional boundaries of class and education. Foxe cites Tyndale telling a learned divine that 'if God spared him life, ere many years he would cause a boy that driveth the plough, to know more of the Scripture than he did' (*The Acts and Monuments of John Foxe*, vol. v, p. 117); and Tyndale's remark was anticipated in turn by Erasmus (drawing in his turn on St Jerome's letters):

I could wish that even all women should read the Gospel and St Paul's Epistles, and I would that they were translated into all the languages of all Christian people, that they might be read and known not merely by the Scots and the Irish but even by the Turks and the Saracens. I wish that the farm worker might sing parts of them at the plough, that the weaver might hum them at the shuttle, and that the traveller might beguile the weariness of the way by reciting them. (Bruce, *History of the Bible in English*, p. 29)

The idealism of Erasmus and Tyndale, who see the vernacular bible as an instrument of freedom and spiritual equality, looks almost quaint, however, in the light of its actual effects within the Tudor state (which will become apparent as the chapter goes on).

Many Catholics, unlike Erasmus, believed that the words of the scripture were intentionally obscure and that to attempt to reduce God's mysteries to the level of plain English for simple people was misguided, if not sacrilegious. The accusation, in the words of a later Catholic writer, was that Protestants 'prostitute the Scriptures . . . as baudes doo theire Harlottes, to the Ungodly, Unlearned, Rascal people . . . Prentises, Light Personnes, and the rifferaffe of the people'. Such riff-raff, according to this view, 'were keapte from the Readinge of the Scriptures by the special providence of God' (Jones, *The Triumph of the English Language*, p. 63).

For Protestants, on the other hand, it was clear that priests, not God, were responsible for keeping the people from reading the scriptures. Latimer, in his famous *Sermon on the Plowers*, appropriates the image of the ploughman for the preacher rather than for the unlearned congregation and argues that the good preacher must use the language of the people if he is to teach them. 'This is the devilish plowing', he thunders, 'the which worketh to have things in Latin and letteth [hinders] the fruitful edification' (*Selected Sermons of Hugh Latimer*, p. 42). Latimer is perhaps here deliberately resorting to metaphor, rather than more specifically naming preaching, since the Catholic church, despite its use of a Latin bible and Latin liturgy, had never in fact habitually preached in Latin except to educated audiences, though, as *Mankind* demonstrates, preachers may have preached in a highly Latinate English. Normally it was the bible or the liturgy that drew the fire of Reformers.

Plain language was not merely the right language for preaching or the bible, and not merely a matter of English as against Latin. It was, for Reformers, the sign by which a truthful speaker was to be known, an aspect of what St Paul had called 'the simplicity that is in Christ' (2 Cor. 11.3), and developed in specific and polemical opposition to the formality and ceremonialism (or corruption, according to the Reformers) of the established church (Knott, *Discourses of Martyrdom*, p. 69). Thus, in a letter written to Henry VIII in 1530, Latimer not only urges the necessity for an English bible on the grounds of its 'freedom and plainness' but pointedly, if somewhat heavy-handedly, constructs his own trustworthiness via the same topos: 'I was bold to write this rude, homely, and simple letter unto your grace, trusting that you will accept my true and faithful mind even as it is' (Knott, *Discourses of Martyrdom*, p. 74). It is a classic appeal to the topos of plain speaking as the guarantee of truthfulness. The guarantee is, however, fraudulent. 'Within ideology', as Simon Shepherd argues, 'plainness becomes a sign of truth. Thus the language of plainness can in turn be appropriated by any authority that presents itself as truth-telling', including the monarch and the state (*Marlowe and the Politics of the Elizabethan Theatre*, p. 13).[5]

ENGLAND AND BABYLON

Appeals to freedom and truth, however, do not tell the whole story of the rise to power of vernacular plainness. These are only two ways of loading the dice. A third and central context for the rejection of Rome is that of nationalism. The developments of the 1530s culminated in 'the formal establishment of an English "nation state", a realm subject to no outside authority' (Smith, *The Emergence of a Nation State*, p. 88), so that Protestant England might from then on justifiably conceive of itself as much in terms of political as of religious difference. As the Act in Restraint of Appeals (*24 Henry VIII, c.12*) proclaims in 1533: 'This Realme of Englond is an Impire' (*Statutes of the Realm*, vol. III, p. 427; see further Ullmann, 'This Realm of England' and Fox and Guy, *Reassessing the Henrician Age*, ch.7). Robert Weimann (*Authority and Representation*) is also centrally interested in the development and representation of authority in sixteenth-century England, and considers the development of a concept of sovereignty at this time to be a virtual 'revolution' (p.54). It is no accident either that the word 'state' comes to acquire the meaning of a 'body politic as organized for supreme civil rule and government' during the same decade (OED; see further Kastan, '"Holy Wurdes"', pp. 269–70).[6]

The 'Babylonical mass', as a Colchester weaver names it (*The Acts and Monuments of John Foxe*, vol. VIII, p. 139), is also made to signify its distance from God by its very foreignness. It should come as no surprise that sixteenth-century writers assumed an identity between Babylon and Babel. This allowed Reformers to link their attack on Latin as the obfuscation of Babel with their figuring of the Pope as the Whore of Babylon, and to construct contemporary Catholicism in terms of fallen language as well as the revelation of Antichrist. The sixteenth century, Margreta de Grazia has pointed out, 'applied the Old Testament connection between sin and babble to its own problems of discourse' ('Shakespeare's View of Language', p. 377). The fallen world seemed to continue to re-enact its own sinfulness in linguistic terms. As Thomas Lodge asked rhetorically, 'What may a man then say of the most part of men's discourses and devices who live in these days? Truly, that it is but babble, that is Babel' (de Grazia, 'Shakespeare's View of Language', p. 377; cf. chapter 1 above).

Rome was conveniently refigured as Babel/Babylon, and the rejection of Latin took its place within a nationalist project underwritten by scriptural authority (St Paul's 'simplicity that is Christ'). As Catholicism was the necessary other against which Protestantism defined itself, so Rome became a necessary other for the definition of England. 'Meaning arises', Richard Helgerson writes, 'not from some central core of identity but rather at a margin of difference. Self-definition comes from the not-self, from the alien other' (*Forms of Nationhood*, p. 22). Latin has to be anathematised in order to validate the honour of the English language for its native speakers, to give them pride in their origins and to empower them to prove that English can compete with any language.

The messenger's opening speech in Rastell's *Four Elements* (1517) laments the low valuation hitherto set on the vernacular, and the trivial nature of the 'toyes and tryfellys' so far printed in the mother tongue. This is not, according to the speaker, due to the inadequacy of English, but to lack of effort on the part of writers. 'Yf clerkys in this realme wolde take payn so', he argues,

> Consyderyng that our tonge is now suffycyent
> To expoun any hard sentence evydent,
> They myght, yf they wolde, in our englyshe tonge
> Wryte workys of gravyte somtyme amonge.   (lines 24–8)

There is a sense of urgency about this passage, a sense that the time has come for English and the writing of Englishness. Only 'now' is the sufficiency of English in place, and that 'now' is a call to arms for the writing of England. The play finds its context within a more widespread interest in publishing in English and on things English. The printing of chronicles in English, for example, begins as early as English printing itself, initiated by Caxton and continued by Pynson; and Rastell, as a printer as well as a playwright, was more widely involved in the remaking of England and English through his ambitious and symbolic project of 'Englishing and printing' the 'Great Boke of Statutes 1530–1533' (Eisenstein, *The Printing Press as an Agent of Change*, vol. i, p. 105). The law, a written text uniquely bound up with the self-definition of a nation, had hitherto been mainly in Latin or Anglo-French. Its availability in the mother-tongue of the land gave new status to the English language, and confirmed the place of language in the making of the nation (see further Helgerson, *Forms of Nationhood*, ch.2).

But the effects of a nation-state united by a single common language are not all liberating. Though the insistence on English is expressed in terms of a community of English speakers, the material effect is one of closer surveillance and more fully centralised control. The 'freedom' to speak and write English looks increasingly like the acceptable face of a project that actually seeks to restrict freedom of speech in the name of England. Cromwell's first Treason Act of 1534 (*26 Henry VIII, c.13*) has become notorious as the law that made it possible to condemn mere words for treason.[7] A sequence of statutes passed through parliament by Cromwell in this year worked to produce a new and tighter relationship between church and state (the Acts are itemised in Dickens, *The English Reformation*, pp. 118–22). The consequence of these statutes was that religious allegiance became more explicitly and inseparably entwined with allegiance to the king, and deviation from the newly established Church of England was legally construed as treachery. Such were the effects of 'freedom' from Latin and the church of Rome.

The practice of religion had always taken material form through participation in a local, a national and an international community; the rift in the church produced a rift in all three communities, preventing the integration of each with the other. Religious choice now meant alignment with one community at the expense of another: many local communities struggled with opposition between parent and child or between priest and parish, while the changes in the English church meant that loyalty to the international community of the Catholic church could signify betrayal of the English nation. And, since the English church did not stand still, but moved now nearer to, now further from, the Roman church throughout the sixteenth century, conformity was an unstable quantity. English Christians, if they wished to remain loyal to England, had to be adaptable rather than firm in their commitment. Any non-conformity or religious difference, whether towards Protestant or Catholic extremes, was a source of anxiety for sixteenth-century governments. Early fifteenth-century legislation, as noted in chapter 1, equated Lollardy with sedition. A glance through the proclamations of Henry VIII shows that the equation of heresy with sedition has become naturalised. The difference is that, with the established religion itself in a state of flux, the adherents of the formerly orthodox church may be cast as the new traitors. Guidelines for orthodoxy now come in the form of legislation from the centre rather than centuries of traditional practice. And the new, legislated orthodoxy cannot tolerate any sign of deviation. The liturgy may have been 'freed' into

English, but those who utter the new English ritual are required to inhabit that apparently free space with extreme care.

How much continuity there was between the Lollards and the early Reformers has been a matter of debate. A proclamation of 1529 refers airily to 'all manner of heresies and errors, commonly called Lollardies' (Hughes and Larkin, *Tudor Royal Proclamations*, vol. I, p. 184), and it is often in areas of known Lollard activity that Protestants are first identified. Concern for the spread of heresy was especially high in England in the early years of the sixteenth century, before Luther had nailed his theses to the door at Wittenberg. Convocation was summoned in 1511 to discuss the suppression of heresy, and Colet's opening sermon described that particular moment in time as 'greved of heretykes, men mad with marveylous folysshenes' (Lupton, *A Life of John Colet*, p. 298).[8] The well-known case of Richard Hunne (Dickens, *The English Reformation*, pp. 90–6; Thomson, *The Later Lollards*, pp. 162–70; Haigh, *English Reformations*, pp. 77–81), which began with Hunne's refusal to pay mortuary dues to the church on the death of his baby son, revealed him to have been the owner of a Wyclifite bible. More importantly, it demonstrated a level of support for him amongst his fellow-Londoners conspicuous enough to provoke Bishop Fitzjames, Hunne's prosecutor, to state his belief that 'if my Chaunceler be tryed by any xii men in London they be so maliciouslie set *in favorem hereticae pravitatis* / that is ar so set apon the favoure of heresie / that they will cast and condemn my clarcke / thowght [*sic*] he was as innocent as Abel' (Thomson, *The Later Lollards*, p. 169).

Heresy trials continue to cite the name of Wyclif down to 1520. Bishop Tunstall's letter to Erasmus in 1523 indicates his belief that there was a clear continuity between the old and the new heresy: 'It is', he writes, 'no question of pernicious novelty; it is only that new arms are being added to the great crowd of Wycliffite heresies' (Dickens, *The English Reformation*, p. 37). The records of Bishop Tunstall's persecution of 1528 would seem to confirm his view. They show that some of those who went to Friar Robert Barnes for a copy of the new Tyndale translation of the bible showed him copies of the Wyclifite translation they already owned (Thomson, *The Later Lollards*, pp. 137–8).

Much clearer than the evidence of actual continuity, however, is the evidence of the Reformist need to demonstrate continuity. The Reformers' claim to represent the 'true' religion rested on a model which presented their church as the direct descendant of the apostolic simplicity of the early church and the Roman church as the deviant latecomer. Challenged to answer 'the question which every papist propoundeth, where was your Church an hundreth yeares past?',[9] they felt a deep need to trace their origins back through an ancestry of protest. Their response to the Roman church was to defy it to reconcile its claim that Protestantism was a jumped-up novelty with the religious persecution that had preceded it. As John Foxe demanded a few decades later: 'And if they think this doctrine be so new that it was not heard of before Luther's time, how then came such great persecution before Luther's time here in England?' (*The Acts and Monuments of John Foxe*, vol. IV, p. 217).

Margaret Aston, who argues ('Lollardy and the Reformation') that early sixteenth-century Lollardy was less a survival than a revival, demonstrates that there was a significant gap in the production of Lollard texts before the Reformers recognised their propaganda value and began printing them. Nor was such printing always a matter of relatively innocent revival; texts were anthologised or even rewritten in such a way as to further the reforming cause. Foxe's belief that Chaucer was 'a right Wiclevian' derives, as Aston points out, from the propagandist project of earlier editors such as Thynne, who added Lollard texts to their editions of Chaucer (see also Dillon, *Geoffrey Chaucer*, pp. 144–5 and n.13). On the other hand, there were also genuine errors in Tudor readings of early texts. The ground was laid for John Bale's attribution of *Piers Plowman* to Wyclif, as we have seen, in Langland's own lifetime (p. 29 above; see further von Nolcken, '*Piers Plowman*', pp. 74–8).

The fear of religious heterodoxy as the root of rebellion was not unfounded in either period, though the fact that it is increasingly singled out as the root that needs attention speaks of the tightening bond between church and state. The English Rising of 1381 followed soon after Wyclif was accused of heresy (cf. pp. 16–17 above), and Lollardy was the self-proclaimed impetus behind the Oldcastle Rising of 1414. Nor did Catholics passively accept Henry's Reformist legislation. The Pilgrimage of Grace in 1536 demonstrated the hostility of the predominantly Catholic North to increasing attempts by government to enforce conformity to the new ecclesiastical legislation. A draft proclamation dating from 1539, with corrections in Henry's hand, shows that he blamed the English bible for the 'murmur, malice, and malignity' among his people. Had this proclamation been issued, bible reading would have had to be performed thereafter '[quietly and with silence] . . . [secretly]', and there would have been no more reading 'with any loud or high voices, [and specially] during the time of divine service or of celebrating and saying of masses' (Hughes and Larkin, *Tudor Royal Proclamations*, vol. 1, p. 285 (Henry's revisions in square brackets); Duffy, *The Stripping of the Altars*, pp. 422–3). Precisely those voices that thought they had been set free by the coming of an English bible would have discovered that the next step was silencing.

Cranmer's preface to the second edition of the Great Bible (1540) demonstrates the ideological project it represented for Henry VIII and his government: 'Herein may princes learn how to govern their subjects, subjects obedience, love, and dread to their princes, husbands how they should behave them unto their wives, how to educate their children and servants, and contrary, the wives children and servants may knowe their duty to husbandes, parents, and masters.'[10] The aim was to construct a people who spoke with one voice. If they could not, or would not, do that, they should be prevented from speaking at all. The bible, briefly fostered by the Tudor state as part of its attempt to produce a unified nation, was gradually to become, in the eyes of that same state, instrumental in the refounding of Babel. Insistence on access to the single authoritative manifestation of the Word before Babel seemed to the Tudor authorities, ironically, parallel with the presumption that had put an end to unitary language.

Tudor governments were fearful not only of public bible reading but of all public performances or gatherings. Any public presentation might whip up discontent on religious or other grounds. A letter said to be from Henry VIII to an unknown Justice of the Peace in York shows both the kind of incident the state feared and the response such an incident might provoke:

Trusty and well-beloved, we greet you well. And whereas we understand by certain report the late evil and seditious rising in our ancient city of York, at the acting of a religious interlude of St Thomas the Apostle, made in the said city on the 23rd of August now past; and whereas we have been credibly informed that the said rising was owing to the seditious conduct of certain papists who took part in preparing for the said interlude, we will and require you that from henceforward ye do your utmost to prevent and hinder any such commotion in future, and for this ye have my warrant for apprehending and putting in prison any papists who shall, in performing interludes which are founded on any portions of the Old or New Testament, say or make use of any language which may tend to excite those who are beholding the same to any breach of the peace. (*Records of Early English Drama: York*, vol. II, pp. 649–50)

One of the earliest attempts to legislate specifically against plays, as opposed to any other kind of ungoverned speaking, was the Act for the Advancement of True Religion (1543). It warned that plays and printed matter should 'meddle not with interpretacions of Scripture, contrarye to the doctryne set foorth by the Kinges Majestie' (*34 Henry VIII, c.1*; *Statutes of the Realm*, vol. III, p. 894). Though religion was not the only matter on which the state sought to silence players, it is symptomatic of the deeply-rooted equation between heresy and sedition (see pp. 82–3 above) that religion is singled out for such attention. State censorship of drama was to become increasingly dominant and more wide-ranging in later Tudor reigns.[11]

The Act was repealed in 1547, at the beginning of the new reign of Edward VI, but two years later a play was apparently the direct trigger for rebellion. Kett's rebellion in the summer of 1549 led to a prohibition of all interludes throughout the realm for two months. A government proclamation of 1551 tried to tighten control over performances by requiring all professional troupes of actors to be licensed and prohibiting plays from dealing with matters of king or government. The proclamation further required the signature of the Privy Council on plays submitted for publication (Hughes and Larkin, *Tudor Royal Proclamations*, vol. I, pp. 514–18). Unsurprisingly perhaps, these measures were directed more against Catholic than Protestant activities, and Protestant propagandist drama could be licensed by claiming to attack a foreign power (Rome) as opposed to dealing with matters of religion (Spinrad, *The Summons of Death*, p. 91). As one Protestant nostalgically described these earlier years, looking back from exile during Mary's reign, 'with God's word was every man's mouth occupied; of that were all songs, interludes and plays made' (*Revels*, vol. II, p. 18). Notably, too, the proclamations of 1549 and 1551 both level the prohibition only against plays or printed matter 'in the English tongue'. Latin plays, privately performed at the universities or for learned audiences in noble households, had a different pedigree altogether, and there were no restrictions on their performance (see further chapters 5 and 6 below). Only the 'free' language needs surveillance.

The exploitation of drama for topical and polemical purposes was hardly new in the reigns of Henry VIII and Edward VI. The Wakefield *Second Shepherds' Play*, with its direct complaint to the audience on the matter of high taxation, is merely the best-known example of a medieval play making reference to issues of immediate concern to a contemporary audience within the differently protected environment of religious cycle drama. We must assume, too, that any really rebellious matter would not be carefully transcribed into a written text either before or after performance, but would be inserted for the immediate occasion and omitted from any written accounts. Even performing before the king, a bold actor might dare to say 'many things against gentlemen, more than was in the book of the play' (*Revels*, vol. II, p. 15).[12]

The church had long recognised the teaching potential of drama in a mainly illiterate society, and used conventional teaching characters, such as the variously named 'Doctor' or 'Expositor' (cf. the discussion of N-Town's 'Contemplation' in chapter 2 above) to expound points of doctrine to the audience. Since the Tudor state after Henry VIII's break with Rome, however, needed to remake rather than confirm the *status quo*, the propagandist nature of its teaching suddenly became much more conspicuous. Drama, the potential rabble-rouser and stirrer of rebellions, could equally be harnessed by the state and paid to work for government masters. Sir Richard Morison, propagandist under the direction of Thomas Cromwell between 1536 and 1539, proposed to Henry VIII that Robin Hood plays, which he saw as inciting not only 'lewdenes and rebawdry', but 'disobedience also to your officers', 'shulde be forbodden and deleted and others dyvysed to set forthe and declare lyvely before the peoples eies the abhomynation and wickednes of the bisshop of Rome, monkes, ffreers, nonnes, and suche like, and to declare and open to them thobedience that your subjectes by goddes and mans lawes owe unto your magestie' (Anglo, 'An Early Tudor Programme', p. 179). This was Cromwell's choice of strategy in attempting to establish the Reformed Church on a firmer footing in England; and it was John Bale, ex-Carmelite and impassioned convert, whom he made production manager of his campaign.[13]

JOHN BALE

A thriving tradition of drama in the monasteries may have shaped not only John Bale, as a writer and actor of plays, but his company.

Bale was not the only instance of a cleric turned player, and he may
have recruited his troupe from amongst other disaffected monks and
friars with experience of staging plays within the old regime.
Records from the Carmelite houses at Maldon and Ipswich, where
Bale was appointed prior in 1530 and 1533 successively, demonstrate
Carmelite involvement in plays and pageants (see p. 32 and n. 3
above).

A different kind of public performance, however, made a significant contribution to the direction of John Bale's writing. As a child
Bale saw a young man burned at Norwich for 'havynge the lordes
prayer in English' and refusing to pray to the saints (Happé, ed., *The
Complete Plays of John Bale*, vol. 1, p. 2). Many years later, after his
conversion to the Reformers' cause and his move from the position
of Carmelite prior to parish priest of Thorndon in Suffolk, he found
himself in the ironic position of hounding resistant parishioners to
learn the Paternoster, Creed and Ten Commandments in English.
Like Tyndale, he constructed his idea of faith on a belief in 'reason',
and could not accept the notion of a faith that functioned in place of
reason. He showed his congregation, he tells us, 'what godly
understanding and remembrance they might have in that being in
English, which they could never have by the Latin. And that where
as no understanding was, nothing could be asked in faith, and that
(which) rose not of faith was sin after St Paul' (Fairfield, *John Bale*,
p. 46). For Bale, the move to English is self-evidently a move to
'understanding'; but for his parishioners, accustomed to an alternative form of understanding, as explained by Princess Mary's
almoner, it must have seemed that what Bale was presenting them
with was compulsion in place of traditional authority. They not only
refused to learn the elements of their faith in English, but openly
identified themselves in their refusal with 'the Northern men'
rebelling during that same year of 1536 (Duffy, *The Stripping of the
Altars*, p. 399).

Despite his acknowledged twenty-four years as a Carmelite friar,
the burning at Norwich clearly remained in Bale's mind and shaped
his later writing. His desire to document the trials of Sir John
Oldcastle, the Lollard rebel executed in 1417, and Anne Askew,
burned for her religious beliefs in 1546, are the clearest examples of
his need to remake the martyrdom witnessed in his early youth,
though his work on Wyclif and many of his prose pamphlets and
plays are also, less directly, related to this same incident. His

expression of the wish that 'some learned Englyshe man' would 'set forth the inglish chronicles in their right shappe' (preface to *Sir John Oldcastle*, cited in Bauckham, *Tudor Apocalypse*, p. 72) was also part of the same mindset, the need to remake the story of the past from the point of view of persecuted protesters, proto-Protestants,[14] in order to challenge the predominantly Catholic ideology of the existing chronicles. Polydore Virgil's *Historia Anglica*, he claimed, told a corrupt version of English history full of 'Romish lies and other Italish beggarys' (Harris, *John Bale*, p. 116). The Oldcastle rebellion, too, he decided to reject as Romish fabrication, since it was at odds with his attempt to cast Oldcastle as 'the prototype of the Protestant saint' (Fairfield, *John Bale*, p. 127).

His *Image of Both Churches*, begun in 1541, three years before the attack on Polydore Virgil, was another attempt to set the record straight, not purely in terms of English history, but in a global and eschatological context. It was a Reformist reading of the Book of Revelation, identifying the pope as Antichrist, 'the first extensive work of apocalyptic interpretation in English Protestantism and the first commentary in English on the book of Revelation' (Bauckham, *Tudor Apocalypse*, p. 21; see further Bauckham, *Tudor Apocalypse*, pp. 21–9). The question of whether Bale (and Foxe after him) regarded England as an elect nation raised above other nations by God has been passionately argued by critics since the appearance of William Haller's study of *Foxe's Book of Martyrs and the Elect Nation* (1963). Richard Bauckham is insistent that Bale illustrated apocalyptic themes from English examples because he had the material to hand and it was of most interest to his readers, not because he believed that England had a 'unique providential role' to play (*Tudor Apocalypse*, pp. 72–3). Nevertheless Bale's strong focus on England is not without nationalist bias. The fact that the *Image* was written in English and about England for English Protestants, as so many of Bale's works were, sets it in a context which binds nationalism and religious reform inseparably together.

The association of the pope with Antichrist in the book, furthermore, was one of Wyclif's themes, and Bale's development of it is a self-conscious alignment of his own position with a heterodox English tradition of anti-papalism and anti-monasticism. Bale wrote two works on Wyclif, *De Bello Wiclivi Contra Papistas* and *An Alphabetical Index to Walden's Fasciculus Zizaniorum Wiclevi*, and worked on preserving and cataloguing Wyclif's works (Harris, *John Bale*, p. 123).

The resemblance between the woodcuts of Wyclif and Bale published in his catalogue of writers, *Illustrum Maioris Britanniae Scriptorum Summarium*, expresses this identification in visual terms, and may be the result of conscious strategy on the part of Bale or his publisher.[15] Foxe's *Acts and Monuments* confirms the alignment between Bale and Wyclif for the next generation: it both recognises the importance of Bale's work on Wyclif (Blatt (*The Plays of John Bale*, p. 59) cites Foxe), and takes on itself 'Bale's reworking of the national myth, making opposition to Rome the central theme of English history' (Fairfield, *John Bale*, p. 106).

Some of Bale's theological views, as his contemporary, Stephen Gardiner, pointed out, were mutually contradictory; but such logical and theological contradictions found a coherence in the common anti-Roman ground they shared (Blatt, *The Plays of John Bale*, pp. 45, 55). His Protestantism is inseparable from his nationalism, and yet at the same time conceived within a framework put in place by Catholicism. For him the purity of the early church was handed down through a line of dissenting martyrs, comparable with the Catholic saints: history was as inescapably theological as theology was historical. Bale's own description of his work, as treating 'both of the heavenly and politicall state of the christen churche' (Blatt, *The Plays of John Bale*, p. 62), is still trapped within the framework of St Augustine's conception of the two cities. It is no accident that, in addition to his explicitly theological writing, the two forms Bale most conspicuously chose to remake in the Protestant image were the history and the morality play. Both are forms that need reworking in order to speak to the Protestant state, yet the very choice of those forms replicates a thinking that is bound into the terms of Catholicism precisely by its reversal of them.

History and morality play are forms not wholly separate for Bale. He moulds history into dramatic form and is quick to see the implicit drama in history. As Ritchie Kendall has shown, many of his non-dramatic works enact a kind of displaced drama. Kendall cites Bale's marginal note on the parallel between Anne Askew's trials and plays well known from the traditional mystery cycles: 'Aforetime hath not been seen such frantic outrage as is now; the judges, without all sober discretion, running to the rack, tugging, hauling, and pulling thereat, like tormentors in a play' (*The Drama of Dissent*, p. 58).[16] On the other hand, however, Bale clearly associates theatricality with lack of seriousness or worse, and has problems coming to terms with drama as a mode of articulation. In the prologue to his play *God's Promises* (1538), Bale warns the audience to expect 'no tryfelinge sporte / In fantasyes fayned, nor soche lyke gaudysh gere', but to look to find instead 'the thynges that shall your inwarde stomake stere' (lines 18–19).[17] The distinction between playful, 'bawdy' theatre and Reformed, conscientious theatre is also explicit in his 'Epistle Exhortatory of an English Christian to his dearly beloved Country', where he berates Catholics for their perverse treatment of players:

So long as they played lyes, and sange baudy songes, blasphemed God, and corrupted mens consciences, ye never blamed them, but were verye well contented. But sens they persuaded the people to worship theyr Lorde God aryght, accordyng to hys holie lawes and not yours, and to acknoledge Jesus Chryst for their onelye redeemer and saviour, without your lowsie legerdemains, ye never were pleased with them. (Collier, *The History of English Dramatic Poetry*, vol. I, p. 133)

King John's sneering at the 'popetly plays' of the clergy in Bale's play of *King John* (1538)[18] (line 415) uses wordplay to link Catholicism with entertainment: the word 'popetly' condemns the church's shows by equating puppets or dolls with the pope and sneering simultaneously at both.

This discomfort with the idea of play is partly due to an association present for him, as for many other Reformers and for Lollards before them, of Catholic ritual with ostentatious theatricality (cf. Tyndale's comparison with conjurers, cited p. 76 above and the discussion of the Lollard *Tretise of Miraclis Pleyinge* in chapter 2; cf. also the quotations assembled by Barish, *The Antitheatrical Prejudice*, ch.6). For the purist Reformers, eager to return to what had to be defined as the plainness of the early church, taking the bible as their only text, the elaborations of church ceremony and written commentary seemed to be the visible manifestation of a corrupt church which had come to substitute empty forms for an absent core of 'understanding'. Both theatre and the Catholic church are seen as manifestations of Babel, proliferating words and forms promiscuously, in opposition to the kind of singleness of meaning the Reformers yearned for. Mockery of the priesthood as charlatans performing well-rehearsed scenes to delude their poor parishioners as to their supernatural powers was a staple of anti-Catholic polemic from the Lollards onwards, and Bale is no exception. Priests, he writes, are like 'daunsing apes, whose natural property is, to counterfet al thinges that they se done afore them, and yet are they never that they seem to resemble' (*The Apology of John Bale Againste a Ranke Papyst*, cited in Kendall, *The Drama of Dissent*, p. 129). The danger implicit in both theatre and the priesthood, as constructed by Reformers, is that both, by representing truth in the way they do, may lead the simple soul to mistake the representation for the truth itself.

The priesthood, 'of all occupacions ... the most folish', is also the butt of Bale's satire because it performs in Latin: the priest, Bale jeers, 'turneth his back to the people / and telleth a tale to the walle in a foren language'. Bale frequently incites hostility in his audience towards the Roman church by targeting its foreignness, and in turn constructing that foreignness as deceitful and exploitative. The gesture of turning one's back is made to seem of a piece with muttering in a foreign language. If the priest turns to face the people 'it is eyther to receive the offering / eyther to desyre them to give him a good wurde / with *Orate pro me fratres* for he is a poore brother of theirs / eyther to byd them God spede / with *Dominus vobiscum* for they get no part of his banket / eyther els to blesse them with the bottom of the cuppe / with *Benedictio Dei* whan all the brekefast is done' (*A Mysterye of Inyquyte*, cited in Blatt, *The Plays of John Bale*, p. 58). The begging succeeds because it fends off questions by proceeding in an incomprehensible language, and the priest has eaten and drunk all the 'banket' while the hungry congregation is distracted. Foreign language is constructed here as the outward sign of a religion that protects a self-seeking and elitist clergy.

Not only do priests, according to Bale, dress up and manufacture illusions as actors do, they also make a puppet of language and wilfully sever its connections with the plain truth. Like the represented images of drama and the priesthood, words can become objects in themselves, signs free of what they represent. Words, in the mouths of Bale's clerics, are deliberately slippery and evasive, as well as dangerously pleasurable and seductive. Their foreignness becomes part of an exoticism which also draws on the native resources of alliteration, rhyme and other sound effects to highlight the materiality of the word rather than its transparency, and can equally exploit dialect speech as a deviation from the plain vernacular.[19] Even English, which is presented, in the thinking about bible translation, as a singleness that unites a community in a mutually shared reading and speaking, turns out to be multiple and unstable.

Such speech becomes an object in itself rather than a glass through which meaning is made visible. As Bakhtin was to argue in relation to the development of the novel, language itself becomes 'the image of language' and a distance becomes visible between language and reality (*The Dialogic Imagination*, pp. 59–60). Though the placing of Latin within this particular discourse is a feature of Protestant drama, the discourse itself goes back to earlier Catholic morality plays, which represented the language of the Vice as similarly opaque and seductive. *Mankind*, as discussed in chapter 3 above, and to a lesser extent the Wakefield cycle, already showed how this discourse might begin to appropriate Latin.

Yet Bale's distrust of theatrical display, as he saw it manifested through the rituals of the Catholic church, is underpinned by a need to accommodate this powerful weapon within the armoury of Protestant propaganda. And Bale's position speaks for the position of the Protestant state. Hence Cromwell appoints Bale to produce the necessary propagandist drama,[20] and Bale valorises his dramatic project by tying it to an explicit and authorised 'mission'. Paul White discusses Bale's connection with Cromwell more fully, noting that *King John* in particular 'treats the issues Cromwell championed during the late 1530s: the royal supremacy, bible reading on a national scale, the dangers of Catholic doctrine and ceremonies' and arguing that Bale's contempt for the rite of confession could not have gone unpunished after 1536 (when Henry VIII refused to proscribe it) without Cromwell's protection (*Protestantism, Patronage and Playing*, pp. 15–19). Evidence suggests co-operation between Bale, Cromwell and Cranmer in creating a Reformation drama: Bale translated Thomas Kirchmayer's *Pammachius*, dedicated to Cranmer; Cromwell paid Bale for writing plays; and all three were apparently involved in a production of Bale's *King John* at Cranmer's residence over the Christmas period of 1538–9, paid for by Cromwell.[21] This production, furthermore, succeeded in arousing the audience against the Roman church, as trial depositions following trouble during the performance show. John Alforde said 'it was a pity that the bishop of Rome should reign any longer, for he would do with our King as he did with King John', while Thomas Brown said that 'King John was as noble a prince as ever was in England, and thereby we might perceive that he was the beginner of the putting down of the bishop of Rome, and thereof we might all be glad' (Gardiner, *Mysteries' End*, pp. 52–3).

One way in which Bale made the necessary accommodation to drama was to emphasise the fact of his drama's vernacular address. He takes care in his Latin catalogues to emphasise that his plays were written in the common tongue ('*in idiomate vulgari*') or mother-tongue ('*idiomate materno*'). This emphasis allows him to see his project as analogous with the apparent liberation and democratisation of a vernacular bible. His project is thus indirectly complicit with the strategies of the Tudor state, just as it is directly complicit with those of the Protestant church (and Cromwell, his protector, was of course actively engaged in making the two inseparable). As Chambers notes, it is his use of the vernacular that marks him as an innovator and sets him 'apart from the other great figures of the Lutheran drama' (*The Medieval Stage*, vol. II, p. 224). Thomas Kirchmayer's *Pammachius*, written in 1538 and translated by Bale some time before 1548, is an example of this Latin Lutheran drama; and the fact that Kirchmayer dedicated it to Cranmer in 1538 is an indication of the direction in which England's religious leaders appeared to be pushing at that time. (Performing it in 1545, however, was another matter. The play provoked both outrage and defence when it was performed at Christ's College, Cambridge, and the correspondence between the Chancellor, Stephen Gardiner, and the Vice-Chancellor, Matthew Parker, suggests the changed climate of Henry's later years of government, with the authorities much more edgy about propagandist drama (Boas, *University Drama*, pp. 22–3; *Revels*, vol. II, p. 17).)

For Bale in the late 1530s, however, making a Protestant drama and making it in English were ideals held with passionate conviction. He is credited with writing the first English history play and the first English Protestant morality play, and there are indications that he was planning a Protestant mystery cycle to oust the extant Catholic cycles (Happé, ed., *The Complete Plays of John Bale*, vol. I, pp. 8, 12–13), again replaying Catholic modes. English is not just the native language of the writer or his audience; it is the language of the godly nation (see further Womack, 'Imagining Communities', pp. 104–5), and is itself part of the justification for the dramatic project. The creation of a new kind of English-language drama at this specific point in time aims to unify the English nation both politically and religiously. Records of performance indicate a range of possible venues for Bale's company (Archbishop Cranmer's household at Canterbury, St Stephen's Church in Canterbury, Thetford Priory, Norfolk, Cambridge and Barnstaple) that further suggests the danger of trying to limit either plays or companies to single specific audiences in this period (cf. chapter 2 above). Part of the function of a propagandist drama, after all, is to spread its message across a wide range of the population, uniting different audiences in a common cause.

The futility of trying to limit plays too strictly to singular audiences, particularly within a new kind of drama, may be suggested by a feature of Bale's play *God's Promises*. Each act ends with an anthem sung in Latin and then either sung or spoken (the stage direction varies) in English. The Latin stage directions make it clear that the actors may choose either the Latin or the English version. It may be that the offer of choice indicates the need to allow the performers freedom to adapt the play to different audiences. The choice may have depended on the proportion of learned to non-Latinate members of the audience; or it may have been a political choice, dependent on whether the performers were playing to the converted or treading a careful line between polemic and their own safety.

On the other hand, it may not suggest anything about the nature of the audience at all, but rather something about the nature of the dramatic engagement. Bale may have wished to retain the option of Latin in order to produce a different mode of engagement in his audience, whoever they might be, at particular moments of the play. The Latin can insist, as medieval drama demonstrates (chapter 2 above), on the significance and *difference* of these authoritative moments, thus clearly marking the transition between acts. The capacity of an unlearned audience to respond to Latin in performance is derived from the centrality of the Latin bible and the Latin mass in vernacular culture over hundreds of years. Much as Bale and the Reformers may have hated the deep-rooted response that Latin could summon, their dramaturgy occasionally continues to exploit it, just as their hostility to Catholicism is ironically framed within the terms of all they reject.

KING JOHN

The idea of remaking the reign of King John in the image of the Reformed church of early Tudor England almost certainly came to Bale through Tyndale and Robert Barnes. Tyndale's *Obedience of a Christian Man* and Barnes' *Supplicacion unto the Most Gracyous Prynce H.*

the VIII, allude to King John by way of addressing themselves to the English king on the subject of the current state of England and the unacceptable face of Rome, as Bale's *King John* does, and both offer a reading of King John as a king of England oppressed and finally overwhelmed by Roman corruption. Bale, as we have seen, looked for the authorisation of prominent Reformers to give his plays a legitimacy which their status as plays might otherwise call into question. As Cromwell was the right choice for patron in the climate within which Bale was writing, so Tyndale and Barnes were politically correct literary sources for the ideological work Bale wanted to do. Accused of heresy, Tyndale and Barnes were both eventually burned for their beliefs. (Barnes had been a friar, like Bale, and Bale wrote an English tract in Barnes' defence.) There could not have been a more apt paternity for a play celebrating a king portrayed as a proto-martyr for the rights of England against the Roman yoke.

King John is the only character in the play who remains a consistent, named individual throughout. Other characters are either allegorical, or shift between allegorical and historical status. The first words of the play are King John's, and they embrace and render indivisible in one stanza the centrality of the bible and the necessity of obedience to a lawful king:

> To declare the powres and their force to enlarge
> The scriptur of God doth flow in most abowndaunce;
> And of sophysteres the cauteles to dyscharge,
> Bothe Peter and Pawle makyth plenteosse utterauns;
> How that all pepell shuld shew there trew alegyauns
> To ther lawfull kyng, Christ Jesu dothe consent,
> Whych to the hygh powres was evere obedyent.   (lines 1–7)

Thus political and theological concerns are entwined from the beginning in a way that sets the tone for the whole play. The rights of the king, the duty of his people and the nature of the godly nation are dictated and monitored by the Word of God.

The political allegory represented by England, the first character to share the stage with King John, is spelled out with absolute clarity. She is a widow, poorly dressed because she has been so badly treated by the clergy (lines 27–39, 58–73), and widowed because her husband, God himself, has been exiled by 'thes vyle popych swyne' (line 107). God, England explains,

> abydyth not where his word ys refusyd,
> For God is his word, lyke as Seynt John dothe tell
> In the begynnyng of his moste blyssyd gospell. (lines 116–18)

Thus neatly do both King John and England enact their own legitimacy by quoting the blessed scriptures and aligning themselves with the Word of God. The plot stresses this alignment of Protestantism with the Word by demonising Rome and the Catholic church as responsible for the absence of God and his Word from the nation of England:

> The Popys pyggys may not abyd this word to be hard,
> Nor knowyn of pepyll, or had in anye regard.
> Ther eyes are so sore they maye not abyd the lyght. (lines 119–21)

This is of course the medieval morality adapted for partisan purposes. As Rainer Pineas points out, the Protestant morality 'was not preaching primarily against man's internal propensity to sin but against a well-organized external force, Catholicism' ('The English Morality Play', p. 165).

The entrance of the third character, Sedition, focuses the propagandist direction of the play with demonic energy. Again, his words immediately denote his status. On seeing King John and England together he gleefully assumes some 'bycherye' (lechery) between them and threatens to 'tell tales' (lines 43–4). His swearing, his fantasy of sin where there is none and his willingness to spread slander in contempt of truth all identify his words as precisely ungodly, and King John's reply makes this explicit for the audience: 'Avoyd, lewde person, for thy wordes are ungodlye' (line 45). The lines are reminiscent of Mercy's rebuke to the Vices in *Mankind* and his warning to Mankind against the dangers of 'ydyll language' (p. 62 above). Sedition's words thus endorse his name and show him deliberately fomenting discord in the realm. When he first announces his name on stage the further equation between Sedition and Catholicism is expressed: 'I am Sedycyon, that with the Pope wyll hold / So long as I have a hole with in my breche' (lines 90–1), and this equation is made explicit at every possible opportunity (see e.g. the superfluous renaming of Sedition at lines 186ff. and Sedition's boasting about his late attempt 'in the Northe' (the Pilgrimage of Grace in 1536) at line 2515). Furthermore, later on in the play, Sedition also becomes Stephen Langton, the Archbishop of Canterbury, appointed by the Pope against the wishes of the King of

England. Cromwell's legislation of 1534, discussed above (p. 82), encouraged this association between refusal to accept the new religion and treason against king and state. The character of Treason in *King John* is a priest, and when King John naively asks, 'A pryste and a traytour? How maye that wele agree?', Treason boasts that he has used the sworn secrecy of confession to produce twenty thousand traitors (lines 1811, 1817–18). References to the treacherous exploitation of the confessional in this way are scattered throughout the play (lines 260–73, 847–62, 1141–90), and may have been partly inspired by Tyndale, who says that papists 'betray all realms' and argues that they put the knowledge derived from the confessional to political and wicked uses (Miller, 'The Roman Rite', p. 821).

On the other hand, Greg Walker cites reports of actual exploitation of the confessional for subversive purposes in the two years immediately preceding the play (*Plays of Persuasion*, p. 214 and n.97), but emphasises that in attacking auricular confession Bale was not following the Tudor state, but rather attempting to lead it. The Ten Articles of 1536 had specifically insisted on the need to confess to a priest and warned the clergy 'in no wise ... [to] contemn this auricular confession which is made unto the ministers of the Church' (*English Historical Documents*, vol. v, p. 799; cited Walker, *Plays of Persuasion*, p. 213). The Six Articles of June 1539, furthermore, explicitly retained auricular confession, despite the campaigning of Bale and other Reformers.

The play clearly insinuates its doctrinal position into a political framework by denouncing the rituals it displays not only as trickery but also as treachery; and it further underlines the equation between treachery and the church of Rome by emphasising national as well as theological difference. The Roman Catholic church is demonised as other not only to the Protestant church, then, but to the English church. The true church of God on earth, according to the play's conception, is a matter of nationality as well as faith, and its opponents are not merely traitors, but foreign traitors. When King John accuses Sedition of being unnatural to his mother England, Sedition utterly denies English descent, and claims his birth 'under the Pope in the holy cyte of Rome' (line 183). His use of French in greeting Dissimulation (line 668) or in describing himself as 'sance pere Sedycyon' (line 817) seems to serve the primary purpose of reminding the audience of his foreignness.

The only other way of interpreting the use of French by a non-

French speaker in this period might be as an indicator of class, since French retained high status as the former language of the English court. Certainly the play identifies the noble and wealthy as traitors, while England and King John remain poor, robbed by the unscrupulous clergy. The other character who is not vicious is Commonalty, the son of England. He too is poor, and blind besides, 'for lacke of informacyon / In the word of God' (lines 1583–4). (Imperial Majesty and Veritas belong to a morality tradition of abstract virtue rather than political status.) The class alignment of the characters of *King John* mimics exactly the strategy of the Tudor state, which was to present an image of the monarch as caring parent, looking to the interests of his/her children and protecting them from exploitation by a self-interested clergy.

Sir David Lindsay's *Satire of the Three Estates*, which seems to show Bale's influence, portrays a similar alignment of monarch and people against clergy, but in his play, as in Bale's, it is highly unlikely that the semi-heroic role of the working people and paupers should be taken as any more than symbolic. Lindsay was, after all, usher to Prince James (later King James V of Scotland), chief herald and poet laureate of the Scottish court. The presence of Commonalty or its equivalent is necessary in both plays, since both share a concern with the nation, which is represented at its most inclusive by the common people. Yet the concern in both plays with clerical oppression, which demands the presence of the common people to represent the object of this oppression, is focused on the nature of the oppression, not the class of the oppressed. The very fact that Bale names his Vice-figure Sedition indicates how little sympathy he would have had towards any movement that took action to empower the oppressed (cf. his attempt to clear Oldcastle of the charge of rebellion, p. 89 above). Both Bale and Lindsay portray the commons as betrayed by the church, but owing complete loyalty to king and country, and indeed looking to the king for protection of their rights.

Though the oppressors come from the clerical and noble estates, more is made of their specific moral failings than of their class positions. Nobility, for example, utters sentiments against Sedition that King John approves:

NOBYLYTE. Syns I was a chyld both hym and his condycyon
          I ever hated for his iniquite.

K.JOHAN.   A clere tokyn that is of trew nobelyte   (lines 330–2) but he is easily persuaded by Clergy to support Holy Church instead of King John because, as he admits, 'I am unlernyd, my wyttes are sone confowndyd' (line 617). The play does not argue that Nobility or Clergy should be done away with, but that they should behave as befits their status in the Reformed state. The nobility should stay loyal to the king to put down sedition, while the clergy should teach the commons the Word of God rather than leave them in spiritual blindness.

A common feature of the vicious, Catholic characters which is foregrounded in the play is their tendency to go under more than one name: Usurped Power is also the Pope, Private Wealth is also Cardinal Pandulphus and Dissimulation is also two other figures, Raymundus and Simon of Swinsett. This doubleness perhaps develops, as White suggests, an idea derived from Tyndale, who compares Antichrist to a player whose nature is 'to go out of the play for a season and to disguise himself, and then to come in again with a new name and a new raiment' (White, *Protestantism, Patronage and Playing*, p. 36). Within the play such instability of character functions as a clear indicator of treachery, as compared with the consistent unity of the non-Catholic characters. Single, stable identity, within the terms of this drama, is demonstrative of truth (the character Veritas (Truth) has also, naturally, a single persona) while doubleness is suspect and deceitful. This links back again to Bale's own anxieties (and those of the Reformers generally) around theatre as deception. It suggests an attempt to develop a whole new aesthetic that approves players who seem to be fused with their parts as against fickle players who make a show of their own facility in changing roles. It is a way of thinking about theatre which seeks to valorise playing that hides its playfulness as opposed to playing that knows and shows its own tricksiness.[22] As 'authorised' playing, commissioned by the state, it perhaps takes its lead from state performance (royal speeches, parliamentary ceremonial, pageantry), a playing that seeks to mask its performed status (see, for example, the opening of chapter 5 below).

The strategy of the play may be compared with Cromwell's public exhibition of sacred images in the marketplace in 1538 and 1539: famous images such as the Rood of Grace were demystified first by being removed from their holy setting, and further by being exposed as fakes to the local people (White, *Protestantism, Patronage and Playing*, pp. 36–7). The device, though itself a piece of theatre, seeks to expose the objects of its derision as 'theatrical' in the sense of fake. In the same way Bale's *King John* incorporates and exposes through parody versions of Catholic ritual, most notably confession and excommunication.[23] In exposing the Roman rites as hollow shows it cunningly distances itself from the negative associations of show and seems to naturalise and neutralise its own status.

Ceremony is repeatedly made an object of derision and explicitly formulated as an alternative to a true religion based on scripture. In adopting this position Bale was again in advance of the state, which had continued to endorse 'laudable customs, rites and ceremonies' in the Ten Articles (*English Historical Documents*, vol. v, p. 804) and which, despite the provision for an English bible in every church in the Injunctions of 1538, was already putting difficulties in the way by April 1539 (see p. 74 above and Walker, *Plays of Persuasion*, pp. 214–19). The rituals of the church are presented as mere empty forms to be discarded by a Reformed religion. King John's words to Private Wealth are among many to make the open opposition between form and substance: 'Take to ye yowre traysh, yowre ryngyng, syngyng and pypyng, / So that we may have the scryptures openyng' (lines 1392–3). Treason, the priest, similarly sees the one as ousting the other:

> In the place of Christe I have sett up supersticyons;
> For preachynges, ceremonyes, for Gods wurde, mennys tradicyons.
> Come to the temple and there Christe hath no place;
> Moyses and the paganes doth utterly hym deface.   (lines 1823–6)

Ceremonial 'gere' (line 1074) is represented as a substitute for the Word, which is why the words of ceremony are deliberately opaque. 'Laten servyce with the cerymonyes many' (line 1078) stands in place of the gospel; 'mattens, houres, masse and evensonge', all in Latin, 'drowne the scriptures' (lines 998–9). The fact that the Roman church conducts its services in Latin is mentioned again and again, both to underline its non-English origins and to make the point that its rituals are deliberately constructed for profit, and can only function in a language that prohibits understanding. The only elements of Christ in a church otherwise dominated by idolatry are 'the Epystle and the Gospell, / And that is in Latyne that no man shoulde it knowe' (lines 1840–1). The point of the prolonged Latin of King John's confession to Stephen Langton (Sedition) (lines 1786–802) is precisely that a large proportion of the audience is expected *not* to understand it. This dramatic method exploits the audience's confrontation of its own ignorance in order to bring it to the realisation of how it has been duped. On the other hand the laboured joke of substituting the Latin for pope, cardinals and prelates in place of God or Jesus Christ and the saints is accessible even to the illiterate amongst the audience, since the Latin ritual of penance would be so familiar as to provoke recognition of any corruption, especially when the missing forms, even in Latin (*Deo, omnipotens Deus, Dominus noster Jesus Christus, omnibus sanctis*), were those most likely to be understood by even the least literate.[24] Though the play may have been performed before audiences who had never understood the literal meanings of the Latin formulae that they heard and uttered in church, they could not fail to notice the insertion of rogue forms and draw their own conclusions. They have already been instructed by Dissimulation that Latin is a trick to draw profits to the church: 'Ther ys no Englyche that can soche profyghtes compasse' (line 717).

The same aesthetic that privileges earnest mimesis over conspicuous playfulness also privileges plain English and controlled utterance over rebellious sound or voices out of control, whether singing, laughing or gabbling Latin. This highly textured, but ultimately chaotic layering of sound is presented as an affront to the orderly simplicity of sound it opposes. As in *Mankind*, playful words that revel in their own materiality and relish the self-conscious display of alliteration, rhyme and other sound effects are unerring signs of sinfulness.[25] The Vice's linguistic priority is pleasure, not truthfulness; and pleasure, as Bale elsewhere says, is dangerous: 'Though the mermaydes songe be swete / yet ys yt full of poyson (as are also your honyed rhetoryckes) and leadeth them unto deathe which geveth them therof the hearinge' ('Epistle Exhortatory', cited in Kendall, *The Drama of Dissent*, p. 99).

As in *Mankind*, song itself is highly suspect, an index of worldliness and fundamental unseriousness. The sequence that leads directly from the prolonged rite of excommunication into an immediate and presumably frivolous song (it is sung 'meryly', at the Pope's instigation (line 1054)) confirms the audience in the view that the excommunication itself is worthless, the work of moral degenerates. The ritual words of the excommunication, possibly chanted, flow almost seamlessly into the frivolity of secular song, thereby illustrating (and by implication rejecting) the promiscuous tendencies of playful theatre, which allows one form of show to collapse into another. The Catholic characters are shown singing merry songs on other occasions too (lines 828, 2086), so much so that an offstage drinking song can become almost readable as the sign that a cleric is approaching. When Dissimulation is heard in the distance singing 'wassayle, wassayle', England's remark that 'He doth seme a farre some relygyouse man to be' (line 2093) is an invitation to the actor to play directly to the audience, perhaps in mock-surprise.

Nor is it only secular song that functions as a sign of degeneracy. Religious song too is capable of being parodied or perverted either by substituting one Latin word for another (lines 764–5; see Happé's note) or by interweaving sacred Latin with English colloquialism (lines 766–7). The Litany, debased in macaronic form, is said to sound like 'sum hoggherd / Callyng for his pygges' (lines 637–8). Whatever the song, it is associated with laughter, whether on the part of the singers themselves or on the part of the audience. But audiences acculturated to the morality tradition of plays like *Mankind* know the need to distrust and evaluate laughter in the context of morality. The more lawless and entertaining the moment, the more likely a trap for the audience. The moment when Sedition and the Cardinal really explode from song to laughter:

> By the messe, Pandulphus, now maye we synge *Cantate*,
> And crowe *Confitebor*, with a joyfull *Jubilate*!
> Holde me, or els for laughynge I must burste   (lines 1692–4)

offers a complex experience of laughter to the audience. They see the wild laughing of cynical churchmen exploiting the unwitting populace with their cheap ceremonies; but they are invited to view that laughter with disapproval, while reserving their own laughter for the ceremonies they have seen exposed as frauds. The play hopes to raise a laugh *outside* the theatre, so that when the audience becomes a congregation in another context it will recognise the absurdity of the moments it has seen desacralised here. Laughter and playfulness are danger signs *within* the play, but the play aims to construct a social response that we might name as 'righteous laughter'.

Another sound effect besides song that blatantly functions to reveal the speaker as sinful is the slip of the tongue (lines 304–5, 512–14). Slippery speakers are shown as literally slipping into words that reveal their true motives in place of those that seek to disguise them. Words that display their own surface rather than behaving as though transparent are always suspect in this play. Though verbal pyrotechnics can be ostentatiously 'vernacular', in one sense of the word (colloquial or even obscene), the type of vernacular speech that identifies the godly (those who care about developing a vernacular for the purpose of biblical translation, for example) is plain. It is the language of the idealised ploughman, not the language of the village pub.

Thus Protestant drama remains trapped within the oppositions of medieval morality even as it reverses them. Though Latin has been transferred from the mouths of holy speakers to the mouths of unholy speakers, and has been replaced by vernacular plainness, holy discourse is still defined by its opposition to Babel. Ungoverned babble remains the unerring mark of sinful speakers. Sedition's literal use of the terms 'bablyng' and 'byble-bable', terms already more widely associated with the construction of opposing truth-claims, is there to call attention to his own wickedness. He uses them in dismissing England's advice to King John on directing the good commonwealth according to the Word of God:

SEDICYON. Of bablyng matters I trow yt is tyme to cease.

K.JOHAN. Why dost thow call them bablyng maters? Tell me.

SEDICYON. For they are not worth the shakyng of a pertre [pear-tree]
Whan the peres are gon; they are but dyble-dable.
I marvell ye can abyd such byble-bable.   (lines 156–60)

A character who explicitly rejects the Word of God as mere bibble-babble (cf. pp. 27 and 74 above) presents his status in a religious drama unequivocally.

The status of Latin, however, is rather less stable than the status of Babel/babble. Perhaps surprisingly, it is not restricted to the function of demonising its speakers as papist schemers, although that is certainly its most dominant function in the play. Bale's use of Latin in *God's Promises* (p. 95 above) is a reminder that Bale knew from his own experience of the Latin liturgy that Latin could produce particular and desirable effects on congregations and audiences, effects too good to discard. And even at a time when translation of the bible elicited such passion on either side, Latin is still the language which most immediately signals to an audience that the bible is being quoted. No English bible had as yet had time to become as familiar and recognisable as the Vulgate. Bale's compromise is to make figures of virtue like England, King John and Imperial Majesty quote the Latin text but also translate it into English (as at lines 83–6, 130–4, 1467–9, 2417–20). Latin also stands untranslated as the language of prophecy when England cites 'Maister Morres' (lines 1899–903). Thus, even within a play that attacks Latin as a means of excluding, deluding and profiteering, Latin retains some of its aura of authority. The audience, while clearly summoned to liberate itself from the exploitation and control that Latin represents, is still called upon to respond to its traditional appeal.

CHAPTER 5

The value of learning

The coronation pageant which marked the beginning of Elizabeth I's reign looked back to the drama of John Bale. The show at the Little Conduit presented two hills, representing 'a decaied commonweale' and 'a flourishing commonweale'. Truth, led by her father Time, stepped from between them to offer the queen an English bible.[1] Elizabeth's performance was one of those that Bale's developing aesthetic sought, where there was no visible distinction between performer and role. There is a structural affinity, too, between Bale's *King John* and Elizabeth's coronation pageant: both present the monarch interacting with the figure of *Veritas*/Truth, and this interaction in turn seems to confirm the sincerity and authenticity of the monarch-performer. Though Elizabeth's response to Truth's gesture may have been rehearsed, or at least premeditated, it was performed to look like a spontaneously gracious act: 'shee as soone as she had received the booke, kissed it, and with both hir hands held up the same, and so laid it upon her brest, with great thanks to the citie therefore' (*Holinshed's Chronicles*, vol. IV, p. 168).

The propaganda potential of such a gesture at such a moment was immense: Holinshed's report of the pageant was in addition to an official printed record (issued twice in 1559 and again in 1604), and the Venetian ambassador also recounted the scene.[2] The impact of Elizabeth's gesture is shown by the way later plays revisit it. Both Heywood's *If You Know Not Me* (1604–5) and Dekker's *Whore of Babylon* (c.1606–7) rework it at powerful moments, Heywood at the end of Part I (itself a complete play) and Dekker in an opening dumbshow. Heywood also reproduces it again in his *Englands Elizabeth* (1631). The gesture was consciously symbolic: it affirmed the queen's rejection of the Marian regime which had just ended, and announced the firmly Protestant direction that her own ecclesiastical legislation would seek. (Significantly, it revived a censored pageant written by Richard Grafton for Philip II, in which Henry VIII was represented as holding 'a booke, whereon was wrytten *Verbum Dei*' (Manley, *Literature and Culture*, p. 249).) It is fitting to note, then, that Bale's *King John* was restaged in 1561, possibly on the occasion of Queen Elizabeth's visit to Ipswich, and was perhaps specifically revised for this purpose (*King Johan*, ed. Adams, p. 24). Its final lines on that occasion celebrate the queen as

> a lyghte to other princes all
> For the godly wayes whome she doth dayly move
> To hir liege people through Gods wurde specyall (lines 2672–4)

and gloat over her subduing of 'the papistes, / With all the ofsprynge of Antichristes generacyon' (lines 2678–9).[3]

FOXE'S BOOK OF MARTYRS

Bale's disciple, John Foxe, became the symbolic figurehead of the new Elizabethan orthodoxy. His *Acts and Monuments* (more commonly known to his contemporaries as the *Book of Martyrs*) was published for the first time in English in 1563 and dedicated to the queen.[4] His letter to the president and fellows of Magdalen, his former Oxford college, calls attention to the importance he attaches to the language of his book, now newly in English, following its two Latin precursors. Acknowledging that a Latin version might have been more pleasing to his academic audience, he nevertheless affirms the importance of publishing the book 'in English, for the good of the country and for the information of the multitude' (cited by George Townsend, 'Life of the Martyrologist', in *The Acts and Monuments of John Foxe*, vol. i, p. 89). The same stance characterises the 'Epistle Dedicatory to the Queen's Majesty', published with the book:

And though the story, being written in the popular tongue, serveth not so greatly for your own peculiar reading, nor for such as be learned, yet I shall desire both you and them to consider in it the necessity of the ignorant flock of Christ committed to your government in this realm of England; who, as they have been long led in ignorance, and wrapped in blindness, for lack especially of God's word, and partly also for wanting the light of history, I thought pity but that such should be helped, their ignorance relieved, and simplicity instructed. I considered they were the flock of Christ, and your subjects, belonging to your account and charge, bought with the same price, and having as dear souls to the Lord as others; and, though they be but simple and unlearned, yet not unapt to be taught if they were applied. (*The Acts and Monuments of John Foxe*, vol. I, p. viii)

This position was self-evidently both nationalist and Protestant. As Richard Helgerson notes, Foxe builds England's royal identity into the structure of his book by dividing it according to English monarchs, where a Catholic would have divided it by papal reigns (*Forms of Nationhood*, pp. 260–1). And though the Catholic church had shown especial concern for the education of the common people during the fourteenth century (see chapter 1 above), the extent to which first Lollards and then later Reformers hijacked the topos of the plain man has already been discussed.[5]

Foxe's text itself is in many instances a rereading of history via the co-ordinates of language. His account of the early church is always ready to highlight indications that it made the scriptures freely available to the laity and worshipped in 'the vulgar tongue', thus laying the foundations for his extensive and polemical treatment of the struggle for an English bible and prayer book in his own century. His narratives of later heresy trials celebrate linguistic opposition between accuser and accused, and he delights in trials such as that of John Aston (or Ashton) the Lollard (*The Acts and Monuments of John Foxe*, vol. III, pp. 35–6) or John Philpot the Marian martyr (vol. VII, pp. 605–86) where this opposition can take centre stage. Aston deliberately violates the Archbishop's insistence that he reply in Latin and calls out to the laity in English, while Philpot interrupts Bonner's Latin prayer to ask the bishop to speak in English so that all may understand (vol. VII, p. 678). Ceremonial, whether manifested practically or linguistically, is punctured in Foxe's representations by plain language. Blunt, colloquial responses to the elaborate forms and language of the Catholic church hold up those same forms for ridicule and in doing so validate themselves. Ridley and Cranmer, for example, respond to the 'abominable and ridiculous degradation' that strips them of their ecclesiastical office as to a meaningless piece of theatre, 'too fond for a Vice in a play' (vol. VII, p. 544). (Foxe prints 'the form of disgrading an archbishop', both words and actions, in full and conspicuous Latin (vol. VII, pp. 77–9).[6]) For Cranmer it is all merely unnecessary: 'I had myself done with this gear long ago' (vol. VIII, p. 79; cf. Bale's use of the word 'gere' in *God's Promises* and *King John* (pp. 91 and 101 above). OED records the depreciatory sense from 1489.). As John Knott comments, 'the contrast is the sort Foxe relished: between the Latin formulae for removing the symbols of ecclesiastical authority and Cranmer's dismissive "this gear" ' (*Discourses of Martyrdom*, p. 73). A new ceremony, whereby the plain man speaks out against ecclesiastical authority, ruptures and disables the old ceremony, making it appear, as Catholic ritual is made to appear in Bale's *King John*, hollow, fake, 'constructed'. And the new ceremony, like the new drama, masks its own constructedness in the act of unmasking another's. Ironically, Reformed performance, specialising as it does in plain speaking and truth-effects, turns out to be even more duplicitous than Catholic performance.

The use of Latin by the presiding bishops is presented by Foxe as a sign of their deliberate exclusion of the laity, an exclusion both scornful and fearful, while the choice of English is made to represent sincerity and openness, truth speaking transparently, with nothing to hide. The very fact that in writing these accounts of trials Foxe is translating the Latin of bishops' registers into English is part of the political statement made by his whole project. It is his aim, as his prefatory letters confirm, to 'reveal' to the *whole* nation truths that have previously been concealed from them. Inevitably, this perspective invites the class polemic inherited from the Lollards: Foxe sees himself as giving a voice to those same 'poor people' compared to swine by Knighton and debarred from reading the bible by Henry VIII's legislation of 1543 (pp. 12 and 74 above). Only a minority of Foxe's Lollard and Tudor martyrs are highly educated churchmen; the rest are parish priests, craftsmen, apprentices, labourers and women. Over half of those executed for Protestantism under Mary Tudor were agricultural labourers (Larner, *Witchcraft and Religion*, p. 122). Lollardy and Protestantism alike produce themselves as antihierarchical: 'every chosen man and womman is clepid a sone or doughtir of this chirche', and even a Whitechapel bricklayer preaching in his own garden earns respect and an audience.[7]

Foxe's anti-hierarchical stance draws predictable hostility from his Catholic opposition: for the Jesuit Robert Parsons Foxe's martyrs are 'a contemptible and pitiful ... rabblement', 'rags and rotten clouts', and the fact that *Acts and Monuments* represents them as capable of defending themselves articulately is read by Parsons as evidence of Foxe's distortion of the truth (Helgerson, *Forms of Nationhood*, p. 265). At the same time, however, this anti-hierarchicalism is complicit with the strategy of Elizabeth I, just as Bale's apparently democratic slant was complicit with the agenda of the earlier Tudor state. The celebration of an alliance between monarch and commonalty against a proud (and foreign) religion directed attention away from the real terms of rule. The degree to which the common people are idealised in Bale's representative figure of 'Commonalty' or Foxe's individual martyrs is immediately apparent by comparison with almost any presentation of 'the mob' in Elizabethan drama (see further chapter 8 below).

Foxe's account of Tyndale shows a clear intention to highlight relations between language and class. Tyndale's project, as Foxe reads it, was as nationalistic and democratic as his own:

> how, by all means possible, to reduce his brethren and countrymen of England to the same taste and understanding of God's holy word and verity, which the Lord had endued him withal. Whereupon ... Tyndale thought with himself no way more to conduce thereunto, than if the Scripture were turned into the vulgar speech, that the poor people might also read and see the simple plain word of God. (*The Acts and Monuments of John Foxe*, vol. v, p. 118)

Significantly, Foxe conceives scripture as simple and plain, like the very people who stand in need of it. The 'descanting upon it with allegories' and 'expounding it in many senses' is presented as part of a conspiracy by the Catholic church to delude the unlearned (vol. v, p. 118). The opposition between English and Latin, then, is once more demonised as a moral conflict between plainness and ornament, aligned respectively with truth and deceit.

This remaking of history via the polarity between Romish fraud and honest Protestant plainness is, as noted in chapter 4, indebted to Bale. When Bale returned to England in 1547–8 he took refuge in the household of the Duchess of Richmond, where Foxe was also living. The friendship between them developed to the point where Bale could speak of Foxe ten years later as having been his 'Achates' throughout those years. Bale and Foxe both went into exile when Queen Mary came to the throne. Their exile was a symbolic act as well as a response to the fact that their lives were in danger. As John Philpot warned his sister, to remain in England was to inhabit 'the confines and borders of Babylon, where you are in danger to drink of the whore's cup, unless you be vigilant in prayer' (vol. vii, p. 695). Both were members of the Frankfurt congregation in 1554, but although they took opposing sides in the rift that divided the congregation, their friendship seems to have continued unaltered, since they were again sharing the same residence in Basle in 1555 (Harris, *John Bale*, pp. 37–9). It is clear that during these years Bale lent books and manuscripts to Foxe, and Margaret Aston has pointed out Foxe's debt to Bale's manuscript, the *Fasciculi Zizaniorum* (see pp. 16–17 above), and Foxe's acknowledgement of Bale as a source.[8] The *Acts and Monuments* should be seen, Aston argues, not merely as Foxe's work, but as 'the completion of a generation's efforts' ('Lollardy and the Reformation', pp. 167–8).

Foxe's project shared Bale's combination of Protestantism with nationalism. His remaking of history was not simply a tale of Protestantism triumphant, but of England as contributing significantly to the struggle to defend God's truth against the idols of Babylon. The dangers of reading this English emphasis as evidence of a belief in England as the elect nation have been discussed in chapter 4 above (p. 89), but, as with Bale, some nationalist perspective cannot be denied to the *Book of Martyrs*. Despite his real awareness, strengthened by years of exile, of Protestantism as an internationally binding force, Foxe is motivated by a need to speak in English to England about its struggle against popery. Patrick Collinson, arguing against Haller, concludes by formulating a paradox: 'Protestantism complicated the religious sense of nationhood even while it intensified it' (*The Birthpangs of Protestant England*, p. 17; see also Helgerson, *Forms of Nationhood*, ch.6.), and Collinson's earlier citation of a range of writers affirming England to be 'the peculiar place of God', including the memorable marginal note from John Aylmer's *An Harborowe for Faithfull and Trewe Subjectes*, written in 1559: 'GOD IS ENGLISH' (*The Birthpangs of Protestant England*, p. 4), confirms the impossibility of avoiding the nationalist face of English Protestantism.

It was because this combination of nationalism with religious fervour was a myth so powerfully in tune with Queen Elizabeth's own myth-making that Foxe's version of English history was given in its own time an official status beyond that of any other book except the bible. Foxe's second edition, published in 1570, was the following year ordered to be set up alongside the bible in churches and other public places so that all could read it.[9] The elevation of Foxe's book to status comparable with the bible was part of a continuing statecraft that sought to fix the allegiance of English subjects by binding it inseparably to the state-approved religious faith. Protestantism was to be seen as allied with the concept of the nation, while

Catholicism was cast as the traitor within: the oath of supremacy (requiring all those holding lay or ecclesiastical office to acknowledge the queen as Supreme Governor of both church and state and to renounce all foreign jurisdiction) was used to deprive the Marian bishops in 1559, and penalties for infringing the oath escalated to the imposition of a judgement of high treason for a third offence. Legislation returned to the subject of the oath of supremacy in 1563 and 1570. The imposition of the royal arms in the place formerly occupied by the crucifix as the primary object of reverence in the parish churches of England was a symbolic gesture, but it was also backed up by the full force of the law.

SECULAR HUMANISM

The line from Bale to Foxe was not, however, the only line of influence joining the reign of Elizabeth to the early Tudor period. The classical tradition formed an equally strong link between the earlier and the later period, a link which, though well documented by recent as well as older scholars, needs brief outlining here. The influence of Plautus and Terence on Tudor comedy and of Seneca on tragedy are truisms of dramatic history. Their presence is so deeply embedded in Elizabethan dramaturgy as to form what Robert Miola has rightly defined as 'a rhetorical and symbolic vocabulary' (*Shakespeare and Classical Comedy*, p. 2). This classical bedrock was deposited via the Tudor education system, which was founded on Latin. Only the self-taught or minimally educated could make a real distinction between literacy and Latinity. Educational institutions, from grammar school upwards, educated their students first and foremost in Latin: *grammar* school implied precisely the study of grammar.[10] From the time of Henry VIII to the end of the century the official Latin grammar, Lily's,[11] was written in Latin, and the use of any other textbook was illegal. Furthermore, since grammar schools themselves sometimes demanded elementary competence in Latin as a condition of entry, petty schools must at least in some cases have been offering the beginnings of Latin. Given that the traditional age of entry to grammar school was seven (Baldwin, *William Shakespeare's Small Latine and Lesse Greeke*, vol. 1, p. 442), the study of Latin was for some beginning almost as soon as they could read. This may be compared with medieval practice, which it would seem was commonly to teach children to read using Latin primers, learning to sound the letters and pronounce the words before they could understand them (Denley, 'Elementary Teaching Techniques', pp. 223–41, esp. p. 226).

In addition, it is important to take account of the fact that schools did not teach only, or even primarily, a capacity to understand written Latin, but aimed first and foremost at cultivating the student's ability to speak fluently and spontaneously in Latin. Lessons were conducted in Latin as soon as the basics had been taught, and it was not uncommon for school statutes to insist that conversation, both at work and at play, be conducted in Latin, with stiff penalties for lapses (Baldwin, *William Shakespeare's Small Latine and Lesse Greeke*, vol. 1, pp. 151, 166, 333, 431). Even when English became the obligatory language of church services, the schools of Winchester, Eton, Oxford and Cambridge were exempted in order to safeguard the students' education in Latin (Edgerton, *Nicholas Udall*, p. 16). As T. W. Baldwin shows, smaller schools all over England were very much modelled on the great and powerful schools, and a fairly uniform curriculum was followed nationwide, except that the small schools sometimes offered only Latin without the addition of Greek and Hebrew, which characterised the upper-school curriculum of well-endowed schools. J. W. Binns, evaluating Shakespeare's Latin, concludes that his education at the Stratford free grammar school gave him a better grasp of the language 'than that attained by the average graduate in Classics today' ('Shakespeare's Latin Citations', p. 119).

The plays of Terence in particular, sometimes with the addition of Plautus, were central to grammar school education all over Europe, and anthologies of selected extracts, such as Nicholas Udall's *Floures of Terence*, were also in regular use. Education was therefore not only strongly Latin-based, but also heavily reliant on specifically dramatic texts; and, predictably, the way drama was studied at school had its effect on subsequent dramatic composition, both in Latin and vernacular languages. Drama was studied first as a linguistic and literary text, with school editions of Terence providing grammatical and rhetorical analysis of scenes, and second as a piece of moral wisdom, offering lessons to be learned by imitation or avoidance (Miola, *Shakespeare and Classical Comedy*, pp. 1–6). Standard commentaries characteristically expounded the lessons of the plays scene by scene, and this in turn contributed to the construction of a body of dramatic theory which rated drama according to its value as moral education. Philip Sidney, for example, sees poetry (within which

category he includes, as Aristotle does, drama) as 'an art of imitation
... with this end, to teach and delight', arguing that its purpose is 'to
lead and draw us to as high a perfection as our degenerate souls,
made worse by their clayey lodgings, can be capable of' (*An Apology
for Poetry*, pp. 101, 104).

Both schools and universities built the performance as well as the
study of plays into their statutes. Such performances were usually in
Latin, with a few exceptions: William Malim, headmaster of Eton,
writing *c.*1560, allowed that the annual Christmas play, performed
'before a popular audience', might occasionally be in English; and
Elizabeth's statutes for Westminster School stipulated that the
scholars were to provide a Latin play annually, while the choristers
could give one in English (Edgerton, *Nicholas Udall*, p. 35; Motter,
The School Drama in England, p. 86). College statutes confirm that the
performance of Latin drama was also built into a university education (Boas, *University Drama*, pp. 16–17). These performances were
aimed at educating the performers as well as the audience, enabling
the actors to practise fluent Latin delivery while providing the elite
audience of the scholarly community with an improving moral
lesson.[12]

Yet even Latin performance was not by definition purely didactic,
and the provision of Sidney's other criterion, that of pleasure, must
not be forgotten. Bruce Smith's description of one of the earliest
recorded performances of classical drama in England, a performance of Plautus' *Menaechmi* before Henry VIII at Hampton Court in
January 1527, demonstrates the way the classical performance was
embedded between a pastoral masque early on in the evening and a
visually spectacular afterpiece, which, as Smith notes, made a
greater impression on the Venetian ambassador's secretary than the
classical play (*Ancient Scripts*, pp. 134–8). Smith argues generally for
the importance of understanding classical 'influence' in England as
more of a 'confluence': a coming together of medieval and Tudor
traditions in both staging and dramatic theory with the texts of
ancient times. As his book emphasises, meanings are made by
particular performances in particular times and places; there is no
single way of signifying that characterises even so apparently narrow
a genre as Latin drama. Despite the necessarily elite feature of Latin
language, such drama cannot always be said to be academic: a
visually spectacular entertainment before the court clearly does not
aim only or primarily to teach or to please purely scholarly tastes.

If this degree of difference must be allowed for between Latin performances, clearly classically influenced or imitative vernacular drama covers an even wider spectrum. Undoubtedly some vernacular dramatists sought to bring seriousness and status to their work via explicit reference to classical models, while, on the other hand, classically influenced dramatic modes such as *commedia dell'arte* or later city comedy were simply appropriating and exploiting the 'symbolic vocabulary' Miola identifies as an available resource for plotting and characterisation. And in vernacular drama a good deal may be inferred from the way the two languages (classical and vernacular) are made to interact as well as from the performance context. Lyly's plays, for example, written for boy actors, for private or court performance, mix Latin and English with an ease that suggests a shared elite culture joining author, actors and audience. In *Mother Bombie* (1587–90), for example, the borrowing of classical comic form, together with the witty and casually frequent insertion of Latin (though it is usually translated and never crucial to understanding the progress of the play), seems to assume an educated audience. The prominence of the clever slave in classical comedy allows Lyly to make the 'page' role, peripheral in his other plays but an obvious device for showcasing the talents of boy actors, central to this play; and the scene in which Candius courts Livia by quoting Ovid's three rules of love in Latin and translating them into English for the benefit of Livia, who is by her own admission 'no Latinist' (line 354), seems created as an invitation to 'the well-educated society audience'[13] at the Paul's private theatre to indulge their reminiscences of Latin lessons alongside their knowledge of Ovid's salaciousness (not referred to in the scene), while submitting to the topsy-turvy pleasure of being instructed by performers who are still themselves students of grammar. The play seeks to affirm the closeness of a relatively small elite community of different ages by emphasising their shared experience of learning and reading Latin.[14]

The registers of classically influenced interludes may be very different from each other. *Jack Juggler* (*c.*1553 to *c.*1558), for example, loosely based on Plautus' *Amphitruo* and the first extant English play to follow a Plautine model, makes obvious concessions to an audience less learned than that of *Mother Bombie*. The gods of Plautus' play are dropped, the figure of Jacke Jugeler owes a clear debt to the Vice of English dramatic tradition and the opening lines of the play introduce Latin only in order to banish it:

Interpone tuis interdum gaudia curis
Ut possis animo quem vis sufferre laborem.[15]
Doo any of you knowe what Latyne is this?
Or ells wold you have an *expositorem*
To declare it in Englyshe *per sensum planiorem?*
It is best I speake Englyshe, or ells with in a whylle
I may percace myne owneselfe with my Latin bigile.

The brief excursus into Latin here, together with the use of
Plautus and the fact that stage directions are in Latin, suggests a
writer consciously addressing an audience less educated than
himself. So too does Jenkin Careaway's insulting reference to the
'many here' who 'smell strong' (line 866). But the play's idiom in
between the prologue and epilogue is conspicuously vernacular:
'to anyone familiar with the affected step-children of *imitare*, with
the painful Latinity of Surrey's *Aeneid* or the pedantic circumlocu-
tions of Newton's Seneca, what strikes the ear in *Jacke Jugeler* is
the liveliness of colloquial English' (Axton, ed., *Three Tudor
Classical Interludes*, pp. 17–18). As Axton goes on to argue, though
the play's roots are classical, it is developed in 'a peculiarly
English way' (p. 18). Nicholas Udall's *Ralph Roister Doister*
(1552–4?), perhaps the best-known English interlude in the style
of classical New Comedy, displays this same emphatic Englishness
and is noted for the vigour, inventiveness and variety of its vernacular speech-forms.

The Englishness of classically influenced plays was not only a
matter of language, of course: plays could also choose classical
subject matter as a cover for consideration of topical matters which
could not be more openly addressed. *Horestes* (1567), for example,
usually described as a 'hybrid' play because of its mixture of classical
interlude with English morality form, uses the classical story of
Orestes to examine the implications for England of events in Scotland following the murder of Mary Stuart's first husband, while
Gorboduc (1562) looks to Senecan tragic drama (and is the only
tragedy to receive Sidney's approval, precisely on account of its
Senecan style) to provide the model for its dramatisation of problems
relating to the English succession.

This kind of Englishness must be kept very separate from the
Englishness of a play like *Jack Juggler*, with its teasing of a
supposedly unwashed and uneducated audience. These plays voice
English concerns which are intended for educated ears only, and

would have been considered far too dangerous for a popular audience. Little is known about the auspices of *Horestes*, but it has been tentatively ascribed to John Puckering, a court gentleman, later Elizabeth's Lord Keeper, and its large cast suggests private performance. It is possible, too, that the play of Orestes performed before Elizabeth in the winter of 1567–8 could have been this play (Axton, ed., *Three Tudor Classical Interludes*, pp. 29–30). *Gorboduc* was certainly first performed at the Inner Temple for the Christmas celebrations of 1561–2 and played before the queen at Whitehall by her own request soon after, on 18 January 1562. As William Tydeman warns, however, we should not assume that her interest was political rather than academic: she may well have been motivated to summon a court performance by her own classical scholarship and her reading (and translation)[16] of Seneca (ed., *Two Tudor Tragedies*, p. 14).

More important than the queen's reasons for commissioning any court performance, however, is the fact that as soon as she came to power she took steps to try to ensure that dramatic performance before a popular audience did not deal with politically sensitive material. Her concern in this area was not a new one in English government, since earlier Tudor legislation also repeatedly attempted to regulate books and plays in order to keep political matters out of the hands of the masses. Henrician and Edwardian statutes implicitly legislated for the class of the audience by legislating for language. Assuming the audience for a Latin play to be a self-selected group largely composed of the governing classes and unlikely to incite riot, their prohibitions and restrictions were limited in application to English-language books and plays. Latin drama could be explicitly polemical, and could occasionally produce a reaction from outside authorities, as the case of *Pammachius* (discussed in chapter 4 above) demonstrates, but it was seen as safe because it was usually performed privately and for educational rather than financial profit.

Elizabeth's proclamation of 1559, passed within six months of her accession, reveals her as even more nervous than her predecessors about the possible effects of dramatic performance. Not only does this proclamation demand for the first time that private as well as public performances be licensed, but it moves from the English-language restriction to a more explicit reference to the class of the audience:

The Queen's majesty [doth] straightly forbid all manner interludes to be played either openly or privately, except the same be notified beforehand and licensed [by mayors, queen's lieutenants or justices of the peace] . . .

And for instruction to every of the said officers, her majesty doth likewise charge every of them as they will answer: that they permit none to be played wherein either matters of religion or of the governance of the estate of the commonweal shall be handled or treated, being no meet matters to be written or treated upon but by men of authority, learning, and wisdom, nor to be handled before any audience but of grave and discreet persons. (Hughes and Larkin, *Tudor Royal Proclamations*, vol. II, p.115)

This increased explicitness may be partly due to the changing conditions of Latin performance, which was now more open to the public. (Frederick Boas says that college productions were apparently always private until the early years of Elizabeth's reign, but his own study documents the existence of at least one earlier play intended for an audience that included townspeople as well as scholars, Nicholas Grimald's *Christus Redivivus*, performed at Brasenose College, Oxford, before 1543 (*University Drama*, pp. 89, 26–7).) Yet Latin nevertheless retained an elite cachet which protected it from much active interference. The high social status of university drama, proudly staged before the queen on the occasions of her three visits (to Cambridge in 1564 and to Oxford in 1566 and 1592), contrasts with the increasing hostility of both universities to visiting players. The distinction is expressed clearly by Leicester, writing as Chancellor of Oxford University following a university statute of 1584 against professional players:

As I ... thinke the Prohibition of common Stage Players verie requisite, so would I not have it meant thereby that the Tragedies, Comodies, and shews of Exercises of Learning in that kind used to be set forth by Universitye men should be forbedden, but accepting them as commendable and great furderances of Learning do wish them in any wise to be continued at set times and increased, and the youth of the Universitye by good meanes to be incouraged in the decent and frequent setting fourth of them. (Boas, *University Drama*, p. 192)[17]

Drama as a controlled activity within the safe parameters of the student curriculum and an elite language was seen as worthy and improving, but the potential subversiveness of public players performing in English for profit was so feared that the universities preferred to pay the players to go away rather than permit them to perform.

But a much more pressing context for Elizabeth's proclamation was the volatility of the religious situation, with a sudden reversion to Protestantism following on the equally sudden return to Catholicism under Mary. As the proclamation makes clear, the other taboo area for public performance besides 'matters of governance' was matters of religion. Elizabeth, despite endorsing a Protestant church settlement, was highly anxious about the Protestant practice of encouraging open discussion of doctrine and the bible. London, she complained, was a city 'where every merchant must have his schoolmaster and nightly conventicles, expounding scriptures and catechizing their servants and maids' so that even maidservants presumed 'to control learned preachers and say that such a man taught otherwise in our house' (Collinson, *The Elizabethan Puritan Movement*, p. 85). Her hostility to Puritan prophesyings and to any forum that encouraged a free exchange of views amongst the lower classes is evidence of just how far removed the Protestant idealisation of commonalty was from the material practice of the Protestant polity.

THE PROTESTANT DILEMMA

For Protestants the whole question of learning was fraught with difficulty and potential contradiction. Their insistence on the need for translated texts (whether of the bible or the classics; see Conley, *The First English Translations of the Classics*, pp. 28–9) was on the one hand evidence of a democratic stand against elitist learning, since it was aimed at allowing printed texts to reach the widest possible audience; while on the other hand that very insistence on the laity's need for books (and above all, 'the Book') rests on the preconception that a greater degree of learning amongst the laity is both desirable and necessary. The Protestant humanist, who has the necessary access to Latin to be able to provide translated texts for his less educated fellows, is therefore in a somewhat paradoxical position, simultaneously attacking and celebrating different kinds of learning. Although it is Catholics who align themselves with learned languages by refusing to acknowledge the need for a vernacular bible, Protestants are the group whose religion is book-oriented. It is Protestantism which demands that its adherents understand the literal meaning of the sacred text, and preferably also learn to read it for themselves. While Catholics may participate in the sacred Word through ritual action, Protestants need to be educated in order to grasp it in the way their religion demands. They are typically, in their enemies' phrase, 'heretics and two-penny book men' (cited Haigh, *English Reformations*, p. 194).

The concept of 'understanding', in opposition to 'babble', continues to construct the accusations levelled at Catholics by Protestants in this period: 'they think that to serve God is nothing else but to deal truly with men and to babble a few words morning and evening, at home or in the church, though there be no understanding' (William Perkins; cited Haigh, *English Reformations*, p. 287). There is a knowing reductiveness about this. Just as Bale's attacks on Latin as obfuscatory babble are in tension with a recognition of how Latin can actually work to produce an intensity of engagement in its audience, so Perkins must have known that the hold of the Catholic form of worship over its adherents went deeper than this. The focus on understanding versus babble is really motivated by a collision between different ways of constructing a religious community: the communal acts of repetition and response that bring together Catholics in their traditional mode of worship look suspiciously easy to a religion that has committed itself to establishing community through a shared understanding of doctrine. The Protestant community can only be constructed through work: education, discussion, perpetual checking on the agreed tenets of faith. The sheer effort necessary to sustain it along the lines of its own principles necessarily predisposes it to regard a community of worship that seems to proceed without all this as facile and superficial.

The Reformers see themselves, in a tradition stretching back to the Lollards, as having a duty to the commonalty, a duty both to elevate and to educate the people, rather than diminishing and defrauding them, as they see it, with cheap substitutes for understanding. A deep source of Protestant anxiety is that ignorance may masquerade as learning, even amongst those of the Protestant faith, and that merely the conspicuous display of a New Testament, for example, may be used to substitute for true learning (see e.g. *Nice Wanton* (1547–53), p.25,[18] a play further discussed below). Protestant and Lollard alike celebrate the natural simplicity of the ploughman together with his right to know. The role of the conventicle (an underground meeting first alluded to in anti-Lollard legislation and continuing as a forum for dissenting worship into Elizabeth's reign and beyond) was to educate and inform its members as well as to pray (see further Martin, *Religious Radicals*, ch.2), and contemporary accounts of 'rustics, women and idiots' searching the bible for texts at open-air meetings (Larner, *Witchcraft and Religion*, p. 122) suggest an engagement with the need for literacy at all levels. One of the most poignant instances of hard-won literacy is an inscription on the flyleaf of a copy of Polydore Virgil's history, written following the 1543 statute restricting bible-reading to the higher classes: 'At Oxford, the year 1546, brought down to Saintbury [Gloucs] by John Darbye, price 14d, when I keep Mr Latimer's sheep. I bought this book when the Testament was abrogated, that shepherds might not read it. I pray God amend that blindness. Writ by Robert Williams, keeping sheep upon Saintbury Hill, 1546' (Haigh, *English Reformations*, p. 161).

Many of Foxe's most memorable narratives, from Lollard to Tudor times, tell stories of men and women of the labouring classes struggling to teach themselves to read, often specifically motivated to do so by their wish to read the bible. William Maldon, in an account of his experience written for Foxe, but omitted (presumably accidentally) from the *Book of Martyrs*, tells how he was inspired to educate himself by the example of poor men of Chelmsford who had bought the New Testament: 'Then thought I, I will learne to rede Englyshe, and then I will have the Newe Testament and rede ther on myself' (Nichols, *Narratives of the Days of the Reformation*, pp. 348–51). Thomas Hudson (*The Acts and Monuments of John Foxe*, vol. VIII, pp. 462–6), a glover, 'a very honest poor man', was taught to read by other Protestants and was subsequently arrested for continually singing psalms and reading aloud from the bible; Rawlins White (vol. VII, pp. 28–33), a fisherman converted to Protestantism and 'a good man ... altogether unlearned', sent his son to school so that the boy could read the bible to him each evening; Joan Waste (vol. VIII, pp. 247–50), a 'poor honest godly woman', blind from birth, paid a prisoner to read to her so that she might 'have printed in her memory the sayings of the holy Scriptures contained in the New Testament'; Dirick Carver (vol. VII, pp. 322–6), a brewer, used the period of his imprisonment for heresy to learn to read. The New Testament, for Protestants, was more than just a text to be read; it was an object to be printed on the memory, written on the body; a book to die for.

This Protestant fusion of text and reader, like the fusion of actor and role (see chapter 4 above) was developed against a view of

Catholicism as a religion that cultivated distance between speaker and utterance. If Catholicism, in Reformed eyes, was the materialisation of Babel, encouraging its congregations to babble nonsense-words that never penetrated their understanding, the way forward for a Reformed religion had to be towards a penetration of reader by text so complete that it might seek to restore prelapsarian singleness and authenticity to the word and allow the worshipper to participate in that restored authenticity.

Like the Lollards, Protestant Reformers urged for wider education of the laity. As one Lollard wrote: 'For the science of God cometh of diligence of reading: truly ignorance of God is daughter of negligence. Truly if not all men reading know God, how shall he know that readeth not?' (Aston, *Lollards and Reformers*, p. 198). This concern was given impetus under Henry VIII by Cromwell's injunctions of 1536, which urged parents to educate their children and encourage them in some honest occupation. As the injunction reveals, Reformist idealism usefully coincided here with the government's own concern to prevent social disorder. 'We may daily see', the injunctions pronounce,

through sloth and idleness, divers valiant men fall, some to begging and some to theft and murder, which after, brought to calamity and misery, impute a great part thereof to their friends and governors, which suffered them to be brought up so idly in their youth; where if they had been well educated and brought up in some good literature, occupation, or mystery, they should, being rulers of their own family, have profited as well themselves as divers other persons, to the great commodity and ornament of the Common-wealth. (*English Historical Documents*: vol. v, p. 807)

These same injunctions of 1536, and those of 1538, ordered English bibles to be set up in parish churches; the connection between the educating and the reforming impulses is clear.

But there was learning and 'learning'. John Shute's defence of a vernacular bible in 1565 suggests this distinction: he argues that the layman has more need of it than the monk, citing pre-Reformation authorities in favour of the view that 'in matters concernyng the fayth, the saying of a laye man oughte to have place, before the saying of the Pope, if hys saying bee more probable, and better authorysed by the olde and newe Testament' (preface to his translation of *The Firste Parte of the Christian Instruction*). On the one hand there is the necessary literacy that allows the plain man to know the bible for himself, without the mediation of untrustworthy clerics;

and on the other hand there is the learning of high-ranking clerics, constructed here as an obstacle between the prelate and that plain knowledge of the bible that seems the natural attribute of the plain man. There was an acknowledged need to educate the illiterate, but what Protestants sought, in the terms of St Jerome (p. 29 above) was 'learned righteousness'. Driven to choose between extremes they would clearly, like Langland, have preferred 'holy rusticity' to 'sinful eloquence'.

Protestants needed to be able to read, but scorned any sign of affectation or showiness in the learning they so highly valued. Such showiness was constructed, in Protestant discourse, as a mere trapping, often covering up for a hollowness where true understanding should be. Latin draws especial fire because it is usable as a mask to cover ignorance. Still primarily the badge of clergy and gentry in Elizabeth's reign, it has an elitist cachet which makes it even more hateful to the non-elite when it is affected merely *as* a badge rather than put to use. Token Latin may function, to the Reformer's disgust, as no more than a ticket to social advancement: 'the world is now come to that passe, that if hee can prate a little Latin, and handle a Racket and a pair of six square bowles: he shall sooner obtain any living then the best learned in a whole Citie, which is the cause that learning is so despised, and bagagicall [worthless, vile] things so much advaunced' (William Baldwin, quoted in Conley, *The First English Translations of the Classics*, p. 15). The neck-verse (discussed in chapter 3 above) was a comparable instance of unearned clerical privilege, much scorned by the lay population, since it allowed felons to claim immunity from the death penalty simply by demonstrating the capacity to repeat a particular Latin phrase.

The records of bishops' examinations of parish clergy reveal a situation that justified this kind of attack on their ignorance: of 311 clergy examined in 1551, 168 could not repeat the ten commandments, 39 did not know the location of the Lord's Prayer in the bible and 34 could not name its author (Dickens, *The English Reformation*, p. 243). Tyndale was similarly appalled by the clerical ignorance of his day, and resentful that men so ignorant should presume to hold an opinion at all on theological matters. Many rural priests, he affirms, are 'full ignorant', 'have seen no more Latin than that they read in their portesses and missals, which yet many of them can scarcely read', and yet 'when they come together to the ale-house, which is their preaching-place, they affirm that my sayings are heresy' (*Preface to the Pentateuch*; *The Works of William Tindale*, pp. 96–7).

The depths of clerical ignorance, together with the clerical tendency to adopt a smattering of Latin as a cover for such ignorance and to protect their own interests, explains the anti-intellectualism which goes hand in hand with the Protestant desire to educate. Protestant conventicles pursued their own discussions of doctrine at the same time as distrusting 'learned men'. Henry Hart, arrested by the Privy Council as leader of the conventicle at Bocking in Essex in 1550, was reported as saying that 'his faithe was not growndid opon Lernyd men, for all errors were broughte in by Lernyd men' (Martin, *Religious Radicals*, p. 24). Alice Driver, brought before two doctors of theology for investigation in 1558, taunts them for their hazy knowledge of scripture and for presuming to pass judgement on her without 'the book of the law', the New Testament, with them. 'I was an honest poor man's daughter', she claims,

never brought up in the university, as you have been, but I have driven the plough before my father many a time (I thank God): yet notwithstanding, in the defence of God's truth, and in the cause of my Master Christ, by his grace I will set my foot against the foot of any of you all, in the maintenance and defence of the same, and if I had a thousand lives, they should go for payment thereof. (*The Acts and Monuments of John Foxe*, vol. VIII, p. 493–6)

It is not by accident that Foxe follows up this passionate statement of faith by recounting that the chancellor reads the sentence of condemnation 'in Latin'. Foxe's aim is to demonstrate that vernacular, Protestant learning, derived from an English bible, proves itself to be honest, committed and true by contrast with the emptiness of Latinity not fully grounded in scripture but parading itself as a guarantee of privilege.

CELEBRATING LEARNING: THREE PLAYS

Given the context described above it is not surprising to find that dramatists use their plays to educate their audience in moral and theological matters (even a witty Plautine interlude like *Jack Juggler* must be understood within a Reformation context);[19] nor is it any surprise to find that Protestant dramatists display an ambivalent attitude towards learning, urging the virtues of education, while also attacking the elitism of an exaggerated or exclusive Latinity. A group of three plays dramatising the education of youth may be considered together in order to highlight parallels and differences between them: *Lusty Juventus* (1547–53), *Nice Wanton* (1547–53) and *The Disobedient Child* (*c*.1559–70). All three are written in English; all focus on the dangers of idleness and equate a refusal to learn with degenerate behaviour; and all present learning as inseparably bound to knowledge of the bible, while rejecting the veneer of Latinity that identifies 'ignorant' (that is, Romish) clerics. Like the more secular plays examined earlier in this chapter, they are indebted in different degrees to classical models,[20] but unlike those classical plays that seek to emphasise their classicism, these ones play down their indebtedness as a consequence of their expressed hostility to Latinity as the signature of Rome. In their very attempt to drive a wedge between the classical humanist and English Protestant traditions they offer evidence of the impossibility of properly unravelling the two.

Protestant insistence on the word and the book creates a drama which focuses with fetishistic intensity on the book as prop. The physical object and the positioning of it in relation to particular characters on stage become the primary index to the moral status of those characters. Just as Queen Elizabeth initiates the reign via the symbolic gesture of kissing the book, and just as Foxe's *Book of Martyrs* presents a sequence of images that repeatedly rework this gesture in their bonding of the book to the body, so these plays return obsessively to gestures that either join characters to, or separate them from, the book. It may be the failure of Protestantism to offer any sensory appeal in place of banished Catholic ritual that drives it to fetishise the book as physical object and to produce a drama that repeatedly speaks of, handles and draws the gaze towards the book.

Two images from these plays stand in emblematic opposition to each other: Lusty Juventus (Youth) with his New Testament tied to his girdle in the play of that name and Ismael and Dalilah tossing their books away in *Nice Wanton*. The first image offers its spectators a model to copy, the second stands as a warning sign. Juventus is given his book, a copy of the New Testament, by the figures of Good Counsel and Knowledge (pp. 12–13). The latter appears in response to Juventus' prayer for 'true knowledge of [God's] law and will' (p. 8) and gives his full name as 'The True Knowledge of God's Verity' (p. 9). His speech is entirely composed of scriptural quotation and paraphrase, and incorporates its own footnotes to guide the audience towards the relevant sources. The perspective is aggressively Protestant, not only in its reverence for the figure of Knowledge (who replaces a figure like Mercy in *Mankind*) but in the discourse Knowledge utters, with its didactic and insistently vernacular emphasis on the centrality of the Word. The sacraments have no place in this drama, though Protestant theology did not reject them entirely. It is a drama rooted in and validated by the Word. A single speech from Knowledge may serve to illustrate the dogged and literal-minded attachment to scripture:

> The prophet David saith, that the man is blessed,
> Which doth exercise himself in the law of the Lord,
> And doth not follow the way of the wicked;
> As the first psalm doth plainly record:
> The fourscore and thirteenth psalm thereunto doth accord;
> Blessed is the man whom thou teachest, O Lord, saith he,
> To learn thy law, precepts, word, or verity.
> And Christ in the gospel saith manifestly:
> Blessed is he which heareth the Word of God and keepeth it;
> That is, to believe his word and live accordingly,
> Declaring the faith by the fruits of the spirit,
> Whose fruits are these, as St Paul to the Galathi doth write,
> Love, joy, peace, long suffering, and faithfulness,
> Meekness, goodness, temperance, and gentleness. (p. 10)

The opposite of this knowledge within the play is, naturally, ignorance, which is the label so frequently used to smear the Catholic church. When Juventus asks Knowledge why his elders never taught him the laws of God, Knowledge offers this reason: 'Because they themselves were wrapped in ignorance, / Being deceived by false preachers' (p. 11). All doctrine which is not God's Word, Good Counsel adds, is false doctrine (p. 11), and the Devil, clearly aligned with the Catholics, announces his specific task as being to fight 'To have the Word of God deluded utterly' (p. 14). The point is underscored yet again in Juventus' long address to the audience following his lapse into sin and reconversion to the gospel. Commenting on his own dramatic function, he addresses the youthful members of the audience: 'All you that be young, whom I do now represent, / Set your delight both day and night on Christ's Testament' (p. 41).[21] The performer, in the aesthetic developing from Bale's drama, is identified with his role, thus guaranteeing his trustworthiness as speaker. And the message is clear: the book is the way to salvation.

Ismael and Dalilah, by contrast, seal their own damnation when they cast away their books and turn their minds to pleasure: 'Farewell our school! / Away with books and all' (p. 97). Like Juventus, they mark their degenerate state in their first appearance on stage by the fact that they come in singing a secular song. The song is not obscene in either case; merely its secularity marks the singer as preferring pleasure to virtue. (When Juventus admits to Good Counsel that he has arranged to meet some minstrels 'To pass the time away in pleasure', Good Counsel sternly informs him that 'there is no such passing the time appointed in the Scripture' (pp. 5–6).) The difference between the two plays is that whereas in each case a virtuous speaker (Good Counsel in *Lusty Juventus*, Barnabas in *Nice Wanton*) directs the pleasure-seeker(s) away from frivolous mirth towards honest and useful labour, Juventus accepts the advice, while Ismael and Dalilah reject it. And, as in *Mankind*, the rejection is framed in terms of rival discourses. Barnabas, brother of Ismael and Dalilah, cites biblical texts via his schoolmaster's good teaching and warns his brother and sister that 'Learning bringeth knowledge of God and honest living to get'. Dalilah's response is to mock his earnestness: 'Yea, marry, I warrant you, master hoddypeak [fool]' (p. 96).[22] Barnabas offers sober reprimand, while Ismael and Dalilah threaten and abuse him, and both parties recognise the other's discourse as representative, and perhaps also productive, of a moral position: 'BARNABAS. Lewd speaking corrupteth good manners, Saint Paul doth say . . . / ISMAEL. Go, get thee hence, thy mouth full of horse-dung!' (p. 97). Like Bale's *King John*, this drama remains framed within a Catholic tradition of dramaturgy: it merely reverses the terms. So while the dramatisation of moral opposition through linguistic conflict is strongly reminiscent of *Mankind*, the 'horse-dung' in the virtuous speaker's mouth is no longer a Latinate, elevated form of utterance, but rather a plain-spoken vernacular, routinely punctuated with reference to biblical sources.

Latin, as predominantly in *King John*, is the mark of Cain. Just as surely as Juventus and Ismael and Dalilah can be pigeon-holed by their merry song, so Hypocrisy can be identified as Catholic and therefore vicious by his first line: '*Sancti amen*, who have we there?' (*Lusty Juventus*, p.16). Protestant polemic identifies irrelevant Latin,

like oaths by the pope and the mass, as the sign of ignorant papistry
as opposed to true learning. The slur is anticipated by Hypocrisy
himself: 'You may say I am homely, and lack learning' (p. 16); and he
too mocks Juventus, as Dalilah mocks Barnabas, for his learning:
'Well said, master doctor, well said! / By the mass, we must have you
into the pulpit' (p. 23). For Hypocrisy, Juventus' learning is a
powerful threat and his book a weapon that fends off 'Popish priests'
by its mere presence. He introduces Juventus as

> a man of the right making;
> And one that hath excellent learning;
> At his girdle he hath such a book,
> That the Popish priests dare not in him look.   (p. 27)

(The conception of the book functioning as magical object, like the
gospel of St John in its little casket (p. 2 above), is strongly suggestive
of Catholic thinking, but it is hard to tell whether this mode of
thinking is a trap the Protestant play falls into or a response to be
associated with the Catholic speaker Hypocrisy.)

Even the foolish Dalilah is mocked for displaying the little
learning she has in a chance use of proverbial Latin. (Again, the use
of Latin here indicates mere surface knowledge rather than real
learning.) When the Latin phrase *'ceteri nolunt'* slips out in conversation with the Vice, Iniquity, he fixes on it in such a way that the
ensuing dialogue allows the accusation of going to school to
degenerate into an insult:

> INIQUITY. Peace, Dalilah; speak ye Latin, poor fool?
>
> DALILAH. No, no, but a proverb I learned at school—
>
> ISMAEL. Yea, sister, you went to school, till ye were past
> grace;—
>
> DALILAH. Yea, so didst thou, by thy knave's face!   (p. 101)

School becomes a dirty word, and Ismael and Dalilah demonstrate
their reprobate natures by attempting to erase all traces of their
education. Without the book, or books of any kind, they cannot
improve their state: Ismael is hanged, Dalilah dies of the pox and
their mother is only prevented from killing herself in despair by
Barnabas' intervention. His final address to the audience advises
parents to be diligent in bringing up their children and children to
apply their learning and obey their elders (pp. 113–14). The play

ends with a song that recalls and revises the secular songs of its
opening by offering to redefine merriment in moral terms:

> It is good to be merry
> But who can be merry?
> He that hath a pure conscience,
>   He may well be merry. (p. 114)

The Disobedient Child resembles *Nice Wanton* in showing its pro-
tagonist damned for rejecting his father's advice to follow his book.
Ironically, he casts his rejection in terms of the Fall:

> For if I should go to my book after your advice,
> Which have spent my childhood so pleasantly,
> I may then seem driven out of paradise,
> To take pain and woe, grief and misery. (p. 47)

It is of course his refusal to go to his book, rather than accept this
duty, which confirms his fall. Towards the end of the play Satan
confesses to the audience that it was he who 'made him refuse / The
wholesome monition of his father dear' (p. 80) and warns children:

> Take heed, take heed of my temptation,
> For commonly at the last ye have the fall,
> And also [be] brought to desperation. (p. 82)

Pleasure now means fallen nature and eternal pain. As the Perorator
tells the audience in the closing speech of the play: 'ye cannot but see
plainly, / How pain and pleasure be knit together' (p. 88). Like *Nice
Wanton* again, the play ends with a holy song to displace the secular
songs that have characterised unholy living.

Unlike either of the other two plays, however, *The Disobedient Child*
has a brief scene offering a kind of comic subplot which revisits the
concern with education in more frivolous form. The scene is
interesting in so far as it seems to offer a perspective on learning
more social than moral, although it is not without a moral dimension, and its function is clearly to point up the moral of the main
plot. The scene shows a man-cook and a maid-cook preparing the
wedding-feast for the young prodigal, who has foolishly chosen to
marry instead of following his books as his father wishes. The maid-
cook sees the true nature of the young man's chosen wife: she 'loveth
too much her pleasure and will' (p. 58). The man-cook, clearly
aligned with the young man seeking his pleasure in marriage, calls
the maid-cook a fool and mocks her for preaching and presuming to

teach young men. Already this begins to suggest the familiar morality pattern of virtuous teaching encountering foolish mockery, although it may not yet be obvious that this is actually the pattern organising the dialogue, since speakers of this status are so unfamiliar in these roles. Cooks, far less women, are not the conventional carriers of reliable teaching, and women are not usually allowed to upstage men in terms of learning (the maid is just the kind of social upstart in terms of both class and gender that Queen Elizabeth so disliked (p. 119 above); just as the established church allowed a select elite to possess English translations of the bible but feared the consequences of its becoming available to all classes, so the educated female was threatening only below a certain class level).

Yet the maid goes on to assert her credentials in precisely the terms authorised by the play's concern with education in youth:

> A fool! mine own Long-tongue! why, call'st thou me fool!
> Though now in the kitchen I waste the day,
> Yet in times past I went to school,
> And of my Latin primer I took assay.

The man turns to the audience to mock her, and a comic dialogue develops:

MAN. Masters, this woman did take such assay,
      And then in those days so applied her book,
      That one word thereof she carried not away,
      But then of a scholar was made a cook.
      I dare say she knoweth not how her primer began,
      Which of her master she learned then.

MAID. I trow it began with *Domine, labia aperies*.[23]

MAN. What, did it begin with *butter de peas*?

MAID. I tell thee again, with *Domine, labia aperies*,
      If now to hear it be thine ease.

MAN. How, how, with, *my madam lay in the pease*?

MAID. I think thou art mad! with *Domine, labia aperies*.

MAN. Yea, marry, I judged it went such ways;
      It began with, *Dorothy, lay up the keys*!

MAID. Nay then, good night; I perceive by this gear,
      That none is so deaf as who will not hear;
      I spake as plainly as I could devise,
      Yet me understand thou canst in no wise!
                    (p. 59)

The man then begs for one more chance and this time finally grasps the phrase, which signals a victory for the maid and confirms her for the audience as the more authoritative speaker, despite the man's witty ripostes. The dialogue is organised along teacher/student and preacher/sinner lines simultaneously and positions Latin according to the older dramatic tradition whereby it identifies an authoritative speaker and its distortions identify a scornful reprobate (a tradition discussed more fully in chapter 3 above). Despite its radical Protestantism, the play eschews the aggressive anti-Catholic tone of *Lusty Juventus* and willingly borrows a linguistic convention from the older Catholic drama (more usually reversed in Protestant plays) in order to drive home the point about education.

The convention, however, is adapted in the borrowing: although the maid-cook's Latin is correct and marks her moral superiority over the ignorant man-cook, it is embedded within a blunt vernacular which explicitly draws attention to its own plainness. This, then, is one form of Protestant dramatic compromise: the maid-cook, if only briefly and comically, becomes a spokeswoman for the virtues of education, so that even as the play endorses the Latinity that necessarily underpins learning in Tudor society, it does so within a context that attempts to marry that Latinity with plainness of speech and occupation and a conscious privileging of the gender least likely to be educated at the time. Though the matching of the maid's competence in Latin with the man's incompetence is primarily a comic routine motivated by sexual rivalry rather than differing views on education, a position on learning is nevertheless endorsed. The contrast between the educated maid and the foolish young prodigal of the main plot who demonstrates the truth of her perception that 'none is so deaf as who will not hear' remains as an afterthought following the laughter.

All three of these plays end with a prayer for the monarch. This suggests increasing awareness on the part of dramatists and players of the need to take account of the state, together with a wish that the state should take account of drama. Increasing state censorship of plays and interludes produces a need for plays to appeal for favour; and where plays deal with matters over which the state has control, such as education and religion, those plays want the state to take note of their advice. Ending with prayers for the monarch may in some cases suggest court auspices; and certainly children's companies and occasionally schools (both possible performers of plays about misspent youth), regularly played at court during this period. *The Disobedient Child* is especially fawning in having stage directions specifying that the players must all enter and kneel to speak the lines of the prayer in turn, but even this degree of fawning is compatible with performance in a noble household, where players might adopt such tactics to please the noble patron. Within a patronage system, drama needs to demonstrate its hegemonic acceptability in order to make space for itself.

Lusty Juventus, with its title-page advice that 'foure may playe it easely', suggests the classic touring troupe, as described by David Bevington (*From Mankind to Marlowe*), which implies that the play may have been performed at popular venues as well as in aristocratic households.[24] Nothing in the content of the plays rules out one audience in favour of another, and evidence suggests that plays first presented at court might then become more widely performed. The title page of *Damon and Pithias* in 1571, for example, states that the text is 'Newly Imprinted, as the same was shewed before the Queenes Majestie, by the Children of her Graces Chappell, except the Prologue that is somewhat altered for the proper use of them that hereafter shall have occasion to plaie it, either in Private, or open Audience'.

THE DOUBLE BIND: *THE LONGER THOU LIVEST THE MORE FOOL THOU ART*

One further play, different in kind from the three discussed above, though written close in time to *The Disobedient Child*, needs to be considered here. *The Longer Thou Livest The More Fool Thou Art* (*c.*1559–68), written by William Wager, resembles the three plays above in taking education as its central theme, but differs from them not only by virtue of its greater length and more sophisticated range of comic technique, but in its approach to the matter of education. Its very title implies its thrust: even education cannot save the unregenerate fool. Thus although the play repeatedly stages attempts to educate Moros, the fool, the effort is shown to be wasted.

Perhaps because the play is so concerned with the *process* of education, and with Moros' resistance to it whatever form it takes, it is also more centrally focused on language than the three plays discussed above, and is particularly interesting to compare with *Mankind*. As in *Mankind*, language is a consistent and reliable index to moral condition, and Wager represents the opposition between different religious and moral viewpoints via the interaction of different discourses. And although the play is so staunchly Protestant in its thinking, it continues to demonstrate some conspicuous points of contact with the earlier morality play. For example, the heavily Latinate ring of its opening words is reminiscent of Mercy's opening speech in *Mankind* (see chapter 3 above):

> Aristophanes, as Valerius doth tell,
> Introduceth Pericles in a comedy
> That he, being reduced [returned] again out of hell
> Unto th'Athenienses, did thus prophesy:
> Bring up no lions in your cities wantonly,
> For, as you bring them up in acts pernicious,
> So in the same you must be to them obsequious.   (lines 1–7)

Importantly, this opening voice is not the voice of any character but that of the Prologue. As such, though it speaks from within the play, it seems to borrow an authority from outside the playworld (inviting comparison with the 'voice of the church' discussed in chapter 2 above).[25] It is not even an allegorical voice to be identified as that of Education, but an unrestricted voice directly addressing the audience on the threshold of their entry into the playworld on matters of import which the play will confront. Mediating between the playworld and the world of performance, it is equipped, by virtue of its occupation of transitional space, to pronounce on the truth of those matters to be enacted by the play. It is free, therefore, to praise rather than to represent education ('O how noble a thing is good education' (line 15)) and to expect its praise to be taken seriously, as authentic utterance rather than 'playing'.

Mercy in *Mankind* operates differently. Though his opening speech at first seems to claim something of the authoritative distance of a prologue, he is soon a character immersed in the playworld, given a name, a costume and an occupation. His voice becomes recognisable as that of an earthly cleric rather than that of pure, untrammelled wisdom and is subjected to the mockery of the Vices. It becomes a voice that has to struggle for authority and, as chapter 3 argues, learn to negotiate a plainer style. In *The Longer Thou Livest* no characterised speakers use such a voice (though they may borrow it, as when they quote 'authorities'). After the direct address of the Prologue it is never used again in the play. Vicious characters speak

with the coarse, colloquial swagger recognisable from earlier morality Vice figures, but virtues speak plainly. Latin is respected, as the
language of education, but it functions in the play precisely as part
of the process of education and is translated on utterance.

The voice of the Prologue, however, remains an implicit presence
in the play, hovering in the pieces of collective wisdom uttered by the
virtues and constructing other utterances as wicked the further they
deviate from this authenticity. Wager's play takes its place within the
developing aesthetic that wants to have play that is not play. As in
the three Tudor plays of education discussed above, and in the
tradition of *Mankind* and *King John*, depravity is signalled via playful
or ungoverned speech and the singing of secular songs. Moros first
enters, like Lusty Juventus and Ismael and Dalilah, singing, according to the stage direction, 'the foot of many songs as fools were wont'
(line 70). The songs, as in the other Tudor plays, are not obscene,
simply frivolous, but the earlier part of the stage direction cited
above states a clear intention that the demeanour of this singing
should indicate the singer's folly: he should enter 'counterfeiting a
vain gesture and a foolish countenance'. Discipline's educational
verses interrupt Moros' singing in order to demonstrate to the
audience the 'song' of virtue. Though the lines are not literally sung,
they enact their own rhythmic formality in opposition to unfinished
snatches of popular song. The very artifice and completedness of
Discipline's verse is testament to its authority here:

> *Gaudet stultis natura creandis*
> (Nature hath a pleasure fools to create)
> *Ut malvis atque urticis et vilibus herbis*
> (As mallows, nettles, and weeds of that rate).   (lines 126–9)

The speech is longer than this, and its pace and length are part of its
effect, but this short quotation must serve to show the kind of
discourse Wager sets up as authoritative. Like Mercy's, it has a
strong Latin element, but unlike Mercy in his initial phase, it
carefully translates the Latin line by line and does not allow Latin to
invade the plainness of its English. Its progress is fetishistically
ordered (as the speaker's name might suggest), meticulously alter-
nating a line of Latin with a line of English and resolutely denying
itself any deviation from that sequence. It is a discourse driven by its
own refusal to play. The speaker who wants his words to sound like
the Word and to suggest incontestable authenticity, can never let his

guard drop against the possible invasion of disorderly play. His discourse is at once cathected and constricted, always holding itself in.

The opposing position, represented by Moros, lets it all hang out. Moros, accused by Idleness in the proverb of the play's title, which runs like a refrain through the play, rhymes 'art' with 'fart':

> IDLENESS. Why, it is true that of thee he said,
> 'The longer thou livest, the more fool thou art.'
>
> MOROS.   Body of God, of him I am so afraid
> That at every word I am like to fart.   (lines 986–9)

As in *Mankind*, *King John* and the morality tradition generally, heightened vernacular, especially with allusions to the body, are the standard form of opposition to official language and teaching. Both the comedy and the moral teaching of the play are structured on the familiar polarity of carnival between official and unofficial, Latin and vernacular, earnest and game.

Latin, as in *Mankind*, is the source of much of the play's comedy, but the laughter is directed not at Latin or at those who speak it, but at failure to understand it. Moros demonstrates his folly by virtue of his consistent refusal to even hear Latin correctly, far less understand it. His moral failure is performed as a linguistic failure: he will never attain to the virtues of Discipline, Piety and Exercitation while he misrecognises them as 'Diricke Quintine', 'Pine-nut-tree' and 'Arse-out-of-fashion'. Notably, this triad of virtues have names which directly transliterate Latin words: *disciplina* (instruction, teaching, learning), *pietas* (dutiful conduct) and *exercitatio* (exercise, practice of duties, occupation). The fact that they are to be understood in their etymological, Latin sense (and hence can only be fully available through education, which makes possible an understanding of the Latin root) measures their distance and difference from the vernacular grotesqueness of Moros' mistranslations.

The stage directions repeatedly instruct the player of Moros to undermine the discourse of his teachers, and the play displays some versatility in the range of oppositional modes it offers. Discipline's long speech outlining the religious education that Piety will provide for Moros is preceded by this stage direction: 'Here let Moros between every sentence say, "Gay gear," "good stuff," "very well," "fin-ado," with such mockish terms' (line 432). This licenses the open disruption of Discipline's formal rhyming verse by punctuating it with arhythmic and colloquial interjections, and at the same time offers the cue to the speaker of Discipline's lines to highlight the rigid and measured patterns of his verse.[26] Elsewhere Moros, again performing his own failure to grasp the cathected shape of Discipline's utterance, undermines it by following his instructions too literally and repeating everything he says, including his instructions and conversation.

Lois Potter sees this mockery of rote-learning as directed against Moros' teachers: 'Wager', she argues, 'is an anti-intellectual writer' (*Revels*, vol. II, p. 199). But this is to misrecognise the dialectic between teacher and pupil, both in terms of the play's structuring of discourses and in terms of the Protestant dilemma regarding learning. The contempt for mere rote-learning without understanding is an aspect of reverence for deeper understanding. It is not the teacher who is at fault here, but the learner, whose responsibility it is to consider the meaning of the verses he repeats, as Piety points out to Moros: 'His meaning you do not consider; / Alone you must say the verses as they be' (lines 352–3). As Potter herself rightly notes, 'it is significant that neither good nor bad teachers can make any impression on Moros; he mislearns the names of both' (*Revels*, vol. II, p. 199). Moros' failure to understand, then, signifies his own depravity, not the inadequacy of his teachers, who recognise his mindless repetition as no mere stupidity, but a deliberate attempt to turn everything into 'a mock and a game' (line 361). In terms of dramatic construction the opposition is by now familiar: it is the attempt to forge authentic utterance out of the rejection of promiscuous play.

That Moros' responses are motivated by a conscious refusal to learn is clear from another of his undermining strategies, one parallel with Myscheffe's strategy in *Mankind*. When Discipline tries again to instruct Moros after a beating, Moros this time perverts rather than repeats his words:

DISCIPLINE. I will love and fear God above all
He might vouchsafe to give me sapience;
I will not cease on his holy name to call
That he may open mine intelligence.

MOROS. I will love porridge, when they be sod, beef and all;
For mutton good sauce is salt and onions.
Up unto the high dish when my dame they call,
While she openeth the pie, I pick the pinions.
(lines 389–96)

Interestingly, Discipline's discourse becomes more Latinate here, and it is its Latinity that points up the parody; but there is no doubt that this kind of Latinate speech continues to occupy an authoritative position, while Moros' parody identifies his reprobate nature.

The kind of Latin which identifies the speaker as fallen is the pat Latin of the Catholic liturgy, which can be repeated without understanding. This, naturally enough, is the kind of 'learning' that Moros has picked up:

> WRATH. You are well-learned it doth appear,
> Can you any Latin to us speak?
>
> MOROS. I can sing *Custodi nos* in the choir,
> And a verse of course, finely broke.   (lines 715–18)

He *can* learn by rote, but cannot learn understanding: hence the title of the play. Wager, just to make sure that this truth is driven home in polemical as well as universal terms, supplies a Catholic Vice called Ignorance (alias Antiquity)[27] as well as the unregenerate Moros.

As in the other Tudor plays of education, the book is again a prop that draws intense focus to itself. Though Piety describes it as a 'testament',[28] it is clear from what follows that it is in fact some kind of primer, and Moros again reveals his inadequacy by looking for pictures. His boastfulness concerning the extent of his learning underlines his imminent damnation through ironic wordplay:

> I may tell you I am past all my crossrows [alphabets],
> I have learned beyond the ten commandments.
> Two years ago, doubtless, I was past grace;
> I am in the midst of God's judgments.   (lines 472–5)

Unlike Ismael and Dalilah and the Disobedient Child, he does not throw away his book; but keeping it, even reading it, cannot redeem him. In a scene parallel to the scene in *Nice Wanton* described above where Iniquity taunts Dalilah with taking school too seriously, the Vices of Wrath, Incontinence and Idleness mock Moros for earnestly reading his book. Yet the stage direction instructs the performer of Moros to 'read as fondly [foolishly] as you can devise' (line 702). This allows both the Vices and the audience to laugh at his reading and prepares the way for Moros to exchange his book for a sword a little further on (lines 834–5).

In between these two moments, Wager finds a striking way of staging the depth of Moros' ignorance: he changes the central prop of the book to a pack of cards. This is a clear indication of depravity in itself, but the comedy, and the moral lesson, consist in deluding Moros into believing that there is no real difference between a book and a pack of cards. Following their discovery that Moros is in fact unable to read a word of his book, the Vices offer him a new 'book':

> IDLENESS. Look what a book I have for thee here.
> [*Have a pair of cards ready.*]
> Cast away that book; it is worse than nought.
>
> (lines 769–70)

Here now, postponed for greater effect, is the moment where Moros throws away his book, demonstrating the hopelessness of his own case by his ready credulity:

> God's days, it is a goodly book indeed.
> Santy amen! here are saints a great sort.
>   . . .
> Teach me this book, I pray you, perfectly to can [know].
>
> (lines 773–85)

The device of exchanging one prop for another allows for a brilliant fusion of comedy and moral teaching, at the same time as making visually clear for the audience what the play of discourses has already demonstrated.

A final surprise in the distribution of learned discourse comes in the figure of People, who enters speaking Latin. This harks back to the eponymous Mankind, who speaks in a Latinate discourse imitative of Mercy when he is pursuing a virtuous course of action, but it is unusual for a play of this date. The demonisation of Latin displayed in Bale's *King John* is generally more familiar territory for later Protestant writers. Yet Wager continues to borrow techniques, as we have seen, from an older tradition, and insists on allowing Latin to retain a revered place in some discourses while offering it up for contempt in others. People's discourse is an interesting mix: like the virtues, he translates his Latin into plain English, but he then goes on to create a virtuoso alphabetical catalogue of abuses in a robust, alliterative mode full of vernacular humour which is more often associated with the Vice:

Sir Anthony Arrogant, auditor,
Bartolmew Briber, bailie,
Clement Catchpole, cofferer,
Division Double-faced Davy...   (lines 1715–18)

This hodge-podge of styles is particularly interesting by comparison with the speech-style of Tenant in Wager's other known play, *Enough Is As Good As A Feast* (*c*.1559 to *c*.1570). Tenant, a figure parallel with People and complaining like him of contemporary social abuses, is directed to speak 'Cotswold speech' (line 969). It would seem that Wager, in confronting the problem of tying discourse to moral type, could not find a consistent way of dramatising an allegorical representation of a category primarily social rather than moral.

Language, used consciously by Wager as expressive of the truth within, also turns back on him to reveal his own uncertainties. The specific chaos of People's speech is only one aspect of an ongoing debate Wager is conducting with himself about the value and significance of learning. His allegiance to two traditions of dramaturgy and two contradictory sets of attitudes towards Latin and the vernacular speaks of a deepening ambivalence about learning at the heart of Protestant thinking as Calvinism becomes a more dominant influence within it. The play shows with absolute certainty that Moros is damned. As he is carried off on Confusion's back his last words anticipate attendance at a different school: that of the devil (line 1858). The choice of metaphor is revealing. It is easy to see that Wager chose it for its irony in relation to the theme of schooling that preoccupies the play; but the irony goes beyond that thematic parallel. It calls attention to a fundamental paradox within the play and within Protestant thought as a whole. Right from the start the ambivalence inherent in preaching the value of education in combination with the doctrine of election is apparent. The play insists simultaneously that education is of value and that it can do no good for those already consigned to damnation. 'Bringing up', as the Prologue announces, 'is a great thing, so is diligence, / But nothing, God except, is so strong as nature' (lines 43–4).

There is a single example of untranslated Latin in the play: *Ipsaque non multo est natura potentior usu* (line 526). We cannot avoid asking why this is the only line of Latin left untranslated by a character who is otherwise rigorous in translating every line of Latin he utters. Discipline's rigour in rendering obscure Latin into plain English seems to be part of Wager's own project in educating his audience, which makes it the more strange that he leaves a line untranslated in this way. Mark Benbow translates this in his edition of the play as 'The nature of a thing is not much improved by use' and goes on to point out that Discipline, who utters the line, qualifies this rather than translates it in his following lines, in expressing the hope that Moros will be improved by conversation with Piety. The line might be differently translated, however, to mean 'Nature itself is not more powerful than prolonged custom.'[29] This would fit more closely with the English lines that follow than Benbow's translation, but stand in blatant contradiction to the Prologue's assertion that nothing except God is as strong as nature.

This potential discrepancy, however, might begin to explain why the line is left untranslated. Translating this line would mean pinning it down to one meaning or another; and while one would accord with the lines that follow and fail to accord with orthodox Protestant thinking, the other would do precisely the opposite. The sense of the line is crucial to resolving the tension that is at the heart not only of the play but of Protestantism itself. Either education is worth pursuing because it brings the soul closer to the possibility of salvation, or it is not worth pursuing because no worldly activity can make any difference to an outcome already decided. To translate the line is to come down in favour of either education or election at the expense of the other. It may be that leaving it untranslated demonstrates Wager's own resistance to confronting that logical outcome.

CHAPTER 6

Shaping a rhetoric

Ambivalence towards learning and learned language carries on throughout and beyond the reign of Elizabeth. In fact the anxiety about language becomes even more evident as English nationalism becomes more dominant, and a flood of rhetorical handbooks bursts into print in the last quarter of the sixteenth century. Richard Helgerson notes the conflict between aspiration and uncertainty that underpins Spenser's rhetorical question in a letter of 1580 to Gabriel Harvey: 'Why a God's name may not we, as else the Greeks, have the kingdom of our own language?' (*Forms of Nationhood*, pp. 1–4). The metaphor renders possession of the language coterminous with possession of the kingdom. The cultural project implies the political project, and the political project seeks affirmation through cultural practice.

The kingdom, as we have seen, was increasingly seeking to consolidate the status of empire, in the primary sense of owing no allegiance to any power beyond itself. The Act in Restraint of Appeals had claimed such status in 1533 (p. 80 above), and the Elizabethan church settlement, together with the beginnings of colonial enterprise, had begun to create the material basis for a claim to 'empire' in both senses (sovereign power and extensive territory). Empires, of course, traditionally need to keep the barbarians and their languages at bay; but the problem for England, as implied in chapter 5 above, was defining the barbarians. Traditionally, Western Europe as a whole looked to the Latin of classical empire as a model of eloquence; but the debate on translating the bible highlighted the extent to which specific aesthetics implied specific religious affiliations. Where secular translations were concerned, and aesthetic considerations were paramount to the texts in question, English was regularly accused of being too 'rude' and 'barbarous' to render the great classical texts adequately. On the other hand the use of the same argument in regard to sacred texts raises moral questions. Given that here the primary consideration is an effect of truth rather than of beauty, the concept of barbarousness becomes a necessary part of the position that casts eloquence aside. To claim English as barbarous is now to claim the moral high ground and thereby to condemn as vain and deluded a use of language that is interested in polished surfaces. The stated aim of Thomas Becon, therefore, in his celebration of 'the glorious triumph of gods most blessed word' (the title of his treatise, published in 1562) is to emphasise substance and wisdom rather than to 'glyster with vayn eloquence of words'. The baser the language of English translation seems, according to Becon, 'the higher doth it excel other, not with windiness and vayne bablyng, but with solidite and grave doctrine' (Jones, *The Triumph of the English Language*, p. 59). Eloquence and substance, for Protestants as for Lollards, are naturally opposed. Barbarism in this context emerges as a variety of plainness. The rhetorical strategy is simple: to link plain language with plain truth.

The Catholic view was precisely opposite. When Queen Mary came to the throne John Standish argued for English scriptures to be removed from 'our new fangled readers', who lacked the 'great fear and reverence' with which 'the mysteries ought to be touched, yea and that only of the learned men' (Aston, *Lollards and Reformers*, p. 132). While Protestants wanted plain language to communicate plain truth to plain men, Catholics put the case that the biblical text was arcane for good reason and should not be reduced to the level of the lowest common denominator (see pp. 78–9 above). In taking this view they were occupying, perhaps unintentionally, the same ground as the humanists (Jones, *The Triumph of the English Language*, p. 62). And it was inescapably elitist ground. The only section of the population equipped to prefer any texts, whether sacred or secular, in a non-English form was the educated class, traditionally restricted largely to the clergy and male members of the gentry class and above.[1]

English writers, whatever their religious conviction, shared a widespread recognition of the need to empower the vernacular to speak for the nation, but this degree of unity is expressed in terms of a division between two possible models of powerful English.[2] One group of writers argues that English should seek to aggrandise itself by adopting a Latinate vocabulary, imitating Latin sentence patterns and even incorporating elements of Latin or Greek wholesale into English writing. Nashe refers to this practice with open scorn in 1589: 'I am not ignorant how eloquent our gowned age is growen of late, so that everie moechanicall mate abhorres the english he was borne too, and plucks with a solemne periphrasis his *ut vales* from the inkhorne' (preface to Greene's *Menaphon*, in Smith, *Elizabethan Critical Essays*, vol. I, pp. 307–8). For Nashe, such language signifies ambivalently: it may denote learning and the class superiority traditionally associated with learning, or it may function as an appropriated discourse, a style affected by a lower class aping its betters. His tone, therefore, is sneering rather than approving. For Richard Mulcaster, headmaster of the Merchant Taylors' school, such language is also an affectation, a mere surface wantonly applied in order to create a false impression. He too sneers at the use of Latin or other foreign languages to give a false veneer of depth to 'slender things … which if theie were Englished, and the mask puld of, that everie man might se them, wold seme verie miserable, and make a sorie shew of simple substance' (*The First Part of the Elementarie*, p. 259). George Puttenham too, like Nashe and Mulcaster, condemns 'inkhorne termes', 'straunge termes', 'darke wordes' and what he calls 'mingle mangle' (the mixing of foreign speech into English).

Puttenham, Mulcaster and Nashe were Protestants, and the determination of Protestants to 'English' both classical and scriptural texts has been discussed in chapter 5 above; but the sudden increase in the production of rhetorical handbooks produced a backlash of resistance from 'the hotter sort of protestants',[3] ever distrustful of rhetoric itself. For Puritan writers, even the nationalist line of Protestant theorists of language like the three above was to be rejected. English was not to be made prouder and more elegant in a way that might allow it to compete with Latin, but was to be kept plain and unadorned. For Puritans, constructing their position within a tradition that looked back to the early Tudor Reformers and before them the Lollards, the important opposition was between transparent expressivity and opaque artifice. Opaque language, language that calls attention to its own functions rather than, or in addition to, its referents, is the object of deep distrust, while transparent language looks like the spontaneous, or 'natural', expression of truth. William Perkins represents the classic Puritan position on the matter of language. Like the early Reformers (p. 79 above), he uses the authority of St Paul to reject eloquence, but cites the first letter to the Corinthians, where St Paul claims that 'my speech and my preaching was not with enticing words of man's wisdom, but in demonstration of the Spirit and of power' (1 Cor.2.4). Perkins insists that sermons must be kept free of 'the words of arts [and] Greeke and Latine phrases and quirkes'. Plain language is the ideal medium for transmitting the power inherent in the Word: 'And I say againe, *the plainer, the better*' (Perkins, cited Lewalski, *Protestant Poetics*, pp. 224–5).

The bible itself, however, as Barbara Lewalski points out, is hardly a model of plain speaking. Its prophetic mode of utterance, in particular, is both highly literary and especially dear to the hearts of Puritans. The Puritan confronts a paradox in conceiving of truth as, on the one hand, naturally linked to plain language and, on the other, the expression of a transforming grace. Religious ecstasy, as Puritans recognised, could transport the self out of everyday concerns and everyday language, and truth could speak in tongues rather than plainly. It follows, then, that if the Holy Spirit is conceived as speaking directly through prophecy, the power to control the nature of that speaking does not lie within the human being through whom it is given utterance.

What really bothers the Puritans about rhetorical handbooks is not their recognition that language can be eloquent, but their humanist implication that eloquence is to be achieved by individual study and endeavour. For the Puritan eloquence is an expression of inspiration and grace; the notion that human beings can or should wilfully cultivate it is misguided and presumptuous, even idolatrous (see e.g. Andrew Hadfield's discussion and citation of Stephen Gosson (*Literature, Politics and National Identity*, p. 117)). As Richard Lanham has argued, a deep-rooted opposition between two attitudes towards language persists throughout Western tradition from the time of the Greeks: on the one hand there is *homo rhetoricus*, the man who takes control over language, seeks out its pleasures and plays with it and on it as on a musical instrument; while on the other there is *homo seriosus*, who distrusts playfulness and beauty and regards language as 'instrumental' in the sense of functional and secondary. The primary focus to which language is secondary in this latter view is truth. Serious man sees truth as the singular validation of speech, while rhetorical man validates speech through the plurality of pleasures it offers rather than its fidelity to any single value outside itself.

It is no mere coincidence that Puritans became more hostile to theatre as they became more hostile to rhetoric.[4] Though Reformers had begun by appropriating the weapon of theatre from the orthodox church (see chapter 4 above), and a Protestant drama had tried to develop a dramatic aesthetic acceptable to *homo seriosus*, there was a growing problem for more extreme Protestants in accommodating the inherent paradox of play that pretends not to play. Puritans were increasingly unwilling to use popular entertainment as a vehicle for serious teaching. The easygoing attitude of early Tudor interludes, which add 'divers toys and gestis ... to make mery pastyme and disport' (*Of Gentleness and Nobility*, c.1527–30), or invite performers to shorten the playing time by leaving out 'muche of the sad [serious] mater' (*The Four Elements*), would be unthinkable for late-Elizabethan Puritans. Though the phrasing of the Tudor descriptions suggests a tendency to think of earnest and game as separable, it also indicates a relative ease about bringing them together. It is characteristic of the later period that the division between purpose and play and between the sacred and the profane has become more entrenched.[5]

The objection to theatre, which becomes so strongly associated with the Puritans from the 1570s, is a development of Lollard and early Reformist hostility to the mass on the grounds that it is an enactment rather than the thing itself. The priest and the actor represent something beyond themselves, but they do so not through the spontaneous and sincere transformations of ecstasy, but through the rehearsed and self-conscious intention to represent. As the Puritan John Rainolds complains of the Catholic church, 'In steede of *preaching the word*, they caused it to be played' (Barish, *The Antitheatrical Prejudice*, p. 163). The burden of contempt carried by the very word 'played' suggests the extent of the distrust it provokes. 'Playing' in both senses is seen as a threat to the Christian commonwealth. Both pleasure and fictional re-enactment are, for some Puritans, dangerously slippery ground: pleasure opposes earnestness as fictionality contests truth. The performance of plays threatens the very root of a faith that is grounded on a continued and spontaneous witnessing to the truth. The act of representation is by definition at a remove from truth and therefore, for the most literal-minded Puritans, a lie. It is precisely this notion of representation as a form of lying that Stephen Gosson expresses in his *Plays Confuted in Five Actions*, published in 1582: players are necessarily frauds, he argues, since they 'by outward signs ... show themselves otherwise than they are' (Mann, *The Elizabethan Player*, p. 95).

Yet to read the more or less violent rejection of theatre as lies and fraud on the part of some Puritans as evidence of mere literal-mindedness is dangerously reductive. Their specific hostility to theatre emerges less out of an incapacity to cope with fiction than out of a recognition that playing out fictions may be deeply compromising. As the Elizabethan state became increasingly repressive towards Puritans it offered them a stark choice between a pretence of conformity and open refusal to conform. What the state demanded was the observance of outward forms (the wearing of vestments by the clergy, regular attendance at the parish church by the individual worshippers), and it made clear that if these outward forms were observed it would not pursue matters of belief too insistently. Puritan worship, however, characteristically took the form of 'prophesyings' and 'exercises',[6] typically open-air gatherings, sometimes on a huge scale, the very public nature of which staged a fearless and unashamed witnessing to the truth which scorned the compromise of appearances that the state demanded. Though the Puritan exercise was a performance, it was a performance based on a singular aesthetic, one that insisted on the public stage as the inevitable demonstration of the spirit within. The state's willingness to accept a performance that would be recognised on both sides as pretence produced the necessity of Puritan rejection of pretence. It is scarcely surprising, then, that so many Puritans found the conscious artifice of theatre compromising and threatening to the integrity of the self.

Even the Latin drama could not remain exempt from this kind of attack on artifice itself. Early treatises, such as John Northbrooke's (1577) and Philip Stubbes' (1583), defended academic drama within strict parameters. Northbrooke lists six conditions within which plays may be allowed:

first, that those comedies which they shall play be not mixt with anye ribaudrie and filthie termes and wordes (which corrupt good manners). Secondly, that it be for learning and utterance sake, in Latine, and very seldome in Englishe. Thirdly, that they use not to play commonly and often, but verye rare and seldome. Fourthlye, that they be not pranked and decked up in gorgious and sumptious apparell in their play. Fiftly, that it be not made a common exercise, publickly, for profit and gaine of money, but for learning and exercise sake. And lastly, that their comedies be not mixte with vaine and wanton toyes of love. These being observed, I judge it tollerable for schollers. (Chambers, *The Elizabethan Stage*, vol. IV, p. 199)

Yet these provisions could not defend dramatic practice against those accusations based on hostility to mimesis itself. Within both Oxford and Cambridge Universities there was increasing controversy regarding the seemliness of staging plays. John Case, in his Latin defence, printed in 1585, and dedicated to the Earl of Leicester, Chancellor of Oxford University, argues, like Northbrooke above and like Leicester himself (cited on p. 118 above), that academic plays are acceptable within certain limits. Dispute became more bitter in the following decade with the open disagreement between two Oxford academics, John Rainolds and John Gager. As F. S. Boas points out, their debate can have had only limited effect as long as it remained in Latin treatises or unprinted letters, but a collection of their correspondence was issued in English as *Th'Overthrow of Stage-Playes* in 1599 and reissued in the following year (Boas, *University Drama*, p. 247). Perhaps the most significant aspect of Gager's defence, in the context of the wider audience reached by an English printing, is that it is based on an emphatic distinction between the professional and the academic stages. The defence for academic drama is precisely that it is not professional drama. Latin drama defends itself by rejecting paid professionals as the barbarians.

ENGLISH AND LATIN IN PERFORMANCE

Such rejection strikes an attitude, but it is an attitude which continually has to compromise. Latin needs its English other to confirm its authoritative status as well as to give it wider currency, just as English needs Latin in order to define its own area of representation. Thus the relationship between English and Latin drama is not simply or always a relationship between two kinds of drama functioning separately from one another, but also, necessarily, sometimes an explicit interchange within a single performance. Pageantry, both in performance and in print, provides a case in point. The mixture of English and Latin in performance is evidence of a variety of aims coming together. The pageant, typically aimed at confirming the authority of the monarch or the Lord Mayor, for example, needs Latin as the language of tradition that brings to the ceremony the knowledge that the ceremonial moment re-enacts and

confirms traditional structures and traditional beliefs. It needs Latin
as the language of the bible, the language of academe, the language
of the ancients, the language of status, authority, formality and
compliment. On the other hand it also needs English as the
articulation of all that the pageant and the subject it celebrates want
to represent for the widest possible audience. It needs English as the
language of the people, the nation and political unity.

In performance, the audience listens to and accepts the different
functioning of the two languages as part of the ceremonial experience. The non-Latinate spectators may listen to the sound of Latin
as they watch a performed spectacle without finding the loss of
verbal comprehension frustrating, since they understand the visual
text, and perhaps even enjoy the aural experience of the Latin in this
context. When the pageant is then printed, however, both the nature
of the audience it addresses and the mode of that address become
more problematic. The performed pageant necessarily addresses a
much wider audience than the printed version, since illiteracy is no
barrier to watching the show. Since the printing of pageants is as
much a form of propaganda as their performance, however, the
printed account has to construct an audience which is in fact literate
and hence tending towards the elite as if it represented the same
wide spectrum of 'the people' as the performed spectacle.

The printed version of the Elvetham pageant of 1591 is interestingly self-aware and explicit about its own project in this respect.
Following the printing of a Latin song it announces its intention to
translate the song: 'Because all our Countrymen are not Latinists, I
thinke it not amisse to set this downe in English, that all may bee
indifferently partakers of the Poet's meaning' (Wilson, *Entertainments
for Elizabeth I*, p. 104). While the printing of the song in Latin
attempts to mediate the ceremonial aspect of the performance, a
'popular' audience is called into being by the printing of a following
translation. The ceremonial and the democratic aspects of political
purpose are here in tension: the Latin both underlines the truthfulness of the printed account (since the song was presumably originally
performed in Latin) and reaffirms the authority brought by its
presence to that performance, while the English attempts to erase
the potential exclusiveness of the Latin in its written form by
ostentatiously gesturing towards the 'popular' audience (not, by
definition, actually reading this account, because still largely illiterate, but an important aspect of the meaning of the pageant). Both

sixteenth-century English plays and sixteenth-century English writing, very different forms of cultural production, offer different purchases on a nevertheless familiar opposition: English establishes its claim to legitimacy through the concepts of nation and democracy, yet it allows the chimera of the Latin other against which it defines itself to remain visible.

This is strikingly apparent in the coronation pageant discussed at the beginning of chapter 5. Though it is a pageant designed to highlight, for political ends, the very Englishness of the English bible, it employs Latin, not only for some of the verses and captions of the pageant, but even for the bible itself, 'upon the which', Holinshed says, 'was written *Verbum veritatis*, The word of truth' (vol. IV, p. 168). Holinshed's citation of the Latin phrase followed by its English translation leaves it unclear whether both Latin and English were inscribed on the bible, or whether Holinshed, like the writer of the Elvetham pageant, has decided to translate the inscribed Latin phrase for his non-English readers. Either way, a double message is clear: English may be the language of the godly nation, but it is visibly authorised here by the language it claims to supersede, which is the traditional language of official ceremony, bringing *gravitas* to the present via the very longevity of the past. (It is notable too that, while English words might be found to do the work approximating to that of the Latin '*gravitas*', none is quite so right as the Latin word, still in current use for precisely the quality that Latin, even now, occasionally supplies in vernacular culture.)

Latin may have signified in certain elitist ways to an English audience, but it was not a language with which only the elite came into contact (see chapter 5 above). Latin and English did not merely coexist in English culture; they coexisted with a degree of contiguity and interchange that it is difficult for us to reconstruct. Though there is no denying the existence of a huge corpus of Latin writing addressed only to the *cognoscenti*,[7] aurally Latin was much more fully present within vernacular culture than is often realised. It was the language of public ceremonial, of oratory, of memorial tributes, of royal and civic pageantry, the language of authoritative culture. It was also, despite Protestant insistence on an English bible and an English prayer book, the language most directly linked in popular consciousness with the supreme and sacramental authority of the Word.

Earlier chapters have already emphasised the degree to which the

Latin mass maintained a high awareness of and receptivity to Latin amongst its participants. This was not an awareness which could disappear overnight with the coming of a Reformed church. Besides the resistance to an English liturgy discussed in chapter 4 (p. 73 above), we must remember that Queen Mary reinstated Latin as the language of the English church during the 1550s, and that congregations were required to worship according to the old use throughout her reign (1553–8). The English bible, contested in different translations with different doctrinal shadings, had not yet achieved the ring of unitary authority that the sound of the Authorised Version came to have for later centuries; whereas the Latin bible, despite its potential evocation of the hated subjection to Rome, had not fully lost its sacramental ring. Unlike foreign vernaculars, which probably specified little more than 'foreignness' to most of the audience, Latin was recognisably Latin, even to the non-Latinate. And congregations familiar with the habit of responding to the Word via the sacrament, through participation in a collective act of worship rather than through intellect and understanding, were also potential theatre audiences ready to respond to language in ways beyond the semantic. The performative ritual of the liturgy celebrated a sacred and social act, literally a communion, in a process that positioned the laity simultaneously as spectators and actors. Their presence was part of the enacted process, but the ritual was also a spectacle, both visual and auditory. And this particular spectacle was one that prioritised other modes of response over the intellectual. The Latin of the liturgy was not uttered so that the congregation should follow its sense, but rather to solemnise and elevate the experience of their participation, to estrange it and to mark its difference from vernacular, everyday life. Such a habit of worship produced auditors who understood that alien language could function to bypass rational processes in a productive way and to specify the deeply invested nature of particular moments in time.

It was at the level of *performance* that the interface between English and other languages was made available to the widest audience. Spectators who could not read, far less read Latin, would nevertheless encounter the sounds of other languages, especially Latin, in performance contexts. Besides accepting Latin as the intermittent language of performance in pageantry and ceremonial, members of the public might have seen whole plays performed in Latin. Many grammar schools, as indicated in chapter 5 above, mounted regular performances in Latin, and these performances were sometimes open to the public. (Boys from these schools, of course, would probably have seen a Latin play performed before they ever witnessed an English one.) An early example of a school opening its performances to the local people is Ralph Radclif's school, founded at Hitchin in 1546. Radclif was a contemporary of John Bale's, and it is Bale's account that provides the only detailed evidence of Hitchin's practice (*John Bale's Index*, pp. 332–4). Radclif built a theatre and composed some of the plays performed there annually by his scholars. It is not clear what language the plays were performed in; T. H. Motter believes that the school offered plays in both Latin and English (*The School Drama in England*, p. 225). Bale's citation of Latin titles cannot be read as evidence of the language of performance, since the language of Bale's text (Latin) may be the determining factor here. The fact that he quotes from the plays in metrical Latin, however, points more strongly to the likelihood of plays actually written and performed in Latin. Though we can prove nothing in this case, the point is simply that performing in Latin to a mixed audience was less improbable than it now seems. The argument that uses a popular audience as evidence that the plays were performed in English fails to take account of the ease with which Latin could be accepted as part of a whole spectacle, even by a relatively uneducated audience.

A document of 1574 records the Merchant Taylors' decision to refuse the use of their hall for any more school performances 'by reasone of the tumultuous disordered persones repayring hither to see suche playes'. The sneering tone of the document indicates the fact that a wider audience than the company thought desirable attended such plays: 'everye lewd persone thinketh himself (for his penny) worthye of the chiefe and most comodious place withoute respecte of any other either for age or estimacion in the comon weale' (Motter, *The School Drama in England*, p. 109). But this kind of audience and this kind of behaviour do not in themselves constitute evidence that the performance must have been given in English.[8]

University productions easily disprove such an assumption. From having been essentially private performances before the accession of Elizabeth, they became after that more frequently open to the public, though still in Latin, and attracted a mixed audience. When Queen Elizabeth attended a Latin play at Oxford University in 1566, the wall that collapsed in the crush killed an undergraduate, a college servant and a town brewer (Binns, *Intellectual Culture*, p. 139). It is perhaps precisely because such performances became available to a wider audience after Elizabeth's accession that the academic drama became subject to attack, and found the need to defend itself against such attack by distancing itself so insistently from the professional public theatre.

Yet the high-level presence of Latin in Elizabethan culture meant that audiences could respond to the meaning and the fact of its presence in a given context, if not to the literal meaning of its words. An interesting reference in a letter by Robert Laneham describing the festivities at Kenilworth in 1575 suggests that Latin could be combined even with bear-baiting if its function was clear. Laneham's account says that the bearward performed a parody of learned dispute with a semblance of 'great wizdoom and gravitée' (*A Letter*, p. 22). Latin is not specified, but would, as L. A. Beaurline comments, be the natural language of learned dispute (note in his edition of Jonson's *Epicoene*, p. 50). The fact that this bear-baiting was presented before the queen, noted for her command of languages, may have stimulated this particular performance, but stage representations of scholars like Faustus, Friar Bacon or Holofernes demonstrate that extended Latin in particular contexts was not uncommon in the public theatres.

Evidently Latin can be functional in a vernacular context, identifying a specific professional group or type. As well as signifying scholars on stage it peppers the speech of stage lawyers, alchemists and magicians. It is also used for certain kinds of utterance, regardless of the character who utters them. At this level it is simply colonised by English culture to perform certain roles within that culture. The audience expects, for example, to hear generalised truths spoken in Latin, and such remarks risk losing their authority if they are not made in Latin. Such brief utterance in Latin within the drama mimics other forms of cultural practice: sermons, ceremonies and written texts frequently cite classical or biblical authority in Latin, and it is no mere coincidence that this kind of utterance is usually known by its Latin name as a *sententia*. Medieval and Renaissance plays regularly cite *sententiae* in Latin, many of which would already be familiar to some of the audience from their schoolbooks. Tudor schoolboys were used to memorising them in Latin and translating them into English. This kind of Latin is understood to be distanced from the speaker. It is understood to be temporarily disconnected, as it were, from the political relations of the speaker's place and time and seems to speak from a realm of universal authority out of time. In a sense its very linguistic difference removes it from the discourse of the speaker, almost from utterance itself, so that it is perceived as transmitting a wisdom that is beyond the here-and-now of the playworld. Though it arises in this form out of direct borrowing from classical drama, it has dramaturgical links with the 'voice of the church' discussed in chapter 2.

Contemporary records of performance suggest that incomprehensible language was less of a barrier to pleasure than it might be to a modern audience. Elizabethan dramatists, as Andrew Gurr points out, distinguished between 'two kinds of playgoers, divided according to the priority of eye or ear' (*Playgoing in Shakespeare's London*, p. 93), and Fynes Moryson's account of the reception of English actors abroad implies a highly gestic style of performance:

> I remember that when some of our cast [i.e. cast off, out of work] despised Stage players came out of England into Germany, and played at Franckford in the tyme of the Mart, having nether a complete number of Actours, nor any good Apparell, nor any ornament of the Stage, yet the Germans, not understanding a worde they sayde, both men and women, flocked wonderfully to see theire gesture and Action, rather than heare them, speaking English which they understand not. (Limon, *Gentlemen of a Company*, p. 1)

Paradoxically, the Latin drama of school and university, while testifying to the centrality of Latin within educated culture, simultaneously offers further evidence that this kind of performance was accessible other than through intellectually understood verbal language. Clearly those non-Latinate townspeople who attended academic performances must have found pleasures unrelated to the meaning (though not necessarily the sound) of the Latin. Similarly, the visits of Italian players to England in the 1570s (Chambers, *The Elizabethan Stage*, vol. II, p. 262) offered English audiences the opportunity to appreciate the relative ease with which language could cease to be a barrier in the highly gestic performance of *commedia dell'arte*.

It would be a mistake to adopt a patronising attitude towards the pleasures available to an audience witnessing performance in an alien language. We don't, after all, patronise the congregation hearing a Latin mass (unless the critical perspective is one that is generally patronising about either the 'medieval' or the 'folk'). Such pleasures are neither wholly non-aural nor wholly non-intellectual. On the contrary, sound can clearly create meanings other than through sense, and meaning is only one of the pleasures available from sound. Similarly, spectacle can communicate meaning as well as other pleasures. Instead of asking whether an inability to make semantic sense of a foreign language was a barrier to response, one might equally well ask whether a capacity to do so blocked other potential modes of response to an alien language.

Plays always offer pleasures beyond the meaning of their words; but Elizabethan plays also demonstrate a specifically dramaturgical dependence on Latin, one that recalls earlier dramatic practice (see chapter 2 above and pp. 95, 104–5 of chapter 4). Late sixteenth-century dramatists still understood that language could be used to invoke deep responses that bypassed any engagement with the sense of the words and allowed particular moments to develop a presence that took them almost beyond the limits of the playworld. And late sixteenth-century audiences were still familiar with encountering Latin at authoritative and heavily invested moments. A group of plays from the 1580s and 1590s will serve to show clearly how strong the emotive address of an alien language can be within a vernacular play. Although the shaping influence of Seneca is central to the dramaturgy of these plays, it is not the classical sources of language, form and content which are under consideration here, but rather the effects produced by the texturing of different languages within a single theatrical experience. All of these plays use the sound of a non-native language, usually Latin, to deepen and focus the engagement with both narrative and non-narrative significance.

Locrine (*c.*1594), like *The Spanish Tragedy* (1582–92),[9] uses the figure of Revenge (in this case Ate, a classical goddess of Revenge) to frame the drama, and opens each act with a dumbshow followed by a line or two of Latin spoken by Ate. The dumbshow and the Latin function together at one level as an emblematic condensation of the narrative unit about to be enacted. Yet these stage images, with their Latin pronouncements uttered by Ate, who stands outside the action, are simultaneously deeply linked with the action and yet separate from it. They perform it at a different level of signification, giving it an alternative form of stage-presence and seeming to link it to some realm of truth that gives its particularity wider significance.

Within the play too, Albanact is given six lines of Latin (lines

895–900) which create the space for fullness of engagement with the significance of his death – the outrageous defiance of Fortune, the heroic courage, the suffering, the injustice, the solemn finality of it and the necessity of avenging it – before he finally thrusts himself through with his own sword. The scene is the battlefield, stage directions indicate alarms sounding throughout and Albanact's speech immediately follows both Thrasimachus' advice to flee and a sounding of the alarm. His speech opens in English, with a refusal to flee: 'Nay, let them flie that feare to die the death, / That tremble at the name of fatall *mors*' (lines 886–7). Latin is introduced almost as an old friend within the vernacular sentence before the move into Latin is made complete. Albanact's English speech makes clear that this is a moment of stillness seized by sheer will out of the chaos of battle, an assertion of self that will make him, by becoming the instrument of his own death, victorious over the forces that seek to triumph over him. The Latin embodies that wilful insertion of the iconic moment; it holds up the surrounding narrative and claims space and time for itself out of the drive towards action, thereby rendering that action, temporarily, trivial and insignificant. Again *gestus* and language intensify the focus together. For those who do not understand the Latin, the change of sound is enough to signal a change in the mode of engagement, while gestures carry the weight of meaning; for those who do understand it, its semantic content is no more than an extra dimension to the charge carried by its difference, its alien prominence.

Sometimes Latin is used once only, to freeze a single moment of this kind, which then stands out in high relief against the vernacular world which makes space for it. This is the case in Thomas Lodge's play, *The Wounds of Civil War* (1586–91). The death of Scilla is heightened first by the introduction of an extra-narrative character, Genius, who appears this once only in order to tell Scilla, in Latin, that his death is at hand, and second, by Scilla's own Latin response, which universalises his personal recognition and acceptance of death (lines 2519–31). In addition the Latin functions to construct conceptions of the historical, indeed the historic, momentarily relocating Scilla in the 'classical' past.

Christopher Marlowe and Thomas Nashe's *Dido, Queen of Carthage* (c.1585–6) freezes two interrelated Latin moments. Dido and Aeneas are first given lyrical and tragic depth and re-anchored in 'antiquity' through their five-line exchange in Latin at the moment of parting (v.i.136–40). Latin encloses them in an intimacy that here appropriately privatises the content of their words, while stimulating the audience, through the sudden change of language and sound, to re-engage with the knowledge of their parting in terms that reach out for mythic significance rather than in terms of the common-sense meanings of localised utterance. Again, even for the Latinate audience, the meaning of the words is less important than the meaning of the moment, given focus by the change of language. The other point where the play moves into Latin is just before Dido throws herself into the flames (v.i.310–11, 313). The sound echoes with the sound of that earlier parting, crystallising the necessary link between Dido's loss of Aeneas and her wish for death. The two moments stand out from the rest of the play as points of plenitude, points at which mythic presence is given full and alien embodiment, originary and untranslated. For the audience, the myth is deeply, if fleetingly, possessed in these moments.

In *Edmund Ironside* (*c.*1590–1600) Latin articulates a moment of sudden clarity of vision: Southampton's eventual recognition of the treachery of Edricus. As Southampton realises that Edricus' defection means certain defeat for the Saxon army, he re-enacts a great historical moment, pronouncing Hannibal's words at the loss of Tarentum (lines 1554–9). Although Southampton himself is not a figure from the Roman classical past like Scilla or Dido, he belongs to a time imaginatively central to the Elizabethans, in their nationalistic nurturing of the myth of Britain, and he is here given *gravitas* and historic stature by the suggested continuity with ancient heroes. *Orlando Furioso* (1591) signals Orlando's recognition of Angelica's faithlessness with a Latin line condemning womankind (ii.i.671), and then presents the onset of his madness via a shift to Italian (ii.i.685–92).[10] Melissa the enchantress later brings the sleeping Orlando back to sanity in a masque-like scene (iv.ii) where satyrs first dance and play around Orlando, causing him to wake and speak before sleeping again. During this second sleep Melissa utters the Latin incantation to the spirits of the wood and the underworld which returns Orlando to his senses (lines 1160–9). As Orlando's sleep and the end of the satyrs' dance signify, the words are uttered within a stage-picture of emblematic stillness. They not only heal his madness, but restore his heroic stature for the audience, showing him worthy of divine intervention, its divinity signalled by linguistic otherness.

Prolonged speech in a foreign vernacular is much less common than in Latin, but several plays offer parallels with the shift to Italian in *Orlando Furioso*. When Joan, the supposed daughter of the King in George Peele's *Edward I* (1590–3), discovers that she is the bastard child of a lecherous friar, she falls grovelling on the ground and begins to speak in an alien language (lines 2871–2). The change of language here represents a crisis in the speaker's sense of identity comparable with the disturbance of Orlando's mind produced by the sudden revelation of unbearable knowledge. A slightly later play suggests the difference travelled in dramaturgical terms between Marlowe and Nashe's *Dido*, in the mid-80s, and the end of the century. John Marston's *Antonio and Mellida* (1599–1600), written, like *Dido*, for a boy company, allows the lovers to express their love in eighteen lines of Italian. The effect may at first seem to bear comparison with the Latin in *Dido*, in that it seals the lovers in a private world and suggests a communion between them that functions at a different level from more ordinary interchange; yet that comparison is held at arm's length by the witty response of the page, who is made to comment: 'I think confusion of Babel is fallen upon these lovers, that they change their language.' The rest of the page's speech extends this distancing of the audience from the lovers: he jokes about women as 'double tongued' and prone to yielding in 'strange language', and even more explicitly invites the audience to think about the acceptability of this perhaps by now dated convention by anticipating its problematic response: ''tis an error easier to be pardoned by the auditors than excused by the authors, and yet some private respect may rebate the edge of the keener censure' (iv.i.189–225).[11] Whereas the Latin spoken by the boy-actors of *Dido* allows them to inhabit their roles very fully and with a stage-presence that demands a deep emotional response from the audience, the Italian of *Antonio and Mellida* is commented on by an actor who steps aside from his role in order to prompt the audience to see the division between actor and role in what has gone before. The choice of boy-actors in the case of *Antonio and Mellida* comes out of a decision to highlight the parodic thrust of the play.

THE SPANISH TRAGEDY

Perhaps the most conspicuous negotiation of other languages in any play of the earlier period, before the changing attitudes of the late

1590s, is that of *The Spanish Tragedy*. It is a play dominated throughout by awareness of other languages, especially Latin, and one that builds to a climax that knowingly names itself as Babel. Latin is present from the opening of the play in the invocation of mythological names that dominates the ghost of Andrea's opening speech. Its sound is both exotic and authoritative. The naming of classical figures and locations not only sets the action within a framework which is distanced from contemporary England or Spain, but invites the audience to perceive the action as having a mythic dimension, a relation to truths and universals greater than the contemporary and vernacular world. The rhythms of 'Minos, Aeacus, and Rhadamanth' (I.i.33)[12] invoke the suspension of aria, the still point which holds up time and narrative to enrich them with iconic significance.[13]

As in medieval drama, Latin functions primarily as the language of truth, whether it takes the shape of quotations from scripture, Senecan *sententiae* or interventions at significant moments in the narrative. Interestingly, the distinction between Seneca and the bible seems to be consciously collapsed; what is important is to recognise both as powerful sources of truth. In Act III, scene xiii, Hieronimo enters holding a book. His first line is a quotation from the Vulgate Bible: '*Vindicta mihi!*'. The Latin functions partly as motto to emblem here, naming the play as revenge tragedy and thereby fixing its outcome. The quotation suggests both that the book he carries is the bible and that its warning that God alone has the right to exact vengeance should be taken seriously. As the speech progresses, however, the citations are from Seneca and seem to point towards the need for human agency in the fulfilment of revenge. Editors usually assume that the book Hieronimo holds is Seneca; yet the quotation from two sources and the attempt to reconcile the bible's directive with arguments justifying disobedience to it look more like an attempt to force a unitary truth out of conflicting authorities, which in turn functions as a reminder that the bible itself has become a conflicted authority. The one unnamed book is made to represent two books; its singleness belies the duality of authority Hieronimo faces in order to legitimate his revenge. Hieronimo's very name works in tension with his role as revenger to underline this conflict of authorities. He shares his name with St Jerome, translator of the Vulgate Bible, and the name itself means 'sacred name'; yet his occupation in the play is that of Knight Marshall, or Justice, of

Spain, and it is his role to fill the absence of monarchical justice or divine retribution with his own revenge.

Other Latin moments are less problematic. They are predominantly gestic moments where action is frozen into quasi-mythic status, given significance beyond the temporary. Stage directions, either explicit or implied, confirm the importance of stage picture at such points. Action becomes icon when Castile praises the King of Spain's victory on his knees (I.ii.12–14), or when the Viceroy of Portugal lies on the ground to indicate the position to which Fortune has reduced him (I.iii.15–17).[14] The comparison with 'Renaissance emblem books in which a Latin motto was illustrated by an engraving and amplified by verses in the vernacular' is suggested by Michael Hattaway;[15] but in fact the Latin does more than merely echo what the stage image already shows. Though Hattaway is right about the emblematic quality of this kind of moment, the comparison with a printed artefact does not fully convey how the staged moment works. The relation between stage picture and verbal text may work in a way that is comparable with that of the printed emblem, but the printed emblem differs by being a static piece, attempting to make its meaning as an object in itself. Its physical context is that of the printed book, and specifically its place on the page in relation to the adjacent emblems in the book. The staged moment, on the other hand, makes its meaning by way of the particular effect of its stillness within surrounding movement, its momentary iconicity. And it is this quality of differentiation that the Latin underlines by virtue of its own textural difference from the surrounding vernacular speech.

Occasionally the Latin moment may be less visually iconic, but it retains its capacity to frame the instance as significant. Hence its occurrence at the high point of the General's battle description (I.ii.55–6): English blank verse, itself heightened into rhetorical patterns which create a stylised picture of 'nearly heraldic formality',[16] moves into even more highly patterned and alliterative Latin verse in order to deepen the audience's investment in the story by striving to fix it momentarily through structures of repetition. The patterns of antithesis already built into the description reach a point of climax in the Latin, which pairs grammatical variants of the same word in thickly textured proximity, pressing the oppositional rhythms on the ears of Latinate and non-Latinate alike: '*Pede pes et cuspide cuspis, / Arma sonant armis, vir petiturque viro.*' The conspicuousness of language as sound here, language as itself the experience rather than the medium by which experience is narrated, is made possible by the move into Latin. It is a move which allows the audience to escape the flow of narrative time and to enter into a different level of engagement with the dramatic action; it is an entry point, in fact, into a different way of being. The Latin couplet which forms Bel-imperia's parting words towards the end of Act III, scene x offers a similar pause for deepening focus.

Most conspicuous and emotive of all the play's Latin focus-points is Hieronimo's lament (II.v.67–80). Stage directions frame the speech with gestic action: Hieronimo 'sets his breast unto his sword' after the first line of Latin and 'throws it from him and bears the body away' when he has finished speaking. In between, the action is held in absolute stillness while the speaking voice as sound takes over from language as sense. Hieronimo himself points out that the speech is a substitute for what should be song, were the death a natural one: 'I'll say his dirge, singing fits not this case' (line 66). An analogy with opera works quite precisely here: the move from recitative to aria is paralleled by the move from vernacular speech as a vehicle for meaning to Latin speech as a mode in which the expressive, emotive and performative functions of language replace the need to communicate content by satisfying a different need. An analogy with Tudor musical composition might be with the change in vocal texture when a single part or voice momentarily breaks free of the surrounding polyphony to sound alone. Here in Thomas Kyd's play the forward thrust of narrative linearity pauses to make room for narrative intensity. The presence of grief is given the space and time it needs, performed to the limit through an extravagance of sound; and it is the fullness of that presence itself that is so satisfying.

Recognition of movement into alien language as a conscious dramatic practice among Kyd's contemporaries should prevent us from being driven to argue that Hieronimo's dirge was probably cut in performance (Edwards, ed., *The Spanish Tragedy*, p. 45), or from dismissing it, as so many critics do, as an admission of failure on Kyd's part, words 'patched together ... when he needed highly-charged emotion and either lacked effective language or was unwilling to use it' (Zitner, '*The Spanish Tragedy*', p. 90). The effective language is precisely Latin, almost as a physical event of speech. The writing of these powerful moments in Latin points to a dramaturgy not yet remotely interested in naturalistic effects, but rather in highly wrought, extravagant fullness. That critics of *The Spanish Tragedy* continue to apologise for the play's 'larger-than-life emphasis', its 'exaggerated and over-theatrical' language and stage-action, is an indication of how much our evaluative theatrical vocabulary emerges out of naturalist and anachronistic preconceptions about theatre.[17] *The Spanish Tragedy*, together with those roughly contemporary plays considered earlier in this chapter, aims to give pleasure by making truth deeply present through high artifice, not by rendering it indistinguishable from ordinary life. Or it may be that it even replaces 'truth' with presence, which feels like the true. (The distance from Bale's aesthetic, with its rejection of conspicuous artifice, is remarkable, though other aspects of the play show some affinity with it; see chapter 7 below.) Gestus and alien sound together produce the most intense moments of a narrative committed to representing truth other than by mimesis. The movement into Latin articulates the recognition that some truths transcend the everyday vernacular.

Foreign vernacular languages, however, are as central to the workings of *The Spanish Tragedy* as Latin, though they function very differently. The play moves towards a climax that stages a re-enactment of Babel, confounding Latin and Greek with French and Italian. In order to understand how the play negotiates this babble of different languages, it is necessary to explore English foreign relations of the period. Englishness and aliens, then, are the subject of the next chapter, which approaches *The Spanish Tragedy* from the perspective of a very different group of contemporary plays.

CHAPTER 7

English and alien

The dating of *The Spanish Tragedy* to the period 1582–92 locates it within a period of great fear and hostility towards Spain and other Catholic nations (see further Mulryne, 'Nationality and Language', Bevington, *Tudor Drama*, ch.14), though the play cannot be fixed with any certainty to either side of the English victory against the Spanish Armada in 1588. Pope Pius V had excommunicated Queen Elizabeth in 1570, and thereby released English Catholics from any duty of obedience to her. Government fears of a rebellion by English Catholics were therefore coupled with fears of invasion by one or both of the great Catholic European powers, France and Spain, or by a suspected Catholic conspiracy united against England.

The queen's immediate response, in 1571, was to pass three new statutes: the Treasons Act, which made it high treason to impugn the queen's right to rule or to speak or write of her as a heretic; the Act 'against the bringing in and putting in execution of Bulls and other Instruments from the See of Rome', which forbade English subjects to bring in any bulls or printed matter from the pope, on pain of high treason, and even prohibited the bringing in of crosses and pictures from Rome; and the Act against Fugitives over the Sea, which imposed forfeit of property on anyone who had gone overseas without licence and failed to return within six months (*13 Elizabeth I, cc.1, 2, 3*). The fear of foreign infiltration, if not invasion, is conspicuous in all of these statutes, and their rhetoric is grounded in the suspicion that movement 'over the Sea' in either direction may be the visible trace of treason. Not only are foreigners entering the country potentially dangerous, but English travellers put their loyalty to the crown in question by spending time on foreign soil, and in particular Roman soil. In the words of Bishop Challoner, the English feared 'lest the Romans should come, and take away both their place and nation' (Tanner, *Tudor Constitutional Documents*, p. 146). 'Englishness' at this point in time is fiercely determined by a demonisation of all that is not English.

Later events of the 1570s did nothing to allay English fears. The discovery of the Ridolfi plot (a conspiracy to replace Elizabeth on the English throne with Mary, the Catholic Queen of Scotland) led to the execution of the Duke of Norfolk in 1571; the St Bartholomew Massacre of French Protestants in Paris in 1572 seemed to warn of the terrible bloodshed that foreign Catholics (or Catholic foreigners – the emphasis made little difference[1]) were capable of inflicting; and the Roman invasion began, not with the landing of an army, but with the secret arrival of priests ordained at William Allen's newly founded seminary in Douai. The first priests reached England in 1574, and their numbers had reached about a hundred when the Jesuits too began to arrive in 1580. The 'invasion' in a sense realised the worst fears of the English. By taking the form of undercover infiltration rather than open warfare, it hid its shape and size, took root in places that were hard to find and created a culture of suspicion strongly focused on the idea of the hidden enemy, who finds clear stage representation in the form of the Machiavellian villain.

Small wonder, then, that English nationalism flourished so aggressively in the 1570s and 1580s, and that it was so insistently tied into the rhetoric of Protestantism in this period. With threats so conspicuous from every form of difference, and religious difference so strongly implicated in racial difference, the English monarch reached out for the powerful weapon of political unity offered by nationalism, and English writers in turn could scarcely avoid addressing questions of nation and nationhood. The outlawing of difference was inscribed in the harshest penalties the law could offer. Seminary priests discovered by the authorities could be executed from 1577. Torture, though illegal, was permitted, as Sir Edward Coke wrote, 'directly against the common lawes of England' in cases of suspected treason, a category which predictably tended to focus on Catholics at this point in time (Hanson, 'Torture and Truth'). The state's perception of religious faith as a danger to national security was starkly displayed in the question commonly asked of Catholics after 1580: in the event of a Catholic invasion, for whom would you fight, pope or queen? The defeat of the Armada in 1588 may look like an ending from this distance, but it did not look like that to Elizabethans. England remained at war with Spain until after the accession of James, and also became involved in the French civil war after 1589. The construction of 'England' remained firmly entrenched in the definition and exclusion of otherness, whether racial, religious or political.

FOREIGN VERNACULARS IN ENGLISH PLAYS

Foreign vernaculars function quite differently from Latin in *The Spanish Tragedy*, and quite differently, too, from the extended use of a foreign vernacular to represent disturbed states of mind discussed in chapter 6 above. In this play they transport the narrative not, as Latin frequently does, out of time and place but specifically into a time and place that are alien, and which the audience is invited to distrust. This distrust, like the respect, even reverence, that Latin invites, is produced by sound rather than sense; it is a response stimulated in both the illiterate and the educated audience. An Elizabethan audience had two bases on which to be able to ground the difference between Latin and other foreign languages: one was the very familiarity of Latin, discussed in chapter 6 above; the other was the audibly different rhythmic organisation of its sound and the slower speed of its delivery, as compared with that of the contemporary vernaculars, Spanish and Italian, that dominate the non-Latin alien speech of this play. It is important, furthermore, that to untrained English ears Spanish and Italian (and to some extent other romance languages such as French) tend to be indistinguishable from each other, while remaining audibly distinct from Latin.[2] And this division in how the audience processes what it hears in turn reinforces its tendency to attribute singularity and authority to Latin, but slipperiness and unreliability to alien vernaculars.

More obviously, of course, foreign vernaculars are heard primarily against English. Political, religious and economic discourses of the period all offer potential perspectives for collapsing foreignness into duplicity, constructing English in the position of strength, firmly allied with plainness and transparency. Spanish and Italian in *The Spanish Tragedy* take the action into a world of swift decisions, calculated treachery and Machiavellian intrigue. The audience is encouraged to summon racist stereotypes to its judgement of Lorenzo, a self-proclaimed villain who plans treachery in secret languages that put an audible barrier between heart and speech and render him opaque and suspicious. The very exclusiveness of an alien language is a knowing part of its function in this instance.

Whether or not the language is recognised or understood, the change of language is designed to provoke a shiver of recognition in the audience, a recognition of foreignness, with attendant fears of danger, secrecy and dishonest dealing. It signals to the audience that this character is a Machiavel capable of different masks, one who cultivates a gap between speech and intentions. Like the villains of Bale's Protestant drama, the Machiavel is both a foreigner (speaking in two or more languages, at least one of which is associated with Catholicism) and an actor.

When Hieronimo drops into Spanish (iii.xiv.118), he too has by now become a double-dealer. Failed by civil justice, he is forced, in his search for revenge, to mask his thoughts and guard his speech. The linguistic echo of Lorenzo's language invites the audience to compare the role Hieronimo is now compelled to adopt with the freely chosen role of the Machiavel. Italian couplets assigned to these same two speakers invite further comparison between them: both Lorenzo and Hieronimo, left alone at the end of Act iii, scenes iv and xiv respectively, close the scenes with Italian couplets. Presumably spoken directly to the audience, these lines paradoxically address the audience primarily to exclude them, guarding their sense from all but a few, while making their statement about the speaker quite clearly. Their sense, for those who understand it, confirms the meaning they communicate to the non-Latinate members of the audience: they identify deception in the speakers. Lorenzo's couplet translates as 'And what I want, no-one knows; I understand, and that's enough for me', and Hieronimo's into the ironically self-reflective 'He who shows unaccustomed fondness for me has betrayed me or wants to betray me' (Edwards' translations (ed., *The Spanish Tragedy*)). Language as mask subverts its own function and exposes its own corruption.

Kyd is representative of his fellow-dramatists at this time in exaggerating the foreignness of his villain and in giving his play of multiple treachery a foreign setting. Barabas and Ithamore in Marlowe's *The Jew of Malta* (c.1589–90) pepper their speech with Spanish; Pedro, the hired assassin in Lodge's *Wounds of Civil War* (1586–91), and Jaques, who plays a similar role in Greene's *James IV* (c.1590), speak in a stage-French dialect; the allegorical figure of Fraud in Robert Wilson's *Three Lords and Three Ladies of London* (1588–90) not only speaks in stage-French, but explicitly calls attention to his own alien status: 'mee un' Forriner' (p. 438). Again and again stage foreigners are presented as murderers, cheats, cowards, rebels or traitors (or some combination of these).[3]

It is unnecessary here to demonstrate the prevalence of anti-alien feeling in late Elizabethan plays, since David Bevington (*Tudor Drama*) has covered this ground so thoroughly already. His chapter 'War Fever' persuasively argues for the rise of the English history play out of a movement towards 'a unifying animosity toward foreigners' gathering force up to and immediately following the Armada crisis of 1588. Elizabeth's attitude, as Bevington points out, masked private connivance with a public stance of outrage; but foreign ambassadors were in no doubt that the staging of anti-Spanish material was part of a deliberate policy (pp. 194–5). Bevington focuses on the plays of Robert Wilson as speaking for 'an especially virulent form of chauvinism, selfishly protectionist, given to crude prejudices, blaming even inner faults on a great vague conspiracy of the entire external world' (p. 191). (Wilson briefly seems to exempt the Jews from that prejudice when he creates the conditions for the audience to sympathise with Gerontus the Jew in *The Three Ladies of London* (*c*.1581),[4] but the absence of any consistent position with regard to the Jews can be demonstrated from *Three Lords and Three Ladies of London* (quoted p. 175 below).) The only expansion of Bevington's discussion requisite here is to note the central role that language plays in constructing anti-alien feeling in the audience.

The climactic confrontation between the English and the Spanish in Wilson's *Three Lords and Three Ladies of London* offers a pointed example. It centres on the opposition between the two heralds, Fealty and Shealty. The names are of course a conscious and polemical foregrounding of racial and ideological difference. Fealty speaks to an English nostalgia for origins, representing loyalty as an entrenched aspect of Englishness rooted in the nation's feudal past, while Shealty, the name of the Spanish herald, is explicitly glossed within the play as 'An Irish word, signifying liberty; / Rather remissness, looseness, if ye will' (p. 470). (Note the casualness with which the play exploits anti-Irish sentiment to intensify anti-Spanish feeling.) The heralds, as Fealty reminds us, are primarily 'trouchmen' (interpreters) conveying messages from one side to the other, so that their very presence is a reminder that different nations also speak in different languages, although their initial exchanges in English lead the audience into the assumption that the different languages must be *imagined* for speakers of different nationalities. As the scene progresses, however, different languages begin to intrude and thereby to direct audience hostility. Pride, a Spaniard, suddenly speaks in Latin prose, arrogantly commanding the English to speak in their native language since the Spaniards all understand it well, though they scorn to speak it. The speech functions similarly to the scattered Spanish and Italian in *The Spanish Tragedy*, since it invites the uncomprehending members of the audience to feel hostile to and suspicious of the speaker, while confirming and specifying that hostility for those who understand it. It is a slippery moment, however, and it is not clear why Latin is chosen rather than Spanish. It may be that Wilson initially wants to suggest Catholicism more strongly than nationality in the first instance, so that audiences react to both triggers of hostility.

Pride's next speech is in Spanish, and Fealty answers him in Spanish:

> PRIDE. *Buena, buena per los Lutheranos Ingleses.*
>
> FEALTY. *Mala, mala, per Catholicos Castellanos.* (p. 466)

The move into Spanish here throws the functioning of the Latin into clearer relief, since several areas in which this exchange invites a different kind of response can be identified. First, the Spanish is so simple and so clear in naming and patterning its antitheses of good and bad, Lutheran English and Catholic Castilians, that it communicates something of its content even to those who have no Spanish. Secondly, the sudden sound of Spanish, and its placing in a clearly oppositional dialogue, seek to elicit a much more straightforwardly racist hostility from the audience than does the Latin. Racism emerges out of the deliberate sneer inherent in reducing a foreign language to a few parroted phrases unable to bear complexity, comprehensible even to those uneducated in this language. The exchange also satisfies a competitive nationalism in that it represents Fealty as able to meet the Spaniard on his own terms and to beat him at his own game (since Fealty has the last word).

The same kind of capping is evident in the Latin exchange between English Policy and Spanish Shealty that immediately follows this one, again showing the same syllabic patterning in the parallelism of the two speech-acts:

> POLICY. *Loqueris Anglicè?*
>
> SHEALTY. *Maximè, Domine.* (p. 467)

It is conspicuous that where Pride, in the previous exchange, enacted his allegorical name by speaking in Spanish, Policy uses Latin, here the appropriately neutral diplomatic language of exchange. The meaning is simply that Policy is checking on whether Shealty speaks English before he gives him the message to deliver. Again, for a comprehending audience, Policy proves himself to be as clever and as linguistically competent as Pride, and perhaps also seems momentarily to shame Shealty, by asking a question that insults his competence as an interpreter; while for an uncomprehending audience it shows at least the first of these points through sound as clearly as sense. Pride is audibly trapped into the format of the double act, upstaged first by a mere herald, then by the triumphant Policy.

The verbal show of battle continues, culminating in the Spanish announcement, in Latin, that the English will soon be their servants, and the English response, in plain English, that 'the Lords of London dare them to the field' (p. 471). Part of the pleasure of the scene is that, after all this formal and static exchange of hostilities through language, which the Spanish perform so arrogantly, the final conflict is presented almost entirely visually. The Spaniards, according to the stage directions, 'make show of coming forward and suddenly depart', then return and 'flourish their rapiers near them, but touch them not'. Finally, and ignominiously, they make 'a little show' of rescuing their shields, then 'suddenly slip away and come no more' (p. 473). The visual sequence is sarcastically constructed as one that shrinks rather than builds. The focus on language before that sequence is carefully designed and paced: while the different languages incite anti-alien feeling as a local effect, the very prominence of language as a preface to the diminished action gradually acquires dramatic meaning: Spanish verbal display and expansiveness is exposed as mere delaying tactics, while English plainness is not only spoken but enacted.

A play which does some thinking about Latin and foreign vernaculars within the same jingoistic frame as used by Wilson, though written later than Wilson's plays, is the anonymous play *The Weakest Goeth to the Wall* (c.1595–1600). Its narrative is filled with opportunities for despising a range of different nationalities. Boastful Spaniards are depicted attacking the weak and cowardly French (as the play's most recent editor points out (Levenson, p. 53), the French were continually dependent on English military intervention against foreign powers in the 1590s), while the unprincipled villain who exploits another's poverty to try and seduce his wife, is described in the words of the oppressed husband as 'Flemish excrement' (vii.62). The central unifying figure is the clown, Barnaby Bunch, who is emphatically English and predictably loyal. His 'failure' to learn French, despite his apparent best efforts, is presented with humorous approval, and his numerous remarks about alien French culture and the miseries of travel serve to point up the superiority of England. England is idealistically represented by the penny pot of ale, available to all, as against expensive French wines, the privilege of a wealthy elite (ii.18–26). The democratising tendency of a nationalist drama and the construction of English plainness, already noted in chapters 4 and 5, are again evident here.

At one point, Lodowick, a French nobleman fallen on hard times as a result of others' treachery, realises he must beg for food or else starve. On his arrival in England, he comes upon one Sir Nicholas, a cleric, and addresses him in Latin in the hope that 'Perhaps for that he'll sooner pity me' (viii.24), since presumably a man of the church might be expected to recognise a fellow-scholar by his use of Latin. The decision to speak Latin, however, has the reverse effect, alienating this plain English cleric on the grounds of both social class and religion:

> This is no university nor school,
> But a poor village, and I promise thee,
> I never could abide this Romish tongue;
> 'Tis harsh, 'tis harsh, and we, I tell thee true,
> Do eat and drink in our plain mother phrase.
> If thou dost want and wouldst have part with us,
> Then do as we do; like an honest man,
> Show thy true meaning in familiar terms.   (lines 37–44)

Nor is the diatribe over when Lodowick speaks in English. Sir Nicholas' reply goes on to make the same point more insistently, more polemically and with more obvious reference to Elizabethan England:

> Why so, now I understand thy meaning.
> Is not this better far than *respice*
> And *precor* and such inkhorn terms as are
> Intolerable in a commonwealth?
> Conjurers do use them, and thou know'st
> That they are held flat felons by the law.

> Be sure, thou mightst have begged till thou were hoarse,
> And talked until thy tongue had had the cramp,
> Before thou wouldst have been regarded once.
> It is not good to be fantastical
> Or scrupulous in such a case as this. (lines 50–60)

What is interesting is the length of time the play dwells on this incident. It is unimportant to the plot, except in so far as Lodowick requires Sir Nicholas' help; but it is clearly central to the project of the play, which is to ally all things English, including language, with truth, plainness, simplicity and justice. To this end, the language Sir Nicholas speaks is also a certain sort of English, which might be described, using terms from the speech itself, as 'plain', 'honest' and 'familiar'. And the speech also contains the terms that might describe that kind of English it abjures: 'inkhorn', 'fantastical' and 'scrupulous'.[5]

FOREIGNERS WITHIN THE FOLD

London in the 1580s and 1590s was becoming home to an increasing number of immigrants, many fleeing from religious persecution in their own countries.[6] As unemployment began to be a problem (from about the mid 1560s) many Londoners blamed conditions on increased competition from aliens and other immigrants. The livery companies too felt threatened by alien workers who settled outside the jurisdiction of the city in order to try to circumvent the companies' controls on trading. There was a clear and hostile demarcation between those working within the city and the company structure, and those offering competition from within the suburbs and the liberties (but see further p. 176 below). Wilson's self-proclaimed 'Forriner' (p. 165 above) defines his own status in opposition to that of Simplicity: 'You be freeman, mee un' Forriner' (*Three Lords and Three Ladies of London*, p. 438). Characteristically, Wilson represents English Simplicity as honest and legitimate, vulnerable to the wicked deceptions of alien wolves.

The city's attempts to monitor the number of aliens throughout the sixteenth century indicate that foreign immigration was seen as in need of controls, and proclamations attempting to deal with the problems of overcrowding and new building suggest a struggle against overwhelming expansion. Certainly London was unique in early modern England in having so many residents from so far away.

The city authorities did attempt to control immigration by monitoring numbers of aliens and length of stay (licences were necessary for long visits) and by the strict enforcement of vagrancy laws, but hostility towards aliens remained high throughout the 1580s and was exacerbated by the extreme hardship of the 1590s. A. J. Hoenselaars notes the eruption of anti-alien hostilities in 1563, 1571, 1576, 1582, 1584, 1586, 1592 and 1595 (*Images of Englishmen*, p. 48).

A digression suppressed in George Puttenham's *Arte of English Poesie* while it was printing in 1589 demonstrates the high level of anxiety about immigrant groups on the part of both Puttenham and the censoring authorities. Puttenham is worried about the policy of admitting Flemish immigrants, who have already rejected the rulers of their own country, fearing their capacity to incite rebellion in their adopted country. 'What likelihood is there', he asks, 'that they should be more assured to the Queene of England, than they have bene to all these princes and governors, longer than their distresse continueth, and is to be relieved by her goodnes and puissance?' (*The Arte of English Poesie*, p. 314).[7] The cancellation of this passage, however, suggests that the authorities were as panicky as Puttenham. The educated elite who would have formed the vast majority of Puttenham's readers are scarcely to be equated with those social groupings most likely to riot against the immigrants. In fact the overreaction of the Elizabethan authorities to anything resembling anti-alien riot, or potential incitement to such, seems to stem partly from the collective 'memory' of 'Ill May Day', a notorious insurrection against the immigrant workforce in 1517, and a continuing benchmark against which Elizabethans measured the anti-alien feeling of their own times. Reporting a near-riot against the French and Dutch in 1586, William Fleetwood, Recorder of London, described it in a letter to Burghley as 'all things as like unto yll May day as could be devised' (Gildersleeve, *Government Regulation*, p. 94). No later sixteenth-century riot was in fact to be as serious as Ill May Day, but Elizabethans were not to know that. The quasi-mythological status of this event continued to determine the responses of both city and Privy Council to public gatherings throughout the Elizabethan period.

Its shadow also hung over the theatre, strongly associated with the possibility of riot by the London authorities. Among the most well-known examples of plays that provoked the censorship of the Master of the Revels is *Sir Thomas More* (*c.*1593 to *c.*1601),[8] a play which seeks at one point to dramatise the events of Ill May Day in 1517. Edmund Tilney's instruction is absolute: 'Leave out ... the insurrection wholy with the Cause ther off and begin with Sir Th: Moore att the mayors sessions with a reportt afterwards off his good service don being Shrive of London uppon a mutiny Agaynst the Lumbards only by A shortt reportt and nott otherwise att your owne perilles' (*Sir Thomas More*, p. 17). Yet the association of the theatres with rioting was only partly to do with the performance of plays. While the city fathers recognised that plays could incite riot, they also knew that certain 'light and lewd disposed persons' resorted to the theatre 'under colour of hearing plays', but really in order to devise 'divers evil and ungodly matches, confederacies and conspiracies' (Gildersleeve, *Government Regulation*, p. 179). Serious riots in London in the summer of 1592, for example, seem to have had more to do with anti-alien feeling and dissatisfaction with the justice meted out by the London authorities, for example, than with grievances raised by the plays performed.[9] The theatres were closed, nevertheless, and an extra watch mounted later in the month in the expectation of further rioting on the traditional occasion of Midsummer.

The following year, on 4 May, the London authorities were obliged to make a count of the total number of foreigners living in London in response to shopkeepers' complaints that foreigners were not content with English goods, but were insisting on setting up their own shops in competition. The next day a warning was found on the walls of the Dutch churchyard:

> Ye strangers that doe inhabite in this lande
> Note this same writing doe it understand
>
> . . .
>
> Since words nor threates nor any other thinge
> canne make you to avoyd this certaine ill
> Weele cutt your throtes, in your temples praying
> Not paris massacre so much blood did spill
> As we will doe just vengeance on you all ...
>
> (Freeman, 'Marlowe, Kyd', pp. 50–1)

More libels were found in the churchyard on 11 May, and this time special commissioners were appointed to apprehend all suspicious persons. It was during this search that Thomas Kyd was arrested and his papers searched. Marlowe, as is well known, was also arrested following Kyd's attribution to him of papers found in their shared lodgings. He may also, as Arthur Freeman ('Marlowe, Kyd') speculates, have been already under suspicion from the first libel, which carries a marginal reference to 'Tamberlaine', as well as including another possible allusion to Marlowe's work in the phrase 'paris massacre' above. (While the first point of reference is obviously the St Bartholomew Massacre itself, so that the phrase belongs within the rhetoric of racism and reprisal, the fact that Marlowe had written a play with this title may also have seemed to implicate him personally.) Both theatres and dramatists, then, fell automatically under the spotlight of investigation when there was an attempted clampdown on riot.

For a period of about two decades between 1586 and 1608, according to Roger Manning, an 'epidemic' of apprentices' riots[10] represented one manifestation of underlying economic, political and social crises (*Village Revolts*, p. 157 and ch.8). The appointment of provost-marshals (the equivalent of martial law) all over southern England after 1588, as an emergency measure for trying to maintain public order, at first excluded London, since it already had some control mechanisms in place. But they were also appointed in London in 1595 following the severity of the apprentice riots of that year. Riot was difficult to control, and both city and state were anxious to nip problems in the bud. Hence the jumpiness about aliens and their relations with the resident population.

Mockery of aliens in its mildest dramatic manifestation takes the form of comic stereotyping. Shakespeare's *Merry Wives of Windsor* (1597) contains a Welshman who 'makes fritters of English' (v.v.143) and a French doctor who abuses 'God's patience and the King's English' (i.iv.5); *Club Law* (1599–1600), a university play, has a Frenchman, a Welshman and a Northerner representing different comic variations of English; and there are many more. Sometimes, however, entire plays seem to exist for the central purpose of mocking and abusing foreigners, and this kind of play is particularly characteristic of the Admiral's Men at the Rose. William Haughton's *Englishmen for my Money* (1598), for example, is plotted around a Portuguese merchant living in England, whose three daughters wish to marry three Englishmen in preference to the Dutchman, the Frenchman and the Italian their father has selected for them. The play never misses an opportunity to present the foreign suitors as ridiculous, and the daughters, pointedly refusing to learn alien languages, use the difference in language as an excuse to remain silent in response to their wooing.

Comic pleasures offered to the audience centre on both foreign languages and foreigners' attempts to speak English. Frisco, the clown, says he must have his mouth full of meat before he can speak Dutch properly (lines 186–9), and later, disguising himself as the Dutchman, announces his plan to 'speake groote and broode, and toot and gibrish' (lines 1415–16). Language, and racially stereotyped modes of speaking are repeatedly the excuse for comic abuse: French is 'this gibberidge, / Or the Pigges language' (lines 846–7) and the Frenchman apparently bows his head, swallows his spittle and 'frissles' his beard when he speaks (lines 976–7); the Dutchman speaks 'rusticke Phrases ... Dutch French tearmes, / Stammering halfe Sentences dogbolt Elloquence' (lines 958–9), talks about the price of cloth in Antwerp and stands still for long periods wondering what to say (lines 960–4); the Italian is openly lecherous, tickling, winking, gaping and 'bawdy too in his discourse' (lines 994–7). The women and the clown openly parody their speech, and several scenes are clearly set up with this object in mind. The challenge is to find new heights of abuse, and the play can be savage as well as comic in this respect. One daughter, for instance, frames her rejection of her foreign suitor thus: 'These horeson Canniballs, these Philistines, / These tango mongoes shall not rule Ore me' (lines 1387–8). Plot and language together encourage the audience in an attitude of triumphant smugness at seeing the foreign competition tricked by three cocky Englishmen and their English lasses.

There is a notable hierarchy in Haughton's play that ranks the participants according to the degree of their Englishness. The alien suitors are made completely ridiculous; the father is seen as suspect in so far as, despite adopting England as his country of residence, he continues to favour foreign husbands for his daughters; while the daughters themselves are allowed the status, it would seem, of fully naturalised Englishwomen. Indeed their status is finally legitimised by the success of their determination to marry English husbands, a dramatic perspective which also legitimises English masculinity as the truest, most unassailable position. This is strikingly at odds with the kind of diatribe against racially mixed marriages offered by Robert Wilson. For him there can be no naturalisation, only racial defilement, altering 'the true English blood and seed, / And therewithall English plaine maners and good state' (*The Pedlar's Prophecy* (1594),[11] lines 343–4). Even second-generation aliens retain their alien loyalties and are potential traitors to England. 'Whatsoever ye do', warns Usury in Wilson's *Three Lords and Three Ladies of London*, 'be not traitors to your native country', and the reply of those to whom the warning is addressed focuses English paranoia at its most extreme: "Tis not our native country, thou knowest. I, Simony, am a Roman: Dissimulation, a mongrel – half an Italian, half a Dutchman: Fraud so, too – half French and half Scotish; and thy parents were both Jews, though thou wert born in London' (pp. 456–7).

David Bevington describes the 'unifying animosity against foreigners' he identifies as developing out of 'a turning away from internal problems of religious conflict' (*Tudor Drama*, p. 187). Yet it is clear from the plays considered above that foreigners were not perceived only as an external threat. The particular threat they posed was double-edged: they fought England abroad, but they also threatened jobs, housing and safety in England. The causes of hostility are clearly outlined in Robert Wilson's plays. In his *The Three Ladies of London* (*c*.1581) he introduces an Italian merchant, who of course speaks a stage-foreigner's dialect, agreeing to carry good English produce overseas and bring back cheap foreign trifles to England (p. 276). Wilson shows the same Mercatore advising Lucre on how to raise extortionate rents:

Madonna, me tell you vat you shall do; let dem to stranger, dat are content
To dwell in a little room, and to pay much rent:
For you know da Frenchmans and Flemings in dis country be many,
So dat they make shift to dwell ten houses in one very gladly.   (p. 305)

Foreigners crowding into London drive up the rent for English residents. Wilson is nothing if not direct.[12] And the particularly insidious quality of the alien threat, as we have seen, was that aliens might pass for English, thus making their treachery all the more difficult to detect. In this way they also tap into all the fears of the Elizabethan state, as demonstrated in the statutes discussed at the head of this chapter. 'The most detestable Barbarians', as Wilson's Pedlar calls them, who continue to arrive daily in London, are more than a mere economic threat: 'Ye shall see them one day play their parts gaily, / When we thinke least, they shall cut our throates' (*The Pedlar's Prophecy*, lines 891, 898–9). Nor does the Pedlar accept the Mariner's humane tolerance towards 'Gospellers', refugees from religious persecution. According to him, the practice of admitting aliens on compassionate grounds is merely 'misusing the word of mans salvation' (line 911). Religious faith is far too dangerous and volatile, as well as far too easily feigned, to be used as a passport to entry. It is 'a cloake to all abhomination' (line 909).

It has already been remarked that foreigners living in London tended to cluster in the liberties of the city,[13] excluded from both the rights and the responsibilities of citizenship. Following the May Day rioting of 1517 both national and city government had to take action to prevent any further such outbreak. Restrictions on the business activities of non-citizens were at first increased in the 1520s, but an act of 1531 adopted a new policy of lowering company admission fees to allow citizenship to a wider range of London's population (Rappaport, *Worlds Within Worlds*, pp. 42–60). Yet strangers were still subject to special regulations, and John Gillies notes the difference between London's treatment of aliens as opposed to that of, say, Venice and Antwerp: 'London', he writes, 'was to be protected from the Babel-like "openness" of Venice and Antwerp' (*Shakespeare and the Geography of Difference*, p. 130). Foreign immigrants therefore had grounds to resent the restrictions placed on them, while native citizens in turn were likely to resent immigrants for managing in some cases to evade restrictions which were in practice difficult to enforce (see further Archer, *The Pursuit of Stability*, pp. 131–40). Relations between aliens and London-born residents might be relatively trouble-free in times of full employment, but economic stress was always liable to put pressure on this tenuous calm. The paternalism of the London companies, which helped to maintain a remarkable level of stability despite the constant threat of riot in this period, was one side of a parochialism that sought to protect a narrowly defined community of residents by identifying its difference from those others who threatened its coherence.[14]

The marginal location of those racial others, then, was both determined by and constructive of their symbolic necessity. In giving definition to the identity of the Londoners who fought to exclude them, they perform a function similar to that of the Moor or the American Indian at a national level. The combined fascination and repulsion of Elizabethans for these more exotic others, their failure to take account of differences between them (they make no clear distinctions between variations of skin colour from 'tawny' to black, for example, though they are meticulous about the differences between those races that may be regarded as rivals to England) while highlighting their collective racial difference from the English, represents the same pattern of self-identification via the exaggeration and demonisation of difference.[15] Certainly the prominence of aliens, both black and European, in Elizabethan drama suggests that plays needed to keep 'playing with' this particular source of anxiety; and it is an anxiety which, naturally enough, is commonly played with in a way that foregrounds language.

It has often been noted that Caliban,[16] possibly the most over-worked example of otherness in the contemporary academy, has a name that invites the audience to hear its anagram, 'cannibal', and that Prospero acknowledges 'this thing of darkness' as his own (v.i.275–6). What tends to be less central to discussions of *The Tempest* (1611), however, is the extent to which Caliban's possession of no language other than the English Prospero has taught him renders him simultaneously knowing and powerless. He is presented throughout the play as English-speaking, and his history, as described in the play, makes it clear that his speech before that has been mere 'gabble' (Miranda's term, i.ii.356). It is unlikely that this 'gabble' should be imagined as a structured foreign language that merely sounds like gabble to English-speakers, since Caliban himself says Prospero taught him names for the sun and moon and Miranda taught him 'language' (i.ii.334–6, 363). The only language he has, it would seem, is that of his conquerors, and he both curses the time he learned it and repents the fact that he loved Prospero for teaching him (i.ii.364–5, 339). It is crucial for the audience's perception of Caliban that he is audible only in the same language as his tormentors, and that he is eloquent in that language, as eloquent in cursing as he is in describing the beauties of the island; as eloquent, in fact, as Prospero. His capacity to learn the civilised virtues throws his brutishness into question; his eloquence prevents him from being dismissed as simply a barbarian. It is this capacity to *equal* his colonisers that makes him most threatening. The other who simul-taneously mirrors and despises the self is far more difficult to accommodate than the unrecognisably alien could ever be.

THE MAKING OF EMPIRE: *HENRY V*

The manoeuvres of empire were neither so far advanced nor so self-aware in the 1590s as they were by 1611, but a breezy confidence that appropriates and manipulates foreignness almost as if it were a commodity is part of the celebration of Englishness offered towards the end of the 1590s by Shakespeare's *Henry V* (1599). This is a play conspicuously full of both English dialects and French, and the conspicuousness of this presence is related to the play's insistent call to, and construction of, Englishness. The Scottish, Irish and Welsh dialects are strategically represented as belonging to soldiers who fight for England and are given only comic and novelty value.[17] The work of Henry's rousing battle-speeches is to erase this difference under the banner of a uniting Englishness. The speech before Harfleur is particularly insistent in its emphasis on England and the English: the siege must be renewed, 'Or close the wall up with our English dead' (III.i.2); the soldiers are 'you noblest English' (line 17) who must take inspiration from the memory of their origins; the yeomen have 'limbs ... made in England' (line 26); and the battle-cry of all must be 'God for Harry, England, and Saint George!' (line 34). The semantic redundancy of all this is the key to its rhetorical necessity. In order to throw themselves into battle the men must be encouraged to erase differences between themselves, and between themselves and their king, and to imagine themselves metonymic beings: pieces of England.

It is immediately following this scene that Fluellen, Macmorris and Captain Jamy are introduced, so that they are, when we first see them, already 'domesticated' by the preceding rhetoric. References to 'nation' in this scene are of an entirely different nature, pointed up by the fact that the Folio speech headings turn from name to nationality just before the entry of Captain Jamy and Macmorris.[18] Fluellen begins to tell Macmorris, the Irishman, that 'there is not many of your nation – ', and is cut off by Macmorris' ranting response: 'Of my nation? What ish my nation? Ish a villain, and a bastard, and a knave, and a rascal? What ish my nation? Who talks of my nation?' (III.ii.122–4). The distracting comedy of dialect empties the concept of nationhood of any seriousness here, and the content of the lines confirms that subversive work by slyly making the Irishman himself voice the terms of abuse levelled at his own nation. This claim to nationhood is invoked precisely in order to be dismissed. England was after all at war with Ireland at this date, trying to subdue Irish rebellion against the English claim to sovereignty in Ireland (cf. the casual anti-Irishness of Wilson's name for the Spanish herald (p. 166 above)). Only the English claim to nationhood is to be presented in earnest.[19]

The French are more carefully worked over. The speech of the

French lords is given in an English peppered with French phrases which may suggest the dominance of English (and the English) in advance of the final battle. If the whole play were rendered in English this would not be so, since English would then function as the conventional language of expression for both native and foreign speakers; it is because the play contains so much French that English becomes noticeable enough to invite more specific interpretation. The only scene in which a Frenchman consistently speaks French is the scene in which Pistol takes a French soldier (iv.iv). The soldier's French then becomes the sounding board for Pistol's dogged Englishness, which consistently renders French phrases into laughable English nonsense. Pistol's failure to understand French, like Barnaby Bunch's failure in *The Weakest Goeth to the Wall*, is turned into a celebration of stubborn Englishness. The sequence of scenes is important here too, since the next scene opens with the French lords admitting defeat. Necessarily, this utterance too is in French, since the foreignness of the enemy needs to be at its most conspicuous at the moment of defeat. French, first mocked and discredited in the mouth of one terrified soldier (and the implication of a Frenchman yielding even to a ranting fool such as Pistol is that French as a discourse is to be perceived as more excessive and outrageous than rant), is passed on to the highest ranks of the conquered as the language in which they acknowledge their collective ignominy.

The ground for that defeat is prepared linguistically, however, in a domestic and apparently trivial scene depicting the attempts of the French princess to learn English (iii.iv). Conducted entirely in French, the only English words are those that the princess is trying to learn, and it is the business of the scene to highlight the fact that apparently innocent English words sound suspiciously like French obscenities. This set of false equivalences between French and English, though primarily a source of humour, also allows the audience to hear something like a conquest going on in this scene. In the first place, one might question why the princess is presented as feeling the necessity of learning English at this premature moment, though the play does not explicitly raise the question. The fact, furthermore, that the scene gets its laughs by outraging the modesty of a foreign princess, by seeming to compromise her in forcing her to utter English words that sound unspeakable to her ears, positions her as unwillingly overcome, even violated, by English. In the context it is hard to avoid the sense that the scene is transmitting, in advance of English victory, English riding roughshod over French sensibility. The English 'obscenity' of this scene is not just a dirty joke extraneous to the main business of the play but part of a project to emphasise Englishness as masculine, robust, direct, plain-dealing, while Frenchness becomes correspondingly (and humiliatingly) feminised.[20]

The scene clearly anticipates the final scene of the play, Henry's courtship of the princess in person. This, the final and most prolonged manoeuvre of English empire-building, follows after the spectacle of victory and explicitly posits this courtship as a problem of language. Henry's first words ask the princess, the language student of the earlier scene, to take on the role of teacher:

> Fair Katherine, and most fair,
> Will you vouchsafe to teach a soldier terms,
> Such as will enter at a lady's ear,
> And plead his love-suit to her gentle heart?   (v.ii.98–101)

The question invites Katherine to solve the linguistic problem, which is one of both register and comprehension, yet the invitation is rooted in bad faith, since the courtship, though it is courteously conducted as though the outcome depended on its processes, is in fact a mask for political necessity. The outcome is politically determined: Henry is the conqueror and Katherine the conquered. She is scarcely free to refuse his advances, and France would be the only loser if she did so. Despite the archness of the dialogue the scene in fact demonstrates an inexorable take-over. Marriage between Henry and Katherine is not the joining of two countries but the appropriation of the one by the other. The apparent suitor is in fact the conqueror imposing his will and his nation on the conquered. His address quickly anglicises Katherine to Kate, and he applauds her worldly-wise distrust of men's deceitful tongues by declaring that such insight proves her 'the better Englishwoman' (line 121). His use of prose in this scene further underlines his adoption of the 'plain Englishman' role here, and the speaker of those triumphs of rhetoric before Harfleur and Agincourt now pretends to be 'such a plain king that thou wouldst think I had sold my farm to buy my crown' (lines 124–6), 'a fellow of plain and uncoin'd constancy' (lines 153–4).

This show of democratic alignment between monarch and commonalty is by now recognisable as a familiar strategy of nationalism, and one that Shakespeare subjects to sceptical enquiry elsewhere in this play. The famous scene before Agincourt where Henry talks to his men, disguised as one of them, produces a resistance from them to the idea that 'the King is but a man' (iv.i.101–2). This resistance is presented more forcefully when Henry takes up his quarrel with Williams in his person as king. Though Williams begs pardon, he leaves the audience in no doubt about the duplicity of the King's pretence of oneness with the common man: 'Your Majesty came not like yourself. You appear'd to me but as a common man ... I beseech you take it for your own fault and not mine; for had you been as I took you for, I made no offence' (iv.viii.50–5). The play here quite openly voices its critique of the claim propounded by popular Tudor myth that the king is a man like other men. On the other hand, since the play itself also uses the strategy of seeking to position its audience as united with the king through manhood and Englishness, this is also a moment that briefly exposes its own methodology as a political gambit.

And yet it returns to that gambit in Act v. When Katherine offers minimal resistance to Henry's courtship in doubting whether she should love the enemy of France, Henry's joking response carries the confidence that a refusal is quite simply not a possible outcome: 'No, it is not possible you should love the enemy of France, Kate; but in loving me, you should love the friend of France; for I love France so well that I will not part with a village of it; I will have it all mine' (v.ii.171–5). His brief venture into French demonstrates him, necessarily, as humorously incompetent (compare the depictions of Pistol and Barnaby Bunch above). It is not the place of the English victor to learn French; the emblem of English masculinity, especially heavily invested in a play written under the rule of an ageing female sovereign, cannot be feminised by conceding too much to either a woman or the French nation she represents.

Furthermore, Katherine's subsequent role in English history, and her importance in legitimating the descent of Henry VII and his heirs via her second marriage, to Owen Tudor, makes it imperative that she is fully anglicised so that she can stand as the authorised mother of England's royal line (see further Herman, ' "O, 'tis a gallant King" '). The English nationalism of 1599 requires a version of history in which Henry V firmly imposes England on France, and there is never any doubt where the power lies in this final scene. Katherine's guarded acceptance, that she will do 'as it shall please de *roi mon père'* (v.ii.247) is countered by Henry's knowledge in advance that it cannot do other than please him. He then overrides the French custom that forbids maids to kiss before they are married by imposing his own Englishness with his kiss. The appropriation moves from linguistic into gestic form. Even the French King's hesitancy over granting the last article of Henry's demands, which requires that when writing to Henry he must address him with formal additions in French and Latin restating his rule over England and France, is easily overcome. The French King simply offers to yield on this last point too, and Henry smugly concludes:

> I pray you then, in love and dear alliance,
> Let that one article rank with the rest,
> And thereupon give me your daughter. (lines 345–7)

Despite the soothing references to 'love and dear alliance', the command form of the syntax makes clear that this is no mutual agreement, but a triumph of force. Englishness asserts its own identity here in a sequence that domesticates, appropriates and finally commands its other.

TRUTH AND FRAUDULENCE: RETURN TO *THE SPANISH TRAGEDY*

Henry's 'failure' in a foreign tongue, taken together with his emotional 'truth', encourages the audience to construct him as a 'true Englishman'. 'Truth' is as important as Englishness here. Earlier chapters have discussed the extent to which the English language, from the late fourteenth century on, was offered as the new language of truth, as opposed to the former language of truth: Latin. In the context of a late-medieval culture, where so much of what was written and dramatised was theological, the contest for truth was necessarily between these two. By the end of the sixteenth century, however, foreign vernaculars have become much more prominent than they ever were in the medieval theatre, and English 'truth' has to define itself against these as well as Latin. Indeed it has become possible now in some polemical contexts to 'regionalise' Latin, reducing it to a sign of 'Romishness' by way of consciously diminishing the authority it characteristically claims (a strategy which emerges out of the context of the 'inkhorn' controversy, in direct opposition to the strategy that seeks to enhance the authority of English via the imitation of Latin; see chapter 6 above).

The facility of English speakers in other languages, though it can be a matter of pride in a competitive context (such as that of Wilson's *Three Lords and Three Ladies of London*, discussed above), tends to be suspect, just as those who have travelled or returned from overseas are constructed as suspect by the legislation of 1571 outlined at the beginning of this chapter. Thus elsewhere in Wilson's same play Dissimulation announces himself as one 'well-seen, though I say it, in sundry languages meet for your lordship, or any noble service, to teach divers tongues and other rare things' (p. 480). Suspicion of facility in languages is linked to the fear that not all those who look and speak English are truly so. Traitors mask their true identity by fraudulent speaking. The punishment for Fraud in Wilson's play is a classic one: that English Simplicity is to 'burn out his tongue, that it never speak more guile'. Fraud, however, like the Spanish, manages to 'slip away' (p. 500). Wilson knows, and stages his knowledge, that there is no easy social remedy for fraudulence.

The need to dramatise fraudulence is one that theatre keeps returning to, since it is itself implicated in such accusations (see e.g. the Lollard treatise (chapter 2 above), the anxieties expressed by Bale and the Reformers (chapter 4 above) and the development of anti-theatrical polemic and Puritan thinking (chapter 6 above)). The Renaissance theatre sought to expose the wearing of masks in everyday life, but was itself complicit with the practice it exposed. And the dramatisation of fraud was open to the accusation of teaching it. The theatre is the place to go, according to Philip Stubbes, 'if you will learn cosenage; if you will learne to deceive; if you will learn to play the Hipocrit, to cogge, lye and falsifie'.[21] As Jean-Christophe Agnew points out, the battle between Puritans and theatre was in part a battle to determine 'the depth of each other's inauthenticity', and it was a battle that was deeply collusive (*Worlds Apart*, pp. 125–6). Just as Puritans agonised over how their claim to authenticity could be reconciled with the theatricality of some of their practices (see chapter 6 above), so theatre too continually worried at the implications of its own theatricality, where some practices were also seen as more theatrical than others.

The promiscuous presence of alien languages, especially alien vernaculars, in English plays of this period is at one level the dramatic expression of this anxiety. Foreign vernaculars, as noted in the discussion of *The Spanish Tragedy* earlier in this chapter, suggest a barrier between heart and speech, a language that conceals rather than reveals, thus subverting its expressive function. While rhetorical handbooks of the period do not suggest expressivity as a primary or even necessary function of language, the theological view of language that takes Babel as the starting point for human languages in all their present forms does. In its biblical context Babel represents above all confusion – a confusion visited on humanity as a punishment for its pride. It presupposes the existence of an originary language deeply bonded to the truths it expresses, because emanating from the same source (God), and therefore unable to pervert those truths. The corollary of the confusion that succeeds this ideal state is not only that language can never again be restored to the bonding with the divine source that made its meaning clear, unambiguous and necessarily true, but also that language, as well as dispersing into a plurality of mutually incomprehensible languages, simultaneously becomes capable of lying, of deliberate *mis*representation.

It is possible now, at last, to return to the climactic scene of betrayal in *The Spanish Tragedy*, the scene that stages the multiple murders through the playlet of *Soliman and Perseda*, and to explore the effects of its estranging decision to stage the playlet 'in sundry languages' (iv.iv.10). There has been a tradition of doubting that the play was in fact performed, as it says it was, with each character speaking a different language. It would seem, however, as S. F. Johnson's seminal essay ('*The Spanish Tragedy*') on the importance of the Babel topos to an understanding of this episode indicates, that the source of this doubt lies in the critics rather than in the playtext, which is full of signs confirming that the playlet was indeed performed in this way.[22] Hieronimo tells the story beforehand (iv.i.108–26) and announces to the performers the plan to have each act his or her part in a different language; Balthazar is made to protest that such a staging 'will be a mere confusion' (line 180); and Hieronimo's reply to him insists that 'It must be so' (line 182). When the play is actually performed, the King and the Viceroy have a book giving 'the argument of that they show' (iv.iv.10), and when it is over Hieronimo explicitly announces the return to the vernacular: 'Here break we off our sundry languages / And thus conclude I in our vulgar tongue' (iv.iv.74–5). It stages, as Johnson shows and as Hieronimo explicitly says it will do, 'the fall of Babylon' (iv.i.195). It is true, of course, that these verbal clues would be exactly the same if the play were in fact performed entirely in English but signalling to its audience that they should understand it as though spoken in different languages; but this is hardly sufficient grounds, it seems to me, for dismissing the printer's note that tells the reader that the play was in fact performed 'in sundry languages' even though it is 'set down in English' for the reader's 'easier understanding' here.

Michael Hattaway, one of the few critics to examine the theatrical effects of such a piece of staging in multiple languages, argues that Kyd 'was trying to see whether he could employ a theatre language that would, to the unlettered at least, communicate by its mere sound ... What an audience who did not understand the dialogue would experience would be the ritual shape of this inset action and perhaps thereby the mythic dimension of the whole play' (*Elizabethan Popular Theatre*, p. 110), but this persuasive analysis leaves questions to be asked. In what sense does language here function to 'communicate'? What does the audience hear? 'Mere sound' or differentiated and specific sounds? Given the culturally specific functioning of different languages earlier in the play, it is important for even the unlettered to recognise at least that what they hear at this point is different – different in so far as it mixes Latin with other languages and deliberately empties all of them of meaning. And if we doubt the audience's ability to hear this episode as a confusion of languages rather than a single alien sound, we know that Hieronimo tells them that this is what it is. There must be no question here of the sacramental heightening of Latin: Latin is changed here, stripped of its authority, forced to become one language among others. And no language is allowed to retain its capacity to communicate, since each is severed from its meaning by receiving a response in another language. In one sense, of course, language does communicate with the theatre audience in that it conveys to them the confusion of Babel, together with the moral judgement that implies. Yet in another sense its most important function is its refusal to communicate, its insistent closing down at a moment when revelations are looked for. The confusion of languages, as sound effect, functions as jarring music might do on film at the moment of a killing, freezing the event as image in order to compel the spectator into a deep engagement with its horror.

Explanation follows image, but the transition to rationality is too abrupt and itself too irrational to be grasped. The audience's sense of the real is so bound to the image that an appeal to reason seems beside the point. There is nothing there beyond the stage-image available for translation into rational discourse. This, at least, seems to be the experience of the onstage audience, who ask for explanation immediately *after* Hieronimo has shown the body of his dead son and given what explanation there is. At this point Hieronimo refuses to speak, insisting that he will not be forced 'to reveal / The thing which I have vow'd inviolate' (IV.iv.187–8).[23] His refusal to speak of things he has apparently (according to 'rational' judgement) already spoken returns us to the experience of the playlet itself, framed in a confusion of languages that functions to mask certain kinds of truth (narrative, political), while hinting at the existence of other, mythic truths that may lie deeper than language. Words, both the playlet and Hieronimo's cryptic utterance imply, may veil and enclose their truth rather than give it up. The untranslated quality of the spectacle brings into being the concepts of secrecy and depth. Hieronimo biting out his tongue becomes an iconic representation of this probing of the inexpressible, focusing the notion of a truth inaccessible through language alone precisely in the form of a speechless image.

Frank Ardolino relates Hieronimo's playlet in sundry languages and subsequent vow of silence to 'the seven-sealed Book of Revelation which is opened – that is, revealed – to those able to comprehend God's secret truths, but which remains closed to the ignorant audience'. For Ardolino, however, the revelation *is* available to the 'elect audience of *The Spanish Tragedy*', and is to be unlocked with the key of contemporary politics. In his view, Hieronimo is the Protestant slayer of the Whore of Babylon, the Antichrist: contemporary Catholic Spain (' "Now Shall I See the Fall of Babylon" ', pp. 105, 106–13). Ardolino's parallel with the Book of Revelation is a suggestive one, but not one resolved, I think, by recourse to Elizabethan politics. *The Spanish Tragedy* probably does make topical reference to relations with Spain and undoubtedly conveys anti-Spanish feeling, but this is not the primary focus of the last act. The play cannot be reduced to a piece of Protestant propaganda, nor is it even a predominantly Christian play, despite its allusion to biblical authority. Apocalyptic references hint at revelation but do not finally offer it. The play leads up to a moment which seems about to become an epiphany, but at the point of revelation, God is not revealed.

Instead the driving force of revenge which has shaped the play to this point seems to go to pieces, though at the same time this breaking-up produces its own, unexpected climax. The rhythm of the revenger's purpose gives way to a confusion of voices and a loss of rhythm and control. The image of slaughter in Hieronimo's playlet emerges fragmentedly and ironically, out of a framework masquerading as fictive, and confronts the audience with a problem of closure. It is an image that baffles by its refusal to suggest a pattern that might offer to help the spectators make sense of its horror, and is in that sense a climax: a non-translatable physical event. Hieronimo's biting out of his own tongue both maintains the insistence on physical event and underlines the refusal to interpret. In place of epiphany the play presents a space that is both full and withheld, open to be engaged with as theatre but closed to the possibility of translation into anything else. Hieronimo's show deepens the audience's investment in potential epiphany, only to deepen its sense of loss at something not revealed, but left unexpressed, 'inviolate'. The dynamic the play seems to set up between alien vernaculars as a sign of bad faith and Latin as a language of compelling truthfulness is overturned by its ending. The bad faith finally exposed is that of language itself, its treachery first revealed through a confusion of different languages and confirmed by the play's final decision to withdraw from language and wrap itself into the untranslated image.

CHAPTER 8

Rebels and outcasts

Those others who needed to be excluded from the definition of England were not all aliens. The imaginary unity of the monarch and her people could only accommodate an idealised commonalty composed of obedient subjects such as the Elizabethan Homilies sought to interpellate. Any subject who did not conform to this model was by definition a threat to the smooth functioning of the polity. The orderly nation naturally seeks to expel any 'dirt' that threatens its orderliness. As Mary Douglas argues: 'Dirt offends against order. Eliminating it is not a negative movement, but a positive effort to organise the environment ... In chasing dirt ... [we] are positively re-ordering our environment, making it conform to an idea' (*Purity and Danger*, p. 2). This work of reordering is very evident in Elizabethan England. A sense of disorder, resulting in a need to strengthen symbolic systems, is particularly visible in the statutes and proclamations of the period, which are preoccupied with reinforcing social distinctions through sumptuary law, controlling or punishing vagrants, witches and conjurers, identifying Catholics and potential traitors to the realm, and restricting free movement from parish to parish for numerous classes of person.

Disorder seems to have reached a peak during the 1590s. 'Everyone is agreed', wrote the Venetian ambassador in 1594, 'that at this juncture England is shaken by religious feuds, by plagues, and other internal troubles' (Bevington, *Tudor Drama*, p. 230). Modern historians also identify this decade as a time of crisis. Apprentice riots and anti-alien riots were particularly frequent, and provost marshals were introduced as an emergency measure in 1588 through most of England and in 1595 in London (see p. 173 above). Rioting was especially severe in London in 1595, and large-scale rebellion broke out at Enslow Hill in Oxfordshire in 1596. The government punished crimes against public order with extreme severity, and new laws permitted riot to be punished as treason in certain circumstances. From about 1587 the government also produced a sequence of social and economic regulations intended to prevent outbreaks of popular disorder: it ordered magistrates to instigate controls over the grain trade; it initiated prosecutions for some enclosures; it passed laws protecting common and agricultural land; and it established a system of poor relief (Manning, *Village Revolts*, pp. 157–8).

It is difficult, of course, to measure the degree of actual disorder against the state's reaction to the *idea* of disorder. Though there was a large increase in the numbers of vagrants arrested in late-Elizabethan London, for example, some of this increase may have been due to greater vigilance on the part of the authorities.[1] More to the point is the increasing visibility of witchcraft. Although the period is notorious for its witch-trials, we cannot deduce from their number that there were more witches, or even more would-be witches, only that there was a growing anxiety around the possibility of their presence. The shaping polarity of order versus disorder produces an emphasis on crimes of status: witchcraft, vagrancy and sectarianism. For the godly nation trying to insist on its boundaries, danger lies in the non-structure, and in the inversion of what the dominant ideology recognises as positive values.

A very clear presentation of these positive values, together with the kind of draconian response to deviation that they encourage, appears in Philip Stubbes' *Anatomy of Abuses* (Part II, 1583). The treatise is in the form of a dialogue between Theodorus, who asks questions about England ('Dnalgne'), and Amphilogus, who answers them. Theodorus asks whether the country is 'quiet, peaceable, and at unitie within it selfe', and receives a eulogy of the peace maintained by Elizabeth over a period of twenty-five years. The only blood shed, says Amphilogus, has been that of traitors, 'who have received but the same reward they deserved'. Amphilogus then goes on to attack 'that man of sinne, that sonne of the divell, that Italian Antichrist of Rome' who has so often conspired against Elizabeth 'by conjuration, necromancy, exorcismes, art magike, witchcraft, and all kind of divelrie besides'. He has sent Catholics to overthrow the realm 'sometime by secret irruption, sometime by open invasion, insurrection, and rebellion' (pp. 4–6). Later in the dialogue, Theodorus asks whether princes' laws are to be obeyed in every instance. Amphilogus answers that they should be obeyed 'in all things not contrarie to the lawe of God and good conscience'; but, in response to Theodorus' next question as to whether subjects may rebel if their prince makes laws contrary to God's, he is categorically negative. Good subjects must lay down their necks on the block rather than disobey God or the prince. They must love their prince as they love themselves. This doesn't, of course, get round the question of the unjust prince, but Stubbes tries to divert the reader's attention from the problem by having Amphilogus express the hope that God will remove from the face of the earth anyone who does not love Queen Elizabeth (pp. 17–19).

This, then, is the good subject of late Elizabethan England: Protestant, fiercely loyal and unquestioningly obedient to the monarch, and anxious to see the harshest possible penalties imposed on all who deviate from this subject position. Failure to fit the definition is always verging towards treason. Though the range of possible deviant types may look wide, what is noticeable about the discourse that demonises them is the tendency to collapse the distinctions between categories. Hence Catholics are pictured as conjurors or witches, witches as rebels, rebels as vagabonds, vagabonds as in league with Satan and all of these as potential traitors to the realm. The wording of the 1581 statute against 'seditious words and rumours uttered against the Queen's excellent majesty' (*23 Elizabeth I, c.2*), for example, shows the way in which witchcraft is conceived as likely to be tangled up with politics:

> If any person ... shall by setting or erecting of any Figure or Figures, or by casting of Nativities, or by calculacion, or by any Prophecieng Witchcrafte Cunjuracions or other lyke unlawfull Meanes whatsoever, seeke to knowe, and shall set forth by expresse Wordes Deedes or Writinges, howe longe her Majestie shall lyve or contynue, or who shall raigne as King or Queene of this Realme of England after her Highnesse Deccase, ... then everye suche Offence shalbe Felonye. (*Statutes of the Realm*, vol. IV, pp. 659–60)

'Conjuration', as Barbara Rosen notes, 'was a useful blanket term both for the mass and for attempts to foretell the future and, as the Jesuits remarked, the government preferred to make accusations not directly connected with the practice of religion' (*Witchcraft*, p. 103). Like the statute, Scot's *Discoverie of Witchcraft* (1584) labours to dissolve the distinction between witches and Catholics. Scot equates 'papistical charms' (*The Discoverie of Witchcraft*, p. 21) with conjurers' incantations, claiming that the only difference between witches and papists is that 'the papists doo it without shame openlie, the other doo it in hugger mugger secretlie' (p. 361). Catholic priests, in his view, are far more deserving of the appellation of 'witch' than those poor old women usually accused by an ignorant populace (pp. 108, 190, 237).

Contemporary writers often quoted the bible to justify the assumption that all witches are potential rebels against the state: 'Rebellion is as the sin of witchcraft' (1 Samuel 15.23). The Puritan William Perkins was more emphatic: 'The most notorious traytor and rebell that can be is the Witch' (Levack, *The Witch-Hunt in Early Modern Europe*, pp. 59–60). Witchcraft, Catholicism and potential rebellion are all apparently interlinked in the St Osyth witch trial of 1582, where it would seem that what the government was really looking for, under cover of a witchcraft investigation, was a Catholic plot: the notorious Richard Topcliff, appointed by the government to seek out Catholics in hiding, was issued with a 'search and seize' warrant immediately after the trial (Rosen, *Witchcraft*, p. 103). The fears surrounding the so-called 'School of Night' show the same interlinking of necromancy, Catholicism and the suspicion of rebellion at a more socially elite level. A pamphlet of 1592 speaks of Ralegh's 'school of Atheisme', which teaches its scholars 'to spell God backwards', and of Ralegh himself as 'the Conjuror that is M(aster) thereof'; the 'Wizard Earl' of Northumberland, a member of the group, was later suspected of involvement in the Gunpowder Plot (Bradbrook, *The School of Night*, pp. 12, 8). Popular suspicion of scholars like Giordano Bruno and John Dee demonstrates the same tendency to link scholarship with necromancy and necromancy with heresy and potential disloyalty to the state.

DANGEROUS/POWERFUL LANGUAGE

Language was central to accusations of disorderliness, whether in the form of witchcraft, Catholicism or rebellion. There was even a language supposedly identifying hardened criminals and vagabonds (cant, or 'Pedlar's French'). Gypsies too had their own language, Romany, from which canting vocabulary borrows (Beier, *Masterless Men*, pp. 60–1). Obviously, ordinary social interaction means that individuals are identified and classified to a large extent by the words they use, so that the use of a particular discourse identifies its speaker as a member of the class to which that discourse belongs. Such identifying discourses correspondingly become available for appropriation by those wishing to be identified with the class in question. Hence the Protestant Antony Munday could infiltrate the English College in Rome and pass himself off as a Jesuit by conversing in the familiar Latin of that community (see his own account of the time he spent at the English College in *The English Romayne Life*). At a very different level of society, a contemporary pamphlet informs us, fraudulent 'cunning men'[2] sought to increase their authority by adopting the pretence of being non-English speakers and larding their speech with exotic-sounding obscurity, whilst employing a servant to 'translate' their wisdom for the poor gulls who came to them. Rogues, in accordance with time-honoured tradition, undermine the bond between language and truth: in the terms of this pamphlet, they 'prate, babble, lie' (Judges, *The Elizabethan Underworld*, pp. 10–12, 8).

Latin, already noted as increasingly identified with Catholics, was also the language of conjurors (see the response of Sir Nicholas to Lodowick in *The Weakest Goeth to the Wall*, p. 169 above). It was the language of magic texts (or at least the translated language in which they were available to English readers at this time), which further explains the connection between scholarship and necromancy in popular thinking. Indeed the very possession of Latin, the necessary language for reading magical texts, uttering incantations and addressing the spirit world, was the link that made it difficult to separate scholars from magicians. In *Hamlet* (1600–1), though Horatio's integrity is not in doubt, he is perceived as having special competence to address the ghost: 'Thou art a scholar – speak to it, Horatio' (I.i.40). Similarly, when Lorenzo challenges Musco, in Jonson's *Every Man In His Humour* (1598), to explain how his (Lorenzo's) son has recognised Musco as his father's man, Musco's reply makes the same equation: 'Nay sir, I cannot tell; unlesse it were by the blacke arte? is not your sonne a scholler sir?' (IV.i.18–19).[3] As one prose writer summed it up in 1600: 'Nowadays among the common people, he is not adjudged any scholar at all, unless he can tell men's horoscopes, cast out devils, or hath some skill in soothsaying' (Thomas, *Religion and the Decline of Magic*, p. 269).

Ralph Ironside's account of the famous occasion on which Sir Walter Ralegh and his brother questioned the existence of the soul raises interesting questions about the connotations of scholarly discourse:

Towardes the end of supper some loose speeches of Master Carewe

Rawleighes beinge gentlye reproved by Sir Raulfe Horsey in these wordes *Colloquia prava corrumpunt bonos mores* [Depraved conversations destroy good character]. Master Rawleigh demaundes of me, what daunger he might incurr by such speeches? wherunto I aunswered, the wages of sinn is death. And he makinge leight of death as beinge common to all sinner and reightuous; I inferred further, that as that liffe which is the gifte of god through Jesus Christ, is liffe eternall: soe that death which is properlye the wages of sinne, is death eternall, both of the bodye, and of the soule alsoe. Soule quoth Master Carewe Rawleigh, what is that? better it were (sayed I) that we would be carefull howe the Soules might be saved, then to be curiouse in findinge out ther essence. (Harrison, *Willobie his Avisa*, pp. 265–6)

The use of the phrase 'in these wordes' preceding the Latin sentence suggests that it was actually spoken in Latin, as does the fact that it encapsulates proverbial wisdom. The context of the account, which is spoken by a cleric, and given before the investigating authorities,[4] would seem to offer no explanation for the Latin other than its having been the actual language of speech at this point. Later in the dialogue the citation of Latin followed by its translation makes it even clearer that Latin, interspersed with English, must have been spoken in the original conversation.

The status of the Latin *sententia*, first made in response to 'loose speeches' and then followed by dangerously heretical English conversation, seems to be that of unassailable truth reproving errant and uncontrolled vernacular babble. Yet the heretical material does not remain all in English, nor is Latin used only to police deviant opinion. As Ironside proceeds with his story, Latin becomes more dominant on both sides of the argument. It is, after all, the natural language of scholars (and necromancers) and, more specifically, the natural language for philosophical argument and the citation of authorities such as Aristotle. Sir Walter Ralegh begins his intervention in the conversation by emphasising his scholarly status: 'I have benn (sayeth he) a scholler some tyme in Oxeforde, I have aunswered under a Bacheler of Arte, and had taulke with divines, yet heitherunto in this pointe (to witt what the reasonable soule of man is) have I not by anye benne resolved' (p. 266), and Latin phrases begin to permeate both his speech and Ironside's from that point on. Thus, though Latin begins, in Ironside's account, by signifying an attempt to control errant speech, its presence gradually becomes more ambivalent and begins actually to license loose talk. Working against the initial intent to privilege Latin as truth-effect is the suggestion that the secret learning of these scholarly men and their private blasphemies are an effect of their access to a relatively 'secret' language.

In case the attention to language here in this consideration of Ironside's evidence to the commission seems unwarranted or excessive, it is important to highlight the almost obsessional attention to language characteristic of official enquiries themselves. One of the things Elizabethan witchcraft trials highlight is the fixation on language as evidence against the accused. Mother Waterhouse, one of the Chelmsford witches examined in 1566, admits to commanding her familiar (a cat called Satan) by saying her Paternoster in Latin (Rosen, *Witchcraft*, pp. 72, 77). When she is questioned as to whether she attends church regularly, the questioning inevitably proceeds to focus on the language of her prayer:

And being demanded whether she was accustomed to go to church to the common prayers or divine service, she said, 'Yea'; and being required what she did there, she said she did as other women do, and prayed right heartily there. And when she was demanded what prayer she said, she answered, 'The Lord's Prayer, the Ave Maria, and the Belief'. And then they demanded whether in Latin or in English, and she said, 'In Latin'.

And they demanded why she said it not in English but in Latin, seeing that it was set out by public authority and according to God's word that all men should pray in the English and mother tongue that they best understood, and she said that Satan would at no time suffer her to say it in English, but at all times in Latin. (Rosen, *Witchcraft*, p. 82)

Latin satisfactorily conflates Catholic practice with witchcraft in the eyes of the investigating Protestant state.

The same insistent attention to language can be seen in Samuel Harsnett's *Declaration of Egregious Popish Impostures* (published in 1603, recounting events of 1585–6). Harsnett's concern is with exorcism, a Catholic ritual presented by the Protestant Harsnett as complicit with its own object of attention, in so far as such ritual practice is itself seen as a kind of conjuration. The pamphlet shows minute attention to language on the part of both Harsnett himself and the Catholics he wishes to discredit, demonstrating the extent to which both Catholic and Protestant thinking fetishise language (not surprisingly, since the spoken language of the liturgy, as authorised by the state, had been liable to change with each change of monarch since Edward VI, and the language of the bible had been a source of contention for much longer). For Catholics a refusal to pronounce liturgical Latin or an interest in the liturgy in English are potential signs of possession; while for Protestants a refusal to pray in English (as in the case of Mother Waterhouse above) or a tendency to mutter Latin or gibberish, are evidence of witchcraft. Harsnett is aware of the fetishism inherent in the thinking of the enemy (whether Catholic or witch), though not, apparently, of his own. He notes the obsession of both witches and Catholics with naming and the proliferation of names for the devil; and he goes on to link this obsession with the Jesuit practice of hiding behind assumed names and the gypsy practice of speaking in agreed gibberish (cant) (*A Declaration*, p. 46).

The theological centrality of the Word in both Catholicism and Protestantism virtually guaranteed an obsessive attention to words, especially once the interpretation of the Word became a matter of controversy. A tendency to fetishise language is present in magical thinking for the same reason: the sacred power of the Word is recognised, even revered, by the necromantic practice that seeks to appropriate it. Neoplatonic magic was deeply influenced by the Christian Cabala. The hundredth chapter of Cornelius Agrippa's *De Vanitate Scientiarum* is '*De Verbo Dei*' (Concerning the Word of God), asserting that the Word of God is the key to all knowledge (Yates, *The Occult Philosophy*, p. 42). Religion and magic, as Keith Thomas has shown, are often barely distinguishable: the Word of God can be spoken, eaten, or worn around the neck (see chapter 1 above). And the equation between magic and religion is made by apologists for magic as well as by attackers of false religion. 'The art of magic', Walter Ralegh argues, 'is the art of worshipping God' (Thomas, *Religion and the Decline of Magic*, p. 320). Those names most sacred to scripture are also those most magically powerful. Calling on the name of Jesus for protection from the devil or on the name of the Tetragrammaton to cast out devils can scarcely be defined as religion rather than magic, or vice versa. Catholicism and magic share an emphasis on the power of words almost as material objects. Whether the speaker understands the words of the prayer or the spell is unimportant. What is important is the words themselves. Hence the fear and awe of exotic names and alien language.

For the Protestant Reginald Scot it is this focus on the materiality of the word, as separate from its sense, that constitutes the unaccep-table face of both witchcraft and Catholicism. But it is unacceptable to him not because words can never of themselves have such force, but because merely human words cannot. The Word of God is the only word in a position to lay claim to power in and of itself. Catholics and conjurors alike, in his view, presumptuously seek to imitate God in claiming such power for their words. Mere human language cannot achieve such privileged status, in Scot's view, and he mocks the notion that it could:

> whence commeth the force of such words as raise the dead, and command divels. If sound doo it, then it may be doone by a taber and a pipe, or any other instrument that hath no life. If the voice doo it, then may it be doone by any beasts or birds. If words, then a parrett may doo it. If in mans words onlie, where is the force, in the first, second, or third syllable? If in syllables, then not in words. If in imaginations, then the divell knoweth our thoughts. But all this stuffe is vaine and fabulous. (*The Discoverie of Witchcraft*, p. 371)

'Words and characters are', in Scot's appropriation of the classic term, 'but bables' (p. 390).

Nevertheless, Scot is fascinated by such power as human language does have, through its sense. 'The true signification of witchcraft', he argues, 'is cousenage [deceit]', and he recognises that it is words which do the work of persuading their hearers to believe lies (p. 109). Words, he grants, 'sometimes have singular vertue and efficacie' and may persuade to salvation or perdition; 'Death and life are in the instrument of the toong: but even therein God worketh all in all' (p. 188). Human beings, Scot sees, achieve power over one another through words, even if God is ultimately responsible for directing those words. And in this perception, despite his hostility to Catholic witchcraft literature and his claim to be writing against 'Sprenger's fables' and 'Bodin's bables', Scot is at one with Saint Isidore, as cited by the much-maligned *Malleus Maleficarum*: 'Enchanters are they whose art and skill lies in the use of words' (Kramer and Sprenger, *Malleus Maleficarum*, p. 180). And both are at one with rhetoricians and rulers, who know in their turn that words are power.

Several modern critics have commented on the fact that language and rhetoric regularly became the locus for anxieties about problems of control (Shepherd, *Marlowe and the Politics of the Elizabethan Theatre*, ch.1; Parker, *Literary Fat Ladies*, ch.6; Mullaney, *The Place of the Stage*, ch.5; Rhodes, *The Power of Eloquence*, pp. 7–12). An explicit interest in how to manage language, as manifested in rhetorical handbooks, or a foregrounding of language in other texts that do not claim to take language as their subject, are often demonstrably indicative of a concern with power, a worry about how one human being exerts

control over another, or over the non-human world.[5] Plays dramatising magic and the summoning of devils are a case in point. Almost
always the moment of power, the speaking of the incantation that
will summon the devil or a spirit from another world, is intensified
by a change of language, a move from the routine vernacular into
the special strangeness of Latin. Often, too, the exotic otherness of
the moment is drawn out at some length. In *Doctor Faustus* (1592–3),
for example, the Latin is extended (in both the A and the B texts)
over six lines of continuous prose (I.iii.244–50), and is added by
Marlowe to his source, which does not present the conjuration in the
form of direct speech, but through a description of the conjuror's
activities of drawing and writing the appropriate characters. Only in
the play is language made as central as gesture. The moment of
gestic significance, representing the point of transgression and the
bid for control, is held still, as it were, by alien language (see the
fuller discussion of this dramaturgical feature in chapter 6 above). It
is no accident that this is the moment singled out for illustration in
the woodcut on the title page of the 1624 quarto of *Doctor Faustus*,
representing as it does a point of deeply memorable engagement for
the audience. Nor is it coincidental that it was at this moment in the
play, 'as Faustus was busie in his magicall invocations' that 'Certaine
Players at Exeter' brought their performance to a sudden stop, 'all
perswaded, there was one devell too many amongst them' (Chambers, *The Elizabethan Stage*, vol. III, p. 424).[6]

Offstage too, the equation between language and power is openly
recognised, sometimes in explicitly symbolic ways. The scholar
Giordano Bruno, finally condemned for heresy after an eight-year
trial by a state long anxious to control him, was led to his death at
the stake with his tongue literally tied. The image of the tongue-tied
heretic neatly demonstrated to the spectators both the cause of
Bruno's condemnation and the power of the authority that condemned him. The Tudor treason statutes and the recurrent struggle
of the Elizabethan Commons for freedom of speech (discussed in
chapter 4 (pp. 81–2 and n. 7 above)) are only two instances of how
the struggle for power was staged in terms of language in England.

REBEL BABBLE

The link between language and issues of control is particularly
marked, not surprisingly, in the discourses of rebellion, whether of

the rebels themselves or of those seeking to control them. The riddling language of prophecy, for example, though it has a long tradition reaching back to the twelfth century in England, becomes subject to a shift in use that constructs it as an incitement to rebellion.[7] Whereas prophecy in the medieval period is often written in Latin and addressed to an elite or scholarly audience, its status begins to change in the fifteenth and sixteenth centuries. Laws passed in 1402 and 1406 begin to link prophecy with rebellion or otherwise attempting to undermine the state. Though prophecies themselves change very little, appealing, as Sharon Jansen (*Political Protest*) has argued, via familiarity rather than originality, the voices that give utterance to them by the 1530s are those of a very different class, opposed to monarch and state. Prophecies are no longer framed by scholars within the safe boundaries of Latin texts, but appropriated as authorities that offer to legitimise resistance to the authority of the Tudor state. The very fact that Henry VIII's government felt compelled to resort to counter-prophecy is itself, as Jansen says, 'a remarkable comment on the contemporary assessment of the value and potency of such predictions' (*Political Protest*, p. 153).

The subsequent legislation of successive Tudor monarchs confirms the continuing pattern of conflict between the official language of government, pronouncing law, and the discourse of popular protest, appropriating prophecy as one of its most characteristic modes. An act of 1542 made prophecy a felony without benefit of clergy. This act was repealed in 1547 but replaced by a new act in 1550, which was then repealed on the accession of Mary in 1553 and reinstated by Elizabeth in 1563 (Taylor, *The Political Prophecy*, pp. 105–6; Jansen, *Political Protest*, p. 19). As Rupert Taylor notes, this last statute (*5 Elizabeth I, c.15*) is interesting for the comment it passes on the causes of its own making:

Forasmuche as sithens thexpiracion and ending of the Statute made in the time of King Edwarde the Syxthe entituled, An Act against fonde and fantasticall Prophesies, divers evill disposed persons, enclyned to the stirring and moving of Factions, Seditions and Rebellions within this Realme, have byn the more bolde tattempte the lyke Practise, in fayning imagining inventing and publishing of suche fonde and fantasticall Prophesies, aswell concerning the Quenes Majestie as divers honourable Parsonages, Gentlemen and others of this Realme as was used and practised before the making of the sayd Statute, to the grete disquiet trooble and perill of the Quenes Majestie and of this her Realme. (*Statutes of the Realm*, vol. IV, p. 445; Taylor, *The Political Prophecy*, pp. 105–6; cf. the 1581 statute cited on p. 190 above).

George Puttenham's anxiety around the topos of what he chooses to name 'Amphibology or the Ambiguous', though probably already familiar to many readers through the work of Steven Mullaney (*The Place of the Stage*, p. 120) and Patricia Parker (*Literary Fat Ladies*, p. 99, citing Mullaney, 'Lying Like Truth' (reprinted and extended as chapter 5 in *The Place of the Stage*)), is cited again here for the directness with which it makes the equation between ambiguous language and conspiracy against the state. This form of speech, 'when we speake or write doubtfully and that the sence may be taken two wayes', is placed last by Puttenham in his chapter on 'vices in speaches and writing'; and he ends the chapter by citing notable examples of the seditious uses to which such riddling speech has been put in the past:

in effect all our old Brittish and Saxon prophesies be of the same sort, that turne them on which side ye will, the matter of them may be verified, neverthelesse carryeth generally such force in the heades of fonde people, that by the comfort of those blind prophecies many insurrections and rebellions have bene stirred up in this Realme, as that of Jacke Straw, and Jacke Cade in Richard the seconds time, and in our time by a seditious fellow in Norffolke calling himself Captaine Ket and others in other places of the Realme lead altogether by certaine propheticall rymes, which might be constred [*sic*] two or three wayes as well as to that one whereunto the rebelles applied it, our maker shall therefore avoyde all such ambiguous speaches unlesse it be when he doth it for the nonce and for some purpose. (*The Arte of English Poesie*, pp. 260–1)

Ambiguous speech, Puttenham is anxious to insist, is always open to the charge of setting out to stir up trouble while covering its tracks. Yet more highly charged is his exception, which seeks to legitimise occasional ambiguous speech, while at the same time carefully leaving the definition of occasion and 'purpose' hanging. As with Harsnett's *Discovery of Fraudulent Practises*, there is a recognition that language is ultimately authorised (or not) by speaker and place. The fact that his examples of illegitimate ambiguity target the foolish common people suggests that the kind of ambiguity he would countenance would issue from the mouths of those in authority and be justified by the 'need' to mislead the commons, though obviously it wouldn't do to spell this out too clearly.

In similar vein to Puttenham, Stubbes' paean to the peaceful commonwealth positions those Catholic enemies who threaten England's peace first and foremost as 'ambidexters', double-dealers whose 'hollowe hearted' nature is of a piece with their seditious intent (*Anatomy of Abuses*, pp. 6–7). Catholics, and Jesuits in particular, were stereotyped by this particular characteristic more than any other throughout the Elizabethan–Jacobean period. Stubbes' 'ambidexters' became the 'equivocators' who escaped their just punishment by manipulating the spoken word.[8] And equivocation, in Protestant rhetoric, was the same as lying.

Rebellious speech is often even more dismissively constructed as mere babble. The voice of the people, especially the voice with which they rebel against their leaders, is regularly presented, in both dramatic and historical writing, as foolish or ill-informed. The familiar dramatic device of having a group of low-class speakers shouting single words or phrases in unison is part of a strategy which aims to present an assembly of people as a 'mob', or what the King in *Jack Straw* (1590–3) calls a 'fowle unrulie crew' (line 680). Simon Shepherd (*Marlowe and the Politics of the Elizabethan Theatre*) identifies as the dominant rhetorical strategy of this play its decision to present the rebels' speech as deviating from the blank verse 'norm' of courtly speakers, thereby classifying their speech as 'disorder and unreason'. It is a strategy that finds its place, Shepherd argues, within a more general tendency in the plays of this period to construct discontent as disordered speech, or 'murmuring' (pp. 10, 30). The word recalls the draft proclamation of 1539, described on p. 84 above, that fixes on the English translation of the bible as the source of 'murmur, malice, and malignity' amongst the people. Inevitably, it seems, unbridled speaking is constructed as malicious 'murmur' by a repressive regime.

The positioning of the audience with regard to the opposition between rebellion and authority in this play is tense and difficult, and the scene where Tom Miller pleads for his life offers an especially problematic purchase on this opposition. His speech represents a failed attempt to ventriloquise elite discourse: it is absurdly verbose, full of redundant and misused phrases and includes a piece of garbled dog-Latin, '*Sursum cordum, alis dictus hangum meum*' (line 821), in which the crucial and recognisably English word 'hang' presumably stands out for an English audience. The measure of his failure to speak the language of the Queen

Mother is made visible through her inability to understand him, and her reliance on the Usher to translate his meaning:

QUEEN. What meanes the fellow by all this eloquence?

USHER. It seemes he feares he shall be hangd,
And therefore craves your Graces favour in his behalfe.

QUEEN. Alas poore fellow, he seemeth to be a starke nidiot.

(lines 831–7 [*sic*])

Yet the audience can guess what Tom Miller is trying to say, which may position the Queen Mother as obtuse rather than Tom Miller as an idiot, and the failure to reproduce elite discourse may give us a laugh at the excesses of the very language it seeks to imitate (Shepherd, *Marlowe and the Politics of the Elizabethan Theatre*, pp. 10–11), just as Barnaby Bunch or Pistol 'failing' to speak French pokes fun at the French more than at its non-speakers (see pp. 169, 179 above). It may be that the speech of the rebels, set against the blank verse of the elite speakers, is temporarily constructed as plainness at this point (though not necessarily throughout the play), where parody positions elite discourse as excessive.

Tom's false Latin may further serve to undermine the workings of the state by reminding the audience that the very exclusiveness of Latin is what gives uneducated people grounds for distrusting their 'betters'. If legal proceedings against them are invoked in a language they do not understand, how are they to be assured of the justice and integrity of those proceedings? If those in power speak in a language that they know to be incomprehensible to those held in subjection by it, aren't those subjects likely to question the need for such secrecy? Those among the audience for this play who share Tom Miller's ignorance of elite language are perhaps more strongly motivated to revile the system that makes a man think he has to plead for his life in an unfamiliar language than to laugh at his failure to do so competently. Though Tom Miller is suspected as a traitor, this moment in the play hints at the knowledge that treachery can work in two directions. The veiled speech of the social elite is as ambiguous and potentially as treacherous as the riddling speech that unites rebels against the state (which Puttenham, with his awareness of 'purpose', knows).

Another play focuses this knowledge more powerfully and explicitly. Mortimer alone on stage in Marlowe's *Edward II* tells the

audience exactly how elite language may be employed to effect
treason while concealing its treasonous intent:

> The king must die, or Mortimer goes downe,
> The commons now begin to pitie him,
> Yet he that is the cause of Edwards death,
> Is sure to pay for it when his sonne is of age,
> And therefore will I do it cunninglie.
> This letter written by a friend of ours,
> Containes his death, yet bids them save his life.
> *Edwardum occidere nolite timere bonum est.*
> Feare not to kill the king tis good he die.
> But read it thus, and thats an other sence:
> *Edwardum occidere nolite timere bonum est.*
> Kill not the king tis good to feare the worst.
> Unpointed as it is, thus shall it goe,
> That being dead, if it chaunce to be found,
> Matrevis and the rest may beare the blame,
> And we be quit that causde it to be done.   (v.iv.1–16)

The speech is extraordinarily careful and detailed in its explanation of
how the unpunctuated Latin is to achieve Edward's death while
protecting his killer. Though the Latin is ambiguous, the words are
precisely chosen, and this precision may be set alongside the faulty
blundering of Tom Miller's Latin. Like the Queen Mother, or
Puttenham's exceptional speaker, Mortimer knows exactly which
words are required and what purpose they are to perform. For the
Latinate members of the audience the ambiguity of the Latin is
offered as an ironic pleasure to savour; for the non-Latinate it is
carefully explained so that its slippery functioning is understood even
though the individual Latin words are not. It is a remarkable moment
that exposes the language of law, church and state as more dangerously open to corruption than any uneducated discourse could be. As
Mortimer opens up the manipulability of elite language for treacherous purposes he plants fear in the hearts of popular and elite alike. All
levels of the audience are made to confront the knowledge that the
centre is both treacherous and vulnerable, and that they themselves
are at the mercy of its secret and suspect workings.

2 HENRY VI (1591)[9]

All the anxieties about language discussed in this chapter crowd
together into a single play burdened with the need to juxtapose as

many manifestations of social disorder as possible against one another: Shakespeare's *2 Henry VI*, entitled *The First Part of the Contention betwixt the Two Famous Houses of York and Lancaster* in the 1594 Quarto text.[10] Within the bounds of this one play witches jostle against fraudulent beggars, conjurors meet with conspirators against the state and popular rebellion is set alongside aristocratic treachery. The play's opening scene demands comparison with the closing scene of *Henry V*, discussed in chapter 7 above. Shakespeare wrote the *Henry VI* plays, as is well known, before turning his attention to earlier historical material in the *Henry IV* and *Henry V* plays. The historical sequence that leads from Henry V's French victories to Henry VI's surrender of those conquered territories to France on his marriage to Margaret of Anjou is reversed by the sequence of composition that moves from the uncertainty and shame of the reign of Henry VI to the conquest and confidence of Henry V over a period of about seven years in the last decade of the sixteenth century. On the other hand, those shames are not forgotten in the later play, where the epilogue acknowledges that despite the greatness of the 'star of England' (Epilogue, line 6), as presented in this play, the victories of Henry V were ignominiously lost in the reign of his son, as 'oft our stage hath shown' (line 13). In acknowledging its dramatic forebears *Henry V* necessarily also acknowledges the sequel to its history.

The rhetorical manoeuvres of *Henry V*, whereby Henry's plain English triumphs over the prettily broken English of his French bride and silences the potential protests of France, are the expression of a need to assert the power of England against the image of English–French relations established by the earlier trilogy. The opening of *2 Henry VI* could not be further from the closing scene of *Henry V*. Margaret of Anjou's English is anything but broken. She addresses Henry VI with bold assurance in verse that shows the same rhythmic and syntactic command as that of the King and his nobles, and the King's first utterance is dedicated to a very public recognition of her 'grace in speech':

> Her sight did ravish, but her grace in speech,
> Her words yclad with wisdom's majesty,
> Makes me from wond'ring fall to weeping joys,
> Such is the fullness of my heart's content.   (I.i.32–5)

Henry's 'weeping joys' ironically anticipate the mourning that his marriage contract will provoke. A formal reading of the contract follows immediately after the exchange of greetings between Henry and Margaret, and its contents reveal the betrayal of England that this marriage constitutes. Its clauses itemise the return of the territories of Anjou and Maine to Margaret's father, the acceptance of Margaret without dowry and, the final humiliation, England's payment of even the costs of Margaret's journey.

The bluff, plain-speaking Englishman of this scene is not the King, who is easily seduced by Margaret's smooth eloquence, but Humphrey of Gloucester, the Protector, whose faltering in reading out the contract is the sign of how deeply England is betrayed by these articles of peace. It is he who is given the long apostrophe to the 'peers of England' expressing a grief that speaks for 'the common grief of all the land' (i.i.75–7) and who explicitly recalls the sufferings endured by his brother, Henry V, in conquering France, his 'true inheritance' (line 82). It is he who, up to his death in Act iii, speaks for England. Those who endanger the state of England are routinely represented as hostile to Humphrey's plainness. According to the Cardinal, Humphrey's plainness is 'too hot' (i.i.137) and 'his railing is intolerable' (iii.i.172); according to Margaret, he is 'insolent ... proud ... peremptory' (iii.i.7–8); according to Suffolk, his 'simple show' is a cover for treason (iii.i.54). And just as Humphrey's plain-speaking is constructed to mark him out as the good ruler, so Henry VI's devotion to the more elite written word is made the mark of his failure. The last line of the opening scene closes on York's denunciation of the reigning King as one, 'Whose bookish rule hath pull'd fair England down' (i.i.259).

The King's bookishness is the measure of his distance from the common people, whereas Humphrey's plainness is part of his claim to protect and care for them. By his own account he has often chosen to take money out of his own purse rather than 'tax the needy commons' (iii.i.116). It comes as no surprise to learn that this idealisation of Duke Humphrey can be traced back to Foxe, who describes him as 'meek and gentle, loving the commonwealth, a supporter of the poor commons, of wit and wisdom, discreet and studious, well affected to religion, and a friend to verity; and no less enemy to pride and ambition, especially in haughty prelates, which was his undoing in this present evil world' (*The Acts and Monuments of John Foxe*, vol. iii, p. 712; see also Bullough, *Narrative and Dramatic Sources*, vol. iii, p. 127). Alongside this unspoken Protestant lineage for Humphrey we may set the depiction of Cardinal Beauford as precisely the kind of 'haughty prelate' the good Protestant seeks to unmask together with the depiction of the King himself as excessively

> bent to holiness,
> To number Ave-Maries on his beads;
> His champions are the prophets and apostles,
> His weapons holy saws of sacred writ,
> His study is his tilt-yard, and his loves
> Are brazen images of canonized saints.   (I.iii.55–60)

The commons, championed by Duke Humphrey, are described by Warwick as 'an angry hive of bees' and a 'rude multitude' (III.ii.125, 135) when they rise up in fury at the news of Humphrey's murder. On the other hand, the very fact that it is Humphrey's murder that provokes them both legitimises their rebellion and distances the audience from any alignment with Warwick. The commons become in fact a very ambivalent force in the play, subject to attack or defence according to the needs and anxieties of the play at different points. The scene that most pointedly presents the commons as a group betrayed by scheming aristocrats and even royalty is Act I, scene iii, where Suffolk and the Queen head off the common people who are waiting to deliver their petitions to the Lord Protector. It is no accident that the first of these is revealed to be a petition against Suffolk himself 'for enclosing the commons of Melford' (lines 21–2). Though no more is made of the subject, even this brief reference to enclosures, a subject of much bitterness and discontent in Shakespeare's lifetime, would have been sufficient to arouse immediate hostility to Suffolk on the part of many in the audience.

The petition which *is* taken up and developed in the play, however, is that of an apprentice, Peter, against his master, Horner, whom he accuses of calling the King a usurper (line 31). In the Quarto text, Peter's claim is that 'the King was an usurer'. As in the scene between Tom Miller and the Queen Mother in *Jack Straw*, Peter fails to express himself in the right words and is corrected by the Queen: 'An usurper thou wouldst say'; but there is an important difference between the credit attached to the two speakers in each play. Whereas in *Jack Straw* the sense of injustice in tension with the comic exposure of the common man's error is not developed, and the final crushing of the rebels is presented as a victory, Peter's comic malapropism in *2 Henry VI* is not only corrected by a Queen already constructed as an enemy to England, which gives a very different edge to their relative status and the potential space for comedy, but is also developed along quasi-heroic lines. Peter is made to defend his charge in a judicial duel which results in his master's confession of treason, and the King's celebration of Peter's own 'truth and innocence' (ii.iii.103).

Yet though this victory is important to the play's insistence on the rights of commons, it is nevertheless ideologically complicit with the centralised power of the state. Peter is part of an established hierarchy that links apprentices to their masters, masters to their guilds and towns, and regional centres to the monarchical centre. Though this little plot may at first glance look potentially radical in so far as it shows an apprentice to be more loyal than his master, the very fact that the accusation is made within this framework and from below emphasises both the endorsement of the social hierarchy by the lowest members of the guild structure and the usefulness of that hierarchy as a system of surveillance. Peter fights not to change the social order but, with the backing of his fellows, 'for credit of the prentices' (ii.iii.71). More importantly, he understands that his first loyalty is to his King, and his centralised reprieve seems to celebrate this relationship as mutual. The King demonstrates his strength in protecting a truly loyal subject (and is grateful for the kind of 'loyalty' that willingly spies for England and the King). The scene is furthermore made to speak of York's treachery as well as Peter's master's, since Peter's accusation is that his master, in denouncing Henry as a usurper, has claimed York as the rightful heir to the throne. (This connection is peculiar to the play; the incident is not linked with any courtly plotting as it is told in the chronicles.) Peter's position, endorsed by Henry's rewarding of his loyalty, is presented as allied with that of the rightful monarch, while his master is aligned with York's treachery. Thus king and commons, the centralised state and its bold young men, are held together in an idealised image that cultivates suspicion of two classes in between, the local masters and the regional nobility. The class binary is bent into a shape that pays homage to the binary that separates traitors from the state, and the image of the monarch feeds off the masculine plainness and youthful vigour of a group here presented as the heart of England.

A comparison between the play's treatment of the apprentice class and its treatment of vagrancy shows the boundaries it draws. The apprentice class, though relatively low in the social order, is very much within a structure that insists on social duty and offers a path for social advancement; vagrants, on the other hand, represent a threat to the social order by virtue of their refusal of its structures. By refusing to give his or her labour, the vagrant roams free of any attachment to the organisation of labour. In another scene grafted on to the chronicle material,[11] the vagrant Simpcox, masquerading as a blind man miraculously cured, is exposed as a fraud by the good Duke Humphrey himself, so that the scene is made to demonstrate the precise limits of Humphrey's sympathy for the commons. Though Humphrey is constructed by the petitioning of Act I, scene iii as a friend to the oppressed, this scene shows his refusal to support the vagrant class whose very existence in the space of non-work enacts its opposition to the ideological basis of the commonweal, where hierarchy is maintained through systematised working relations. Humphrey's sympathies extend to those whose place in the social order exposes them to exploitation or injustice, not to those who place themselves outside the social order altogether. His only interest in Simpcox is to see him punished. The plea of Simpcox's wife, 'we did it for pure need' (II.i.154) is met with clear instructions from Humphrey to operate the penalties laid down by the Elizabethan poor laws: 'Let them be whipt through every market town, / Till they come to Berwick, from whence they came' (lines 155–6).

The historical anachronism of the punishment here emphasises how clearly the play speaks from and to its own late Elizabethan world. Whipping was not introduced as a punishment for vagrancy until a statute of 1531 laid down that offenders should be tied naked to a cart, then dragged and beaten with whips until they were bleeding. Prior to this statute, in the time when the play is set, masterless men would commonly have been held in the stocks, a detention which gradually came to be perceived as a punishment. The scene presents Simpcox's small-time fraud and its punishment as a demonstration and justification of the statutes by which the (Elizabethan) state protects its interests and maintains its definition of the good commonwealth. The good Duke Humphrey and the obedient and hard-working commons whose Protector he is are here aligned with the law that punishes and expels ideological misfits with their treacherous and wasteful language, their invented stories and fabricated miracles devised as a substitute for honest work.

Betrayal of the ideals of the good commonwealth, however, is not merely or mainly the prerogative of social outcasts like Simpcox. The ironic praise of Duke Humphrey's 'miracle', in making the lame 'to leap and fly away' (lines 157–8) is brusquely ended by Buckingham's entry announcing a far more serious threat to the safety and well-being of the state. The terms in which Buckingham outlines the threat are important:

> A sort of naughty persons, lewdly bent,
> Under the countenance and confederacy
> Of Lady Eleanor, the Protector's wife,
> The ringleader and head of all this rout,
> Have practis'd dangerously against your state,
> Dealing with witches and with conjurers,
> Whom we have apprehended in the fact,
> Raising up wicked spirits from under ground,
> Demanding of King Henry's life and death,
> And other of your Highness' Privy Council. (lines 163–72)

The emphasis on witchcraft as a danger to the state is again tied up with the thinking of Elizabethan statutes not in place at the date of the play's setting.[12] The detailing of the offence refers indirectly to the act of 1581 (cited on p. 190 above), with its anxiety about those who use conjuring to find out answers to questions about how long the monarch shall live or reign. As in the Simpcox episode, wrongdoing is defined as contravention of the (Elizabethan) statutes and exploited as an opportunity to endorse the rightfulness and necessity of the statutes. Error is constructed not primarily in religious terms, as sinfulness, but in political terms, as felony and potential treason.

This play, like several other contemporary plays, has a scene representing the act of conjuring. The scene is expanded and altered from a mere hint in Hall, who merely reports the conviction of Eleanor Cobham and her associates, specifying that they 'devised an image of waxe, representyng the kynge', with intention to destroy it and him (*Hall's Chronicle*, p. 202). But where in *Doctor Faustus*, for example, the corresponding scene (i.iii) represents this action in terms of outrage against the spiritual order, in *2 Henry VI* it is represented primarily as an outrage against the political order. This perspective is prepared in advance of the conjuring scene. Eleanor's interest in Margery Jordan, the witch, and Roger Bolingbrook, the conjuror, is presented not in relation to Eleanor's soul but in relation to her political status and ambitions. John Hume, her intermediary, reports back to her that the witch and the conjuror have promised

> to show your Highness
> A spirit rais'd from depth of under ground,
> That shall make answer to such questions
> As by your Grace shall be propounded him. (1.ii.78–81)

Hume is given a soliloquy immediately following his brief exchange with Eleanor that places Eleanor's scheming within the framework of a prior political plot of which she is unaware, a plot devised by Suffolk and the Cardinal to entrap her. (As in the case of the apprentice accusing his master, Shakespeare adds the detail that links the scene to the treachery of noblemen. Hall says nothing to indicate that Eleanor is set up.) The conjuration, then, is already established within two competing frameworks of plotting against the state before it is represented on stage.

The conjuring scene opens with more machinations, this time on the part of the conjuror, who disposes his accomplices as for a show, thus manufacturing one of those moments, familiar from Bale and Protestant drama, where theatre tries to define its real self in opposition to show: 'it shall be convenient, Master Hume, that you be by her aloft, while we be busy below; and so I pray you go in God's name, and leave us. [*Exit Hume.*] Mother Jordan, be you prostrate and grovel on the earth. [*She lies down upon her face.*] John Southwell, read you; and let us to our work' (1.iv.7–12). This piece of visible stage management on the conjuror's part makes what follows very uncertain in signification. The stage direction outlines a sequence that gives nothing away as to whether this conjuring is fact or fraud: '*Here do the ceremonies belonging, and make the circle. Bolingbrook or Southwell reads* Conjuro te *etc. It thunders and lightens terribly; then the Spirit riseth*' (line 22). The signs are contradictory: while Bolingbrook's arrangements suggest that the four participants are consciously conspiring to stage the mere show of a spirit's appearance, there is nothing to help an audience determine whether the terrible thunder and lightning are to be understood as real thunder and lightning or as effects staged by the characters. Since they are of course by definition stage effects, there is nothing about the mode of representation that can clarify how they are to be understood. The audience is ambiguously positioned with regard to what it sees. Knowing that the thunder and lightning are manufactured, but accustomed to accept manufactured effects as representing the real thing, it has no way of knowing whether it is being asked to incorporate its knowledge of the mechanics of representation into its understanding of the represented event.

The verbal text is equally ambiguous. Drawing the circle and speaking the Latin incantation, as *Doctor Faustus* demonstrates, would be the expected way of calling up a real spirit; the spirit that appears responds in Latin to indicate its obedience ('*Adsum*' [Here I am] (line 23)); and Margery Jordan addresses it by the exotic name of 'Asnath', an anagram of Sathan.[13] The presence of these details makes the status of the conjuration indistinguishable as either genuine or fake. More importantly, the Spirit goes on to answer Eleanor's questions with the classically riddling replies that are exactly what an audience would expect from a real spirit, yet, equally, so recognisably part of the discourse of spirits as to be easy to fake, though nothing within the diegesis reveals who's doing the faking. And, like the whole process of conjuring, the prophesying riddles are added by the play to the source. Hall only makes reference to one prophecy, and that is not linked with Eleanor's conjuring, but slipped unobtrusively into his report of the death of Somerset, 'who long before', he says, 'was warned to eschew all Castles' (*Hall's Chronicle*, p. 233).

Since the Dukes of York and Buckingham break in at the precise moment that the Spirit descends, the question of whether the conjuror and the witch are charlatans is never resolved. They are guilty of the crime of conjuring in the eyes of the state, which is unconcerned as to whether they truly raised any spirits or not, since its agents set them up in the first place. The distinction between true and false conjuring is not one the state needs to concern itself with. It is looking for victims, and duly punishes its victims according to their status. The witch is burned; Bolingbrook and the two priests are hanged; and Eleanor herself is condemned to public penance followed by perpetual banishment.

The incident dramatises two of the more extreme forms of linguistic deviancy (Latin conjuration and riddling prophecy), but at the same time frames them as in fact subordinate to political scheming. (Both kinds of foregrounding, of linguistic deviancy and political scheming, are absent from the chronicle source material and specific to the play.) This makes the apparent deviancy difficult to read. Though the associations of the deviant discourses in question are such as to stimulate an audience to disapprove of those who utter them, ironically the possible fraudulence of their status reduces the effect of deviance. Fake conjuring and fake prophecy are less threatening both to the soul and to the state than the real thing. What is foregrounded is the treason of those who set up the fakery, Suffolk and the Cardinal. And precisely because they escape punishment, they continue to represent a danger to the state that remains the more dangerous on account of its invisibility and its evasion of punishment. On the other hand, although the threat of overmighty subjects is so difficult for others within the play to see, the object of the play is to make it very visible to the audience. Shakespeare foregrounds incidents that reveal their set-ups and machinations: Hall's brief reference to York's part in setting up Jack Cade to incite rebellion is pointed up in a long soliloquy given to York at the close of Act III, scene i, which also hints at his part in Duke Humphrey's death; and the involvement of Suffolk and the Cardinal in entrapping Eleanor is Shakespeare's own addition to the chronicle material. These plots are themselves both real and fake, ambivalent shows; they are the product of scheming noblemen, whose 'work' in producing these dangerous shows is implicitly set alongside the real work of the commons.

Though the question of whether the witch and the conjuror are charlatans is not pursued in the play, the riddles they conjure up become embedded in its shape. When York and Buckingham break in, York reads the paper and openly scoffs at the ambiguous syntax that allows the prophecy to be 'true' whatever the outcome:

> Now pray, my lord, let's see the devil's writ.
> [*Reads.*] What have we here?
> 'The duke yet lives that Henry shall depose;
> But him out-live, and die a violent death.'
> Why, this is just
> '*Aio te, Aeacida, Romanos vincere posse*'. [I affirm that you, descendant of Aeacus, can conquer the Romans / I affirm that the Romans can conquer you, descendant of Aeacus]
> (I.iv.57–62)

He reads on to repeat the prophecies concerning the Dukes of Suffolk and Somerset, that the first shall die by water and the second should shun castles. Part of the effect of this, of course, is that the audience hears each of the prophecies twice, so that, despite York's scepticism, the prophecies themselves are given extraordinary prominence. More importantly, but predictably from the shape of this scene, the prophecies are proved 'true', and in each case the prophecy is explicitly recalled at the point of convergence. Suffolk meets his death at the hands of Walter (pronounced 'water') Whitmore, whose name Suffolk immediately construes as one 'in whose sound is death' (iv.i.33); while Richard, Earl of Warwick, kills Somerset under an alehouse sign of the castle, which is not only given stage presence as a visual sign, but echoed in Richard's formal acknowledgement of Somerset's death 'underneath an alehouse' paltry sign, / The Castle in Saint Albans' (v.ii.67–8). Since these two noblemen, through their liaison with the Queen, represent a greater threat to the state than any mere conjuror, whether genuine or fraudulent, there is a nice irony about the fact that their deaths are made to coincide with the prophecies issuing from a plot initiated by one of them to frame another nobly-born schemer.

Though the play calls for a hostile reaction to a range of outcast figures, such as the witch, the conjuror and the false beggar, its hostility to treason in high places is even more marked. It is continually setting threats to the state from the margins of society against threats to the state from the centre, and apparently even excusing to a degree some of the marginal threats as effects of machinations at the centre. It is important, then, to look closely at how it stages rebellion to see where its sympathies lie, accepting that, whatever its sympathies are, they cannot transcend the contradictions of its position.

Like the conjuror and the witch, the rebels are the tools of schemers at the centre, and again we are given this information before the rebels themselves are brought on stage. It is the Duke of York who in this case confides to the audience that he has

> seduc'd a headstrong Kentishman
> John Cade of Ashford,
> To make commotion, as full well he can.   (iii.i.356–8)

He goes on to recount Cade's boldness in battle and his craftiness as qualities that make him suitable to stir up rebellion. York's words leave the audience in no doubt that they should read Cade as no more than a mechanism for York: 'This devil here shall be my substitute' (line 371). As noted above, York's involvement is Shakespeare's addition to his source.

This framing of the audience's perspective on the rebels is put in place well before the first appearance of the rebels in iv.ii; but the material immediately preceding the entry of Jack Cade also merits consideration. The scene opens with a conversation between two unnamed rebels.[14] Geoffrey Bullough calls them 'two comic workmen' (*Narrative and Dramatic Sources*, vol. III, p. 95), a reminder of how often the unnamed figures of Shakespeare's drama have been unthinkingly dismissed in this way. (What's comic about them? Can the servant who tries to stop Cornwall blinding Gloucester in *King Lear* be dismissed as comic because he is unnamed?) The absence of names highlights their representative status: they are not figures who function by virtue of personality, but rather as spokesmen for a position, like the unnamed gardeners of *Richard II* or the scrivener of *Richard III*. And their conversation is important in terms of the way it predisposes the audience to think about issues of class and the commonwealth:

[FIRST WORKMAN]. I tell thee, Jack Cade the clothier means to dress the commonwealth, and turn it, and set a new nap upon it.

[SECOND WORKMAN]. So he had need, for 'tis threadbare. Well, I say it was never merry world in England since gentlemen came up.

[FIRST WORKMAN]. O miserable age! virtue is not regarded in handicrafts-men.

[SECOND WORKMAN]. The nobility think scorn to go in leather aprons.

[FIRST WORKMAN]. Nay more, the King's Council are no good workmen.

[SECOND WORKMAN]. True; and yet it is said, labour in thy vocation; which is as much to say as, let the magistrates be labouring men; and therefore should we be magistrates.

[FIRST WORKMAN]. Thou hast hit it; for there's no better sign of a brave mind than a hard hand. (IV.ii.4–20)

The conversation raises general issues via spokesmen whose words do not need to be weighed against their characters, since characters are not developed for them. Instead they speak as representatives of a perspective. They give voice to the view that the commonwealth is in need of overhaul and repair and they blame its deterioration up to this point on the rise of gentlemen who scorn first-hand acquaintance with honest labour. In their view there should be no gap between manual labour and any other kind of labour: those who work for the good of the commonwealth should learn through experience to understand and honour the place of craftsmen in that collective labour. In this way, their decision to fall in with Cade and his men is made comprehensible rather than being exposed as folly.

Cade's entrance, however, shifts the audience from a position of sympathy, however brief, for the rebels' cause to one that exposes the rebel leader as unworthy to head them. As Cade's speech proceeds through a sequence of pretentious claims as to his marriage and descent, it is regularly punctuated with asides from Dick the Butcher exposing them as false. Cade is thus discredited from two directions simultaneously: not only is his claim to be the descendant of a Mortimer and a Plantaganet revealed as a foolish lie, but his right to represent those honest craftsmen whose discontent with the commonwealth was given some positive moral status at the opening of the scene is alienated by his rejection of the class position of craftsman as not good enough for him.

The presentation of Jack Cade undoubtedly sets out to discredit him. His discourse needs to be emptied of force as soon as he appears, in order to emphasise his subjection, his status as the mere tool of a more authoritative villain, of true aristocratic descent: York. Dick's references to Cade's father's imprisonment for vagrancy and Cade's own past whippings for beggary and branding for sheep-stealing (all details added in the process of dramatising the chronicle material) construct him as more deviant than Simpcox. As Arthur Freeman has demonstrated in the introduction to his edition of the play, the distance between Hall's Cade and Shakespeare's Cade shows an evident intention on Shakespeare's part to malign Cade:

> In line either with official policy, or his own predilections, or both, Shakespeare's Cade scarcely resembles the 'youngman of goodly stature and pregnant wit', the 'subtle captain,' and audacious field-general Hall portrays; rather he stands for rampant ignorance, executing a clerk for his ability to read and write, and Lord Say, as much as for anything, for his cultural accomplishment. (Freeman, ed., *Henry VI, Part Two*, p. xxxii)

Yet, while Cade himself is demeaned in this way, there is another perspective on the rebels that Freeman does not allow for. Rebellion, like conjuring and prophecy, is represented through a foregrounding of opposing discourses; and, as the rebellion develops, the contradictory positions already made available to the audience via the unnamed rebels and Jack Cade respectively continue to compete.

The encounters with the clerk and Lord Say are not merely encounters between Jack Cade and individuals who can read and write; they are also encounters between the rights of the illiterate and the oppression of the elite. The opposition is not just between individuals but between discourses representing access to and exclusion from power.

As a messenger reports, the targets of Cade's band of rebels are the educated elite: 'All scholars, lawyers, courtiers, gentlemen, / They call false caterpillars, and intend their death.' (iv.iv.36–7). Their education is no mere frill, as the rebels perceive, but the basis of their hold on power and their exclusion of the illiterate from such power. As long as the law, for example, exists in the form of written records, it can be known and used only by those able to read and write. Hence Cade's decision to hang a clerk 'with his pen and inkhorn about his neck' (iv.ii.109–10, again a scene invented for the play out of a mere phrase in Holinshed's account of the 1381 rising)[15] is no mere representation of an aspect of Cade's character, his 'rampant ignorance', but a symbolic attack on the learning that limits the rights and powers of labouring men while creating the conditions for those in power to leech on the labours of their underlings. The murder of the clerk is of a piece with Cade's determination to destroy all written records and put the spoken word in their place: 'Away, burn all the records of the realm, my mouth shall be the parliament of England' (iv.vii.13–15). The opposition between speech and written record represents the opposition between the disempowered and the traditions of power. In attacking the Savoy Palace and the Inns of Court the rebels are attacking institutions that house aristocratic parasites on the commonwealth and reproduce the dependence on written texts that underwrites the exclusion of the illiterate from the government of the commonwealth.

The targets of the rebels' anger, furthermore, while functioning symbolically within the dramatic structure of the play, have some historical foundation, but not in the description of the fifteenth-century rebellion Shakespeare is describing. The rebels of 1381, according to Thomas Walsingham, destroyed the Savoy and the Inns of Court, burned university archives and legal records and made teachers swear to stop teaching children Latin grammar (see p. 10 above).[16] This last focus of attack, on the possession of grammar as the barrier between oppressors and oppressed, finds an analogue in the play's representation of the death of Lord Say. As in the case of the clerk, the political attack is focused through language, and again the emphasis is peculiar to the play, diverging significantly from Hall's account of Say's execution.[17] In one breath Cade accuses Lord Say of 'gelding' the commonwealth and denounces him as a traitor because he can speak French. Cade's logic and rhetoric are blatantly foolish: 'Nay, answer if you can. The Frenchmen are our enemies. Go to then, I ask but this: can he that speaks with the tongue of an enemy be a good counsellor, or no?' (iv.ii.169–72), yet his words have a resonance beyond the immediate circumstances. As in the case of the clerk's murder, there is more to be said about these lines than that they display Cade's 'rampant ignorance'. When the question is asked, perhaps directly of the audience, their response can scarcely avoid the comparison with Queen Margaret, working for the interests of France throughout, even from the point where she first worms her way into Henry's affections through her command of English, and consistently counselling him against the best interests of the English state.

When Lord Say is brought on stage to face his accusers, Cade is given a lengthy diatribe against him that again collapses political crimes with devotion to education (iv.vii.24–47). Giving up Normandy is placed on a par with 'traitorously corrupt[ing] the youth of the realm in erecting a grammar school'; and hanging poor men that could not read (and hence could not escape, as elite offenders did, by claiming benefit of clergy) is set alongside having 'men about thee that usually talk of a noun and a verb'. Lord Say's reply to the question of what he thinks of Kent: 'Nothing but this; 'tis "*bona terra, mala gens*" [a good land, bad people]', is a reply guaranteed to affect his unlearned accusers in terms of language rather than content, and Cade's response is instant and decisive: 'Away with him, away with him! he speaks Latin' (iv.vii.57). Interestingly, in the Quarto text the response is shared amongst Cade and his followers:

> CADE. *Bonum terum*, sounds [zounds] what's that?
> DICK. He speakes French.
> WILL. No 'tis Dutch.
> NICKE. No 'tis outtalian, I know it well inough.

Yet the response is still one focused on language, though here bewilderment is more conspicuous than rage.

Lord Say is now given a long and eloquent speech in his own

defence. Problematically for the audience, who have been taught to see Henry VI's bookishness as a failing by comparison with Duke Humphrey's common touch, Lord Say makes no apology for his endowment of scholarship and calls attention to the fact that it was his learning that preferred him to the King (line 72). Cade responds to his pleading with remorse; yet, paradoxically, it is the very persuasiveness of Lord Say's speech in his own defence that decides the issue: 'He shall die, and it be but for pleading so well for his life. – Away with him, he has a familiar under his tongue, he speaks not a' God's name' (lines 106–8). Even as he is moved to remorse by Lord Say's command of language, that very experience reminds Cade of the advantage that those who have power over words have over those who are at their mercy. His claim that Lord Say's speech is inspired by the devil comes across as no more than a pretext for his decision, which, as the early part of the scene has made clear, emerges out of an entrenched hostility to scholarly privilege.

This is a deeply unsettling moment in performance. The power of the performer and of theatre itself is behind Lord Say, because it is the skills of the performer that must mediate the force of his eloquence; while the inadequacy of Cade, already York's puppet, is, within the fiction, the inadequacy of one who knows he cannot perform and resents those who can. In terms of performance skills it aligns the Chamberlain's Men with the aristocratic class who are their patrons, challenges them with the contemporary attacks on theatre as empty show and distances them from the social class to which, as working men, they belong. What they are negotiating, in a sense, is their awareness of the contradictions of their own position. Materially, they straddle a newly emerging place as the theatre turns professional. Their name claims them as allied to a noble patron; the law condemns them as vagabonds if they try to perform without this guarantee of authority; and between those two poles their day-to-day business situates them as doing a job for pay, a pay that comes directly from an audience that includes both noblemen and apprentices. Imaginatively, the particular work they do situates them as apprentices one moment, kings the next. Their work is to represent all classes of society from within the contradictory material pressures on them and to defend that work of representation against the claim that it is mere fakery. In such a situation it is scarcely surprising that scenes presenting confrontations between rebels, apprentices or conjurers and great lords are uncertain in tone.

From the audience's point of view the whole scene between Cade and Lord Say recalls the earlier scene (IV.i, again an elaboration expanding on a few sentences in Hall) in which a member of the educated aristocracy attempts to escape death at the hands of a social inferior. The gap between the Duke of Suffolk and the Captain whose prisoner he becomes is nothing like as wide as that between Jack Cade and Lord Say, but Suffolk's own pride leads him to centre on the class difference between them as he insults the Captain:

> Obscure and lousy swain, King Henry's blood,
> The honourable blood of Lancaster,
> Must not be shed by such a jaded groom.   (lines 50–2)

As always in this play, social and political difference is quickly focused as linguistic difference, in this case the difference again between writing and speech. Suffolk concludes his insistence on the difference between them by summoning this polarity: 'This hand of mine hath writ in thy behalf, / And therefore shall it charm thy riotous tongue' (lines 63–4). Suffolk's command over written text is set against the Captain's unruly speech. Whitmore, who captured Suffolk, offers to stab him at this point, but the linguistic duelling is to be drawn out at much more length than this:

> CAPTAIN. First let my words stab him, as he hath me.
>
> SUFFOLK. Base slave, thy words are blunt and so art thou.
>   (lines 66–7)

Both speak verse, and both cite Latin, so that the linguistic opposition is very different from that between Cade and Lord Say, but the situation is the same in so far as the lowlier of the two has power over the life of his social superior, and a parallel interplay between power and language is invoked. Suffolk, unlike Lord Say, will not stoop to plead for his life. His response to the First Gentleman's suggestion that he should 'entreat him, speak him fair', is proud, refusing even the directness of the first-person pronoun:

> Suffolk's imperial tongue is stern and rough,
> Us'd to command, untaught to plead for favour.
> Far be it we should honour such as these
> With humble suit.   (lines 121–4)

But the Captain's response to his speech is the same as Cade's response to Lord Say's for different reasons: 'Hale him away, and let him talk no more' (line 131).

While Lord Say's pleading incites Jack Cade to cruelty via remorse, Suffolk's expression of a refusal to plead incites the Captain's cruelty by a more direct route. In each case the scene presents social status as allied with rhetorical power, and shows that combination as one guaranteed to provoke resistance. Jack Cade's ignorance is a politicised ignorance that constructs its opposite as equally inadequate. Bookish kings and proud or scholarly noblemen are not what the commonwealth needs to return to order. The prescription for the good commonwealth is based, as it was again to be based in *Henry V,* on the ideal of plain-speaking. Plain English, as spoken by Duke Humphrey and Peter the apprentice, each in their appointed place in the social order but united across the class divide by their ability to speak directly to one another and, of course, to put the interests of the commonwealth above their own, is the cement that is to bring the nation together.

Conclusion

To stop at 1600 is not to reach the end of the argument, but rather to stop at a major point of transition. The end of the century and the end of Elizabeth I's very long reign (1558–1603) do not represent an end to the staging of non-English voices in English drama; but they do coincide with notable changes to the context of that staging which suggest a whole new area of study. The accession of a Scottish king to the English throne, for example, a king with the concept of a united Britain on his agenda, is only one very obvious aspect of how England's assertion of Englishness is very differently determined after 1603.

Other languages remain central to English Jacobean drama, and the Babel/Babylon topos remains a conspicuous one across different discourses, including anti-theatrical discourse. As William Crashawe thunders in a sermon preached at Paul's Cross in February 1608: 'The ungodly Playes and Enterludes so rife in this nation; what are they but a bastard of Babylon, a daughter of error and confusion, a hellish device, (the divels owne recreation to mock at holy things) by him delivered to the Heathen, from them to the Papists, and from them to us?' (Crashawe, *The Sermon Preached at the Crosse*, p. 170). For this preacher, as for Bale, theatre is deeply linked with heathen and Catholic degeneracy by its predisposition to 'mock at holy things'; and because this tendency towards mockery is, in Crashawe's view, so deeply-rooted in the theatrical act as to be a defining characteristic of theatre, the only solution is to destroy theatre: 'happie hee that puts his hand to pull downe this tower of Babel' (p. 172).

The image of the Tower of Babel, as earlier chapters have shown, changed in use during the course of the fifteenth and sixteenth centuries. Its fifteenth-century prominence as an image for heterodox or heretical speaking, often used against Lollards, moved during the course of the sixteenth century to ironic realignment with the

Reformist cause, so that it became, as Babylon, a figure for the church of Rome. At the same time, too, the image gathered secular force; as the English church became the domain of a separatist English state, the image of Babel also came to stand more widely for the dangers of ungoverned speaking.

During the seventeenth century, however, the Tower of Babel became more strongly associated with economic than with theological or political conditions, and was in popular use almost exclusively as an image of the contemporary marketplace (Agnew, *Worlds Apart*, p. 86). In a parallel development, the anxiety about theatre, characteristically framed in theological terms from the *Tretise of miraclis pleyinge* to the fulminations of John Bale, became more commonly addressed from within an economic framework. As companies acquired theatre buildings and professional status, and theatre became an increasingly firmly established economic enterprise, so the contradictions of that position explored by the Lord Chamberlain's Men in the 1590s (p. 217 above) developed new emphases within a growing commercial awareness. Theatre, which had once looked like religious ritual and produced anxiety on that account, increasingly looked more like economic exchange, and produced a different kind of anxiety. As Thomas Dekker put it in *The Gull's Hornbook*: 'The theatre is your poets' Royal Exchange upon which their Muses – that are now turned to merchants – meeting, barter away that light commodity of words for a lighter ware than words – plaudits' (Dekker, *The Wonderful Year, the Gull's Hornbook*, p. 98). Money is nowhere explicit but everywhere present in the vocabulary of exchange, barter, merchants and commodities. Words, says Dekker, have become commodities to be exchanged for applause; but the real commodity is theatre, which is now understood as offered for sale. It is that more than anything else which changes the conditions of Babel for the seventeenth-century theatre.

Notes

1 'VERBUM DEI' AND THE RISE OF ENGLISH

1 The authors do elsewhere give fuller consideration to the legitimacy of these practices, citing earlier doctors of the church on the question, and come to the conclusion that there is no harm in wearing sacred writings as charms so long as there is nothing about them 'that savours of an invocation of devils', and no unknown names are included in the charm (Heinrich Kramer and James Sprenger, *Malleus Maleficarum*, p. 182). Pope Innocent VIII's bull of 1484, *Summis desiderantes affectibus*, authorising Kramer and Sprenger as witchcraft inquisitors, was published as a preface to the *Malleus* and thus circulated with it.

2 Though the Authorised Version (1611) postdates the period of this book, I have chosen to cite its translations routinely throughout rather than select one out of the many contested and contemporary translations which feature in the arguments of the book. This does not imply, of course, that the 1611 translation is above dispute, but rather that its familiarity, together with the fact that it is later than the parameters of this study, remove it to some extent from the particular disputes under consideration here.

3 This discussion is indebted to Eric Jager, *The Tempter's Voice*, esp. ch.2, 'The Genesis of Hermeneutics'. Jager cites Augustine at much greater length, including the quotation given here (p. 53).

4 Christian writers were not the first to worry about relations between language and a higher reality. Plato's *Cratylus* argues that 'the power which gave the first names to things is more than human, and therefore the names must necessarily be correct' (*Cratylus*, p. 183).

5 I diverge here from Jager, who argues that Babel 'did not emerge as a major literary topos until after the Renaissance, with the decline of Latin as a "universal" language' (*The Tempter's Voice*, p. 1). Though I think he is right to relate it to the decline of Latin, this decline started in the late medieval period and was a matter of debate throughout the Renaissance, as I hope this book will show. Articles by S. F. Johnson, '*The Spanish Tragedy*', Margreta de Grazia, 'Shakespeare's View of Language' and A. J. Hoenselaars, 'Reconstructing Babel in English

Renaissance Drama', demonstrate the familiarity of the Babel topos during the period of the English Renaissance.

6 Peter Burke speculates as to whether the mock liturgy of the Feast of Fools was experienced by the congregation as 'not only a festive reversal of the everyday but also a criticism of the unintelligibility of the liturgy to the layman' (*Popular Culture in Early Modern Europe*, p. 124).

7 See M. T. Clanchy, *From Memory to Written Record*, p. 212 and plate xiv. For a fuller discussion of the relations between Latin, French and English, see Elizabeth Salter, *English and International*, ch.2 and Janette Dillon, *Geoffrey Chaucer*, ch.4.

8 See further Malcolm Richardson, 'Henry V', on Henry V's conscious fostering of the vernacular.

9 Clanchy, *From Memory to Written Record*, ch.7, discusses this question more fully. He notes that although there is evidence conflicting with 'the medieval axiom that laymen are illiterate and its converse that clergy are literate', medieval terminology 'preserved intact the appearances of these fundamental axioms while acknowledging the realities of daily experience, where some clergy were ignorant and some knights knew more of books than brave deeds' (p. 226).

10 D. W. Robertson, Jr asserts that peasants of villein status paid the fee and obtained this permission 'often' ('Who Were "The People"?', p. 11), but it seems unlikely that many were able to overcome the combined obstacles of wealth and status. R. N. Swanson, *Church and Society*, pp. 37–8, points to the limited evidence of former serfs becoming clerics and argues that most of those who managed to finance education with a view to a clerical career for their children in this period would be of middling economic standing. On the question of the politics of literacy, see further M. E. Aston, *Lollards and Reformers*, pp. 193–217.

11 On the importance of written documents to the rebellion and the ideology informing their destruction see Steven Justice, *Writing and Rebellion*. Justice points out that the notion that such destruction was simply the expression of illiteracy's rage against the written word was the view of the chroniclers, themselves at the centre of elite written culture. The rebels, Justice argues, were familiar with another form of written culture in the shape of the documents that recorded their landholdings, the services due to their lords and so on. The burning of legal documents was not a rejection of written forms but a symbolic appropriation of them, an assertion of rights through the authoritative medium of written record. For a more extended consideration of rebels and learning see my discussion of *2 Henry VI* in chapter 8 below.

12 For further discussion and examples of the movement towards the vernacular devotional and instructional material discussed in this paragraph, see Aston, *Lollards and Reformers*, pp. 101–34, Vincent Gillespie, 'Vernacular Books of Religion' and Eamon Duffy, *The Stripping of the Altars*, ch.2. There are also earlier examples of such initiatives, but

the point here is rather how much more widespread they became in the fourteenth century.

13 '*Unde quia volui materiam communicatem clericis et laicis, collegi et communicavi triginta tres conclusiones illius materie in li[n]gwa duplici*' (Aston, 'Wyclif and the Vernacular', p. 287). Aston's note 17, following this quotation, cites two other instances in Wyclif's Latin works where he mentions having made the same point in more than one language. She demonstrates that Wyclif undoubtedly used English to put forward his own views, despite the fact that the only extant writings certainly attributable to him are in Latin.

14 '*qui volunt dampnare scripta tamquam heretica propter hoc quod scribuntur in Anglico et acute tangunt peccata que conturbant illam provinciam*'; *De Triplici Vinculo Amoris*, ch.2; cited in Anne Hudson, *The Premature Reformation*, p. 30; my translation. The Latin word *provincia* must refer here to the whole area where English is spoken. Latin was not totally and immediately rejected by the early Lollards, however, just as English was not totally rejected by the orthodox church in the same period. John Aston disseminated his views on the eucharist on flysheets in English and Latin, while *The Lantern of Light* gives its quotations first in Latin and only afterwards in English (see Hudson, '*Laicus litteratus*'; these examples cited pp. 230–1).

15 '*clericis et ecclesiae doctoribus, ut ipsi laicis et infirmioribus personis, secundum temporis exigentiam et personarum indigentiam, cum mentis eorum esurie, dulciter ministrarent*'. The translation of *infirmis* and *dulciter* is somewhat ambiguous, but the context seems to highlight Knighton's belief in the self-evident superiority of the clergy over the laity and in the ability of clerks to determine how much it is right for the weaker to know.

16 '*transtulit de Latino in Anglicam linguam non angelicam, unde per ipsum fit vulgare et magis apertum laicis, et mulieribus legere scientibus, quam solet esse clericis admodum literatis et bene intelligentibus, et sic evangelica margarita spargitur et a porcis conculcatur*'.

17 Aston's essay, 'Lollardy and Sedition, 1381–1431', is also reprinted in Aston, *Lollards and Reformers*.

18 See Ronald Waldron, 'John Trevisa and the Use of English', p. 174, n.9. Trevisa held a fellowship at Queen's Hall, Oxford between 1376 and 1379, at about the same time as Wyclif and Hereford were there, but there is no evidence that he was accused of Lollard leanings at the time, though his name was later associated with the Lollard Bible (see David C. Fowler, 'John Trevisa and the English Bible'; Waldron, 'John Trevisa and the Use of English', pp. 178–9; Hudson, *The Premature Reformation*, pp. 395–7).

19 Lauren Lepow, *Enacting the Sacrament*, p. 66, cites examples.

20 '*sicut magister eorum Wyclyf potens erat et validus in disputationibus super caeteros, et in argumentis nulli credebatur secundus: sic isti licet recenter ad sectam illam attracti nimis efficiebantur eloquentes, in omnibus versutiis atque verbosis colluctationibus caeteris praevalentes; validi in verbis; in garulis fortes; in sermocinationibus*

praepotentes, in litigiosis deceptationibus omnes superclamantes. Et sic quod non poterant recta ratione quasi pugnanti impetuositate cum voce clamosa et turbida et altisonis verbis supplebant.' Myers' translation treats 'magister' as Wyclif's title ('Master John Wyclif') but the Latin clearly indicates that Wyclif is being identified as the 'master' of the Lollards, which is slightly different. All subsequent translations from *English Historical Documents*, vol. IV, are Myers'.

21 '*qui mutaverunt Evangelium Christi in Evangelium aeternum, id est, vulgarem linguam et communem maternam, et sic aeternam, quia laicis reputatur melior et dignior quam lingua Latina*'.

22 The Middle English version reads as follows: 'Yit worldli clerkis axen gretli what spiryt makith idiotis hardi to translate now the Bible into English, sithen the foure greete doctouris dursten nevere do this. This replicacioun is so lewid that it nedith noon answer, no but stilnesse eithir curteys scorn. For these greete doctouris weren noone English men ... But thei ceessiden nevere til thei hadden holi writ in here modir tunge of here owne puple' (reprinted in Hudson, ed., *Selections from English Wycliffite Writings*, p. 70).

23 By the sixteenth century, however, Lollardy was upwardly mobile again (Susan Brigden, *London and the Reformation*, pp. 96–7).

24 The Prologue to the Wyclifite Bible makes the same point about Latin bibles, arguing that many of them are 'ful false' and 'han more nede to be correctid ... than the English bible late translatid' (Hudson, ed., *Selections from English Wycliffite Writings*, p. 69).

25 The conditions in which the extant manuscripts of a sermon by Thomas Wimbledon, preached in 1388, survive demonstrate the hardening of a semi-automatic equation of English-language texts (especially on theological matters) with Lollardy. The Latin manuscripts are found in collections of 'apparently unquestioned orthodoxy'; the English version is bound with Lollard treatises (G. R. Owst, *Preaching in Medieval England*, pp. 229–30).

26 Claire Cross, ' "Great Reasoners in Scripture" ', p. 367, has pointed out that the pretence of illiteracy among women investigated for heresy is a significant factor impeding our attempts to measure female literacy in the period. If such pretence was common, literacy could have been much more widespread than we can now prove.

27 '*scripsit tales profundas materias in Anglicis, quae magis aptae erant laedere legentes et audientes quam illis proficere ... et ideo novum cimbolum magnum et longum in Anglicis verbis composuit*' (Thomas Gascoigne, *Loci e Libro Veritatum*, p. 213; cited in Hudson, *Lollards and their Books*, p. 160).

28 The memorandum is cited from Michael Sargent, ed., Love, *Mirror of the Blessed Life of Jesus Christ*, p. xlv. See further Sargent's detailed discussion of 'The Anti-Wycliffite Stance of *The Mirror of the Blessed Life of Jesus Christ*', ibid., pp. xliv–lviii.

29 Janet Coleman, *English Literature in History 1350–1400*, pp. 233–5, 253–6,

offers further comment on Langland's attempt to adapt English for discussion of theological and scholastic matters, previously restricted to Latin. One such discussion, cited by Coleman, prompts the listener within the poem to remark on the other speaker's language: 'Englisch was it nevere' (p. 254).

30 Quotations are taken from the B-text. There are numerous comparable passages that move freely between English and Latin. Two that spring to mind are the move into Latin to expand on the figure of Piers himself ('Piers the Plowman, *Petrus id est christus*', xv.212) and the description of the crucifixion, which renders each moment of direct speech in Latin ('*O mors ero mors tua... Crucifige! ... Tolle, tolle! ... Ave, raby... Consummatum est*', xviii.35–57).

31 This is a recurrent opposition in the poem, but is particularly clearly expressed in the discussion between Study and the Dreamer in Passus x and in Imaginatyf's teaching in Passus xii.

32 References to cycle plays throughout the book are given in the form of play number followed by line numbers.

33 The phrase is David Lawton's ('Voice, Authority, and Blasphemy', p. 98). Lawton also makes the parallel below with Kempe's glossing of the Latin text. For Lawton, this evidence suggests that Kempe was herself both literate and Latinate, despite her claim to illiteracy. The evidence of learning and Latinity in *The Book of Margery Kempe* could of course be the result of scribal mediation, but Lawton is dismissive of this possibility. See further John Hirsh, 'Author and Scribe in *The Book of Margery Kempe*', Lyn Staley Johnson, 'The Trope of the Scribe', and Dillon, 'The Making of Desire in *The Book of Margery Kempe*'.

34 Not only does the incident record a member of the laity offering an interpretation of scripture, but that layperson is also a woman, and Lollards were known for encouraging women to teach and preach, against the prohibitions of the orthodox church.

35 See also Julia Bolton Holloway's ('Crosses and Boxes') discussion of the gendering of Latin as the Vatersprache and the vernacular as mother-tongue, and cf. Walter J. Ong, 'Latin Language Study'.

36 Margreta de Grazia notes that this was also the Elizabethan etymology for the word 'babble' ('Babbling Will in *Shake-speares Sonnets*', p. 121).

37 Again, there may be an influence here from Langland, whose dreamer is 'yrobed in russet' (xi.1; the phrase also occurs in the A and C texts). See further Pamela Gradon, 'Langland and the Ideology of Dissent'.

38 On the question of relations between *Piers Plowman* and Wyclifite thought, see Gradon, 'Langland and the Ideology of Dissent' and Hudson, *The Premature Reformation*, pp. 398–408. As both point out, it was still possible at this time to put forward ideas which might have been shared by Wyclif without embracing wholesale heresy. Later generations, however, unable to date the poem so precisely, assumed Langland to have been, as John Bale puts it, '*ex primis Iohannis Wiclevi*

discipulis' (one of John Wyclif's first disciples) (Gradon, 'Langland and the Ideology of Dissent', p. 179).

39 Both Walsingham and Knighton refer to this letter, which is reprinted in full in Kenneth Sisam, *Fourteenth Century Verse and Prose*, pp. 160–1.

2 STAGING TRUTH

1 Although a general notion of the cycles as popular drama seems hard to dislodge, earlier scholars did not in fact so simplify it themselves. V. A. Kolve, for example, is cited (e.g. Staines, 'The English Mystery Cycles', p. 93) as saying that 'the cycles addressed themselves above all to the unlettered and the un-Latined' (Kolve, *The Play Called Corpus Christi*, p. 3); but Kolve in fact goes on to note that 'they work at several levels, speaking to a heterogeneous assembly', citing the Chester *Judgement*'s direct address to the clergy and N-Town's self-consciousness about its different functions as teacher to the unlearned and preacher to the learned (p. 4). He even specifically warns against the dangers of a reductive view: 'we must forgo thinking of the drama as addressed only to simple, unlettered men. Its true use was to all Christians, whatever their theological learning' (p. 5).

2 There is evidence to indicate that the N-Town cycle was not initially composed as a cycle, but put together from separate plays: the Mary Play, the Passion Play and so on. Alan J. Fletcher, 'The N-Town Plays', suggests Thetford as an alternative to Bury St Edmunds for the source of the N-Town compilation.

3 Paul Whitfield White (*Protestantism, Patronage and Playing*, pp. 19–20) makes this suggestion, pointing out that Bale was not the only writer of interludes to emerge from a monastic background, and noting further connections between the Carmelites and civic drama.

4 Though Latin is adopted simply as the customary language of stage directions, so that its use in this context is primarily functional, its presence nevertheless suggests clerical authorship by virtue of the old equation between Latinity and clerical training. While a small fraction of the non-clerical populace was Latinate, it is still statistically more likely, even in the fifteenth century, that those capable of employing Latin were themselves in clerical orders.

5 William Tydeman translates this phrase as 'both for the common people and the literate'. While this is certainly a possible correct translation, it ignores the more commonly understood meaning of this frequent pairing: 'laity and clergy'. The extent to which literacy was understood to be bound up with clerical status in the medieval period is discussed in chapter 1 above.

6 For explanations of the development and performance of this trope see e.g. Glynne Wickham, *Medieval Theatre*, pp. 30–40 and John Wesley Harris, *Medieval Theatre in Context*, pp. 27–31.

7 Anne Hudson notes that it is not a subject that seems to have attracted much attention from the Lollards. She includes it, she writes, 'not because of its representative nature in the movement, but because it has attracted modern discussion as an unusual contemporary criticism of the plays' (*Selections from English Wycliffite Writings*, p. 187). Marianne Briscoe, ('Some Clerical Notions of Dramatic Decorum') notes Rosemary Woolf's suggestion that the *Tretise* may represent a now lost body of polemic concerning the merits of drama, and calls attention to other clerics' views on the subject (William Melton, Reginald Pecock, Alexander Carpenter).

8 I refer to Stephen Spector's edition for the EETS (1992), from which quotations are also taken. References, both to this cycle and to the Wakefield cycle, cite play number, followed, where relevant, by line number.

9 What Catherine Dunn actually says about English is that it 'is still in an experimental stage of the alliterative poetic revival (perhaps about 1375)' ('The Literary Style of the Towneley Plays', p. 489). The manuscript, of course, does not date back to the fourteenth century, but to the late fifteenth century, or even the early sixteenth century (Cawley and Stevens, ed., *The Towneley Cycle*, p. ix and n.19). Dunn was perhaps thinking in terms of earliest possible performance dates, without properly acknowledging the gap between early performance and extant manuscript evidence. Nevertheless, her general point about the 'difference in elevation' remains valid.

10 Dunn is particularly interested in Sepet's *Origines catholiques de théâtre moderne* (Paris: L. Lethielleux, 1901), and has developed these ideas over a number of articles. See further her 'Voice Structure in the Liturgical Drama: Sepet Reconsidered', and the other pieces of her own she lists in note 42 (p. 54) of that article.

11 Gail Gibson notes the absence of any critical attention to Contemplacio as 'the personification of contemplation in the technical sense of monastic prayer and withdrawal' rather than an ' "exposytour in doctorys wedes" ' (*The Theater of Devotion*, p. 128). I think this distinction is less absolute than Gibson suggests. While the naming and costuming of Contemplacio may identify him closely with monasticism, thus making him more specific than the classic Doctor or Expositor, his role nevertheless continues to include an expository function. Gibson's comments on the figure of Contemplacio (pp. 128–31) are, however, both illuminating in themselves and a persuasive part of her general argument for the play's monastic auspices.

12 Dunn also sees in this 'language of static reference' a gesturing towards a higher reality. She describes this reality as 'the subjects or themes talked about – perhaps we can say, the reality imitated by the speech' ('The Literary Style of the Towneley Plays', p. 484).

13 Elizabeth Salter, however, rightly refuses to name this as 'realism'. As

she argues, we have no way of knowing 'whether the new shepherd materials are part of a total plan, possessing a sacred, symbolic significance, or whether they reveal artistic inventiveness running riot' (*English and International*, p. 288).

14 Cf. the Chester shepherds (*The Chester Mystery Cycle*, 7: lines 376–407), though the episode is differently developed there.

15 Cf. the miraculous powers of understanding granted to the German priest in *The Book of Margery Kempe* (p. 24 above).

16 Gail Gibson discusses this contrast at more length, and links it to the recurrent concern of the N-Town cycle with learning itself (*The Theater of Devotion*, pp. 131–2). Martin Stevens, in his discussion of the cycle's concern with learning (*Four Middle English Mystery Cycles*, pp. 213–20), goes on to make the crucial point that the child Mary is characterised as a prodigious scholar in this cycle, and that her scholarship must be understood as true learning, by comparison with the false learning of the doctors. Nevertheless, her access to God's wisdom, as Stevens points out, is also expressed through the 'obtrusive Latinisms' (p. 219) of her language.

17 Stevens, in a study limited to the plays of the Wakefield Master, suggests Wyclifite authorship ('Language as Theme in the Wakefield Plays', p. 105; cf. *Four Middle English Mystery Cycles*, p. 163), whereas Lauren Lepow (*Enacting the Sacrament*), more on the basis of the cycle's treatment of the sacraments than its linguistic concerns, argues for its counter-Lollard intention and effect.

18 While I am in sympathy with Martin Stevens' rejection of the designation 'Wakefield Master' on the grounds of its embedded critical judgement ('Language as Theme in the Wakefield Plays', p. 100), I find his phrase 'Wakefield Author' too ambiguous for use in a discussion of the whole cycle as opposed to only those pageants usually attributed to a specific author.

19 Stevens has moved to this position himself in his more recent work (*Four Middle English Mystery Cycles*, p. 158).

20 For a comparison of all the extant English shepherds' plays see Rosemary Woolf, *The English Mystery Plays*, pp. 182–93.

21 'Weme!' and 'tord!' are expressions of impatience.

22 N-Town stage directions are very explicit about costume, and Annas and Cayphas use words like 'prelat' and 'primat' to describe their own status (26: lines 165, 209). At one point a stage direction directs the council house to 'sodeynly onclose schewyng the buschopys, prestys and jewgys syttyng in here astat lych as it were a convocacyon' (27: line 76).

23 In fact Christ speaks Latin only twice in this cycle: once when he heals the soldier whose ear is cut off by Peter ('*In nomine patris*, hole thou be!' (20: line 715)) and again in the Harrowing of Hell, when he utters the familiar command to open the gates: '*Attollite portas, principes, vestras et elevamini porte eternales, et introibit rex glorie*' (25: lines 121, 189).

24 Stevens cites a much fuller list of the play's nouns of agency denoting misusers of language (*Four Middle English Mystery Cycles*, p. 163).

25 The first of the two lines of Latin translates quite straightforwardly: 'Tutivillus collects the fragments of their words', but the second seems to degenerate into nonsense. Stevens notes A. C. Cawley's suggestion that 'if *algorum* be interpreted as "of colds, fevers," then *belium doliorum* could mean "of belly aches" (with – *um* stuck onto the English *belly*, and with a comic play on the *beli* of *belial* and *belium*)' (Stevens, *Four Middle English Mystery Cycles*, pp. 164–5, n.75). This kind of pseudo-Latin, made by putting Latin endings on to English words can be paralleled elsewhere in medieval drama, most conspicuously in *Mankind* (see chapter 3 below). As so often with Latin in vernacular plays, the meaning is less important than the sound and its associations. Here the main function may be what Stevens calls 'diabolic litany' ('Language as Theme in the Wakefield Plays', p. 106), where the emphasis is on the fact of Latin and its rhyming chant, rather than on coherent content.

26 Robert Weimann's consideration of the Wakefield Master's plays in terms of their arrival at a dramatic form of plebeian self-awareness and self-representation leads him to see potential links with Lollard heresy from this angle of analysis too (*Shakespeare and the Popular Tradition*, pp. 92–3).

3 THE VOICE OF GOD

1 I reject the use of the word 'aureate' for this kind of English, since it implies stylistic elaboration for predominantly aesthetic reasons, which is not how I understand its dramatic use. On the use of different languages to identify different dramatic functions, see further Rainer Pineas, 'The English Morality Play', Robert Weimann, *Shakespeare and the Popular Tradition* and G. C. Britton, 'Language and Character in Some Late Medieval Plays'.

2 The names of these virtuous characters are a pointer to clerical costume in plays of this period, and dialogue often confirms their clerical status. To an audience, of course, their clerical status would be visible through costume from the character's first appearance. See T. W. Craik, *The Tudor Interlude*, pp. 55–6 and Robert Potter, *The English Morality Play*, p. 39). A character such as Imagination in *Hick Scorner*, who sits in the pub boasting of his sins, yet claiming that he and his friends are clerks, and will thus escape hanging by knowing their neck-verse (*Two Tudor Interludes*, line 266) seems to me likely to represent that class of men who had received the first tonsure but taken no steps towards ordination, and hence were not members of the practising clergy. They seem to have existed in some numbers, for reasons not now clear (R. N. Swanson, *Church and Society*, p. 41).

3 The transgressive pleasure of seeing virtue mocked is briefly discussed

in chapter 2 above (pp. 42, 49). This pleasure, I argue, creates the space for viewing virtue from a different and more sceptical angle, but does not actually question its status as virtue.

4 N. F. Blake (*Non-Standard Language*, p. 69) cites this example from Skelton, together with an example of Flemish speech from *Fulgens and Lucres*, but notes that although Skelton is clearly using French for comic effect, Medwall's use of Flemish indicates the difficulty of establishing the intended tone of foreign references in this earliest period of their appearance in English drama.

5 This belief also emerges in other heresy trials (John A. F. Thomson, *The Later Lollards*, pp. 39–40). See chapter 1 above for discussion of Lollard appropriation of the 'plain man' topos.

6 A less challenging, more formal, fixed, relationship between Latin and the vernacular can be observed, for example in *Youth*, where the virtuous figure of Charity maintains a much tighter division between the two languages, using Latin only to cite the word of God, and introducing each quotation with the distanciating formula, 'It is written'.

7 MED gives only the meaning 'idle talk' for 'dalliation', citing *Mankind* as the single source; but the word must be related to the verb 'dalien', for which MED documents the two contradictory meanings of talking politely, intimately, even frivolously, or, alternatively, seriously or solemnly. Lee Patterson has further suggested to me a submerged pun on the Latin term *dilatio* (or *dilatatio*), a technical term in preaching. For further discussion of the term see Patterson, ' "For the Wyves love of Bath" ', pp. 675–6 and n. 37.

8 Kathleen Ashley also notes that the metaphor of corn and chaff stands 'not merely for the worthy man and the sinner, but for the kind of words to which each gives his allegiance' ('Titivillus and the Battle of Words', p. 132).

9 Several critics have explored the parallel between Myscheffe and Mercy; see e.g. Mary Philippa Coogan, *An Interpretation of the Moral Play, Mankind*, pp. 64–5; Weimann, *Shakespeare and the Popular Tradition*, p. 117; Ashley, 'Titivillus and the Battle of Words', pp. 132–3.

10 The text is not translated in the play, but is, as G. A. Lester (*Three Late Medieval Morality Plays*) points out in his note to this line, very familiar from tombstones and adapted from Job 34.15.

11 For example, they describe 'Master Woode of Fullburn' as a *'noli me tangere'* (lines 511–12; John 20.17) and allude to death via the metonymic *'in manus tuas'* (line 515; Luke 23.46).

4 THE CONTROLLING STATE

1 The following account is largely indebted to F. F. Bruce, *History of the Bible in English*, A. G. Dickens, *The English Reformation* and S. L. Greenslade, *The Works of William Tindale*.

2 The quotation comes from a chapter that considers at more length the impact of the English bible on the class excluded from reading it by the 1543 statute.

3 Despite their attacks on glossing as getting in the way of plain scripture the Reformers also provided marginal glosses; and these glosses were often more inflammatory than the translations themselves. The struggle for 'possession' of the text is fought precisely in the margins (see further Evelyn Tribble, *Margins and Marginality*, ch.1).

4 Cf. Ritchie Kendall (*The Drama of Dissent*, p. 23), who argues that: 'Perhaps the failure of Lollardy stemmed not from the power of its enemies or the miscalculations of its leaders but from its premature vision of a Gutenberg galaxy, its worship of the written word in an age of handwritten texts and massive illiteracy.'

5 I am indebted throughout to Simon Shepherd's discussion of 'Language and Power', *Marlowe and the Politics of the Elizabethan Theatre*, ch.1.

6 J. W. Lever makes the important point that most of the connotations of the word 'state' challenged 'the traditional view of a divinely sanctioned order... it was a Renaissance coinage derived from the idiomatic Italian phrase *lo stato*, which might be rendered in our own idiom as "the set-up"' (*The Tragedy of State*, p. 6).

7 The wording of the Act may be consulted in *Statutes of the Realm*, vol. III, pp. 508–9. A. G. Dickens (*The English Reformation*, p. 122, n.18) cites the work of I. D. Thornley and G. R. Elton against such an interpretation of the Act, but it continues to be seen as a significant landmark. Freedom (or repression) of speech remained a focus of struggle between the state and its subjects. As Alan Smith points out (*The Emergence of a Nation State*, pp. 129–30), the question of free speech was central to the parliaments of 1566, 1576 and 1587, but no extension to the Commons' rights was granted, and Peter Wentworth was imprisoned for his disrespectful words about the queen. For a fuller discussion of how the controls of the Elizabethan state in particular may be exposed through contemporary linguistic theory and language use, see Shepherd, *Marlowe and the Politics of the Elizabethan Theatre*, esp. ch.1. Chapter 8 below discusses the language of treason in the sixteenth century and the tendency of later Tudor writers to regard linguistic ambiguity as socially and politically dangerous.

8 Colet preached the sermon in Latin. In the original language, this section reads: '*Infestamur etiam hoc tempore ab hereticis hominibus mira stulticia insanientibus*' (Archbishop Laud's copy, unpaged).

9 The quotation is from George Gifford's sermons on the Apocalypse, published in 1599 (Richard Bauckham, *Tudor Apocalypse*, p. 118).

10 The extract from Cranmer's preface is quoted by Evelyn Tribble within a fuller discussion of the Great Bible's attempt to produce 'a docile readership'. She draws attention to the pointing hand in the margin warning the reader of passages he must not dare to interpret without

official guidance and discusses the way Holbein's frontispiece presents an image of the circulation of the bible as one of orderly control from the top down (*Margins and Marginality,* pp. 24–6).

11 The question of dramatic censorship has been the subject of two recent books, by Janet Clare ('*Art Made Tongue-Tied by Authority*') and Richard Dutton (*Mastering the Revels*), but neither offers any discussion of this early period, which is much in need of fuller study. Norman Sanders summarises the legislation in *Revels,* vol. II, pp. 24–30.

12 The play in question was performed before Henry VIII in 1537 and aimed to teach him 'how he should rule his realm'. See further Greg Walker, *Plays of Persuasion,* pp. 31–2, who rightly stresses that the anxiety about it was due not to its content in any absolute sense, but to the presentation of that content before a popular audience in the period immediately following the Pilgrimage of Grace.

13 Paul White (*Protestantism, Patronage and Playing,* pp. 12–15) offers fuller discussion of Cromwell's exploitation of the stage as an ideological weapon, highlighting the point that, in turning to stage-plays, Cromwell was appropriating an ideological weapon from the Roman church. Richard Morison, cited on pp. 10–11 above as noting the power of this Catholic strategy, was Cromwell's secretary.

14 The first recorded use of the word 'protestant' in this generic sense, according to the OED, is in 1553, but later writers use it anachronistically of Lollards by way of asserting continuity with the past. The late Elizabethan play of *1 Sir John Oldcastle* (1599), for example, uses the term at scene ii, line 20.

15 Thora Blatt (*The Plays of John Bale*) reproduces the two pictures.

16 John Knott (*Discourses of Martyrdom*) also looks at Bale's work in his study of how prose texts 'dramatise' martyrdom, retelling them in terms of dialogue, ritual and stage directions.

17 References to Bale's plays throughout this chapter are to Peter Happé's edition, *The Complete Plays of John Bale.* As Walker demonstrates, Bale's use of the dramatic medium to parody the ritual of Catholic worship leads him to provide his non-Catholic figures with lines that virtually 'define [them] out of existence' by stressing the unrepresentability of what they represent (*Plays of Persuasion,* pp. 190–94).

18 For a discussion of dating see further Barry Adams' edition of *King Johan,* pp. 20–4. Adams demonstrates the flimsiness of Jesse Harris' argument for an earlier date of 1533–4. Both Adams and Happé take the B-text as the basis of their editions, much of which seems consonant with performance in 1538–9, despite the addition of later material, including the final stanzas thanking God for Queen Elizabeth, which cannot have been added before 1560 (Adams, ed., *King Johan,* pp. 6, 24). For a fuller discussion of the two texts and material specifically topical to the earlier date see Walker, *Plays of Persuasion,* pp. 170–8).

19 See e.g. Bale's *Three Laws.* The subject of the connotations of dialect

speech is too big to develop here. Suffice to say that dialect can be a hallmark of villainy, foolishness or plain-speaking honesty, and certain dialects are more readily associated with one character-type than the other. Any dialect that savours of foreignness is more likely to indicate an untrustworthy character in this period. See further chapters 6 and 7 below and N. F. Blake, *Non-Standard Language*. Blake also comments on the importance of dialect speech to the development of the Vice.

20 'Balle and his felowes', as most critics since J. H. P. Pafford have agreed, are almost certainly to be identifed with 'Lord Cromwell's players' (Pafford, ed., *King Johan*, p. xvii; White, *Protestantism, Patronage and Playing*, pp. 16–17; *Revels*, vol. ii, p. 114). Cromwell twice intervened to have Bale released after charges of heresy had been brought against him, and Bale's own account attributes Cromwell's intervention to his sympathy for Bale's plays ('*ob editas comoedias me semper liberavit*'; *Illustrum Maioris Britanniae Scriptorum Summarium*, cited Blatt, *The Plays of John Bale*, p. 13).

21 Though most critics accept the probability that the play performed on this occasion was Bale's *King John*, there must remain some doubt about this equation, as about the equation of 'Lord Cromwell's players' with Bale's company. See further Sydney Anglo, *Spectacle, Pageantry, and Early Tudor Policy*, pp. 268–9).

22 As David Kastan has argued, the play 'always threatens to collapse its fundamental opposition between godly rule and papal duplicity in the very condition of its enactment. If papal untruth is presented in terms of its manifest "ipocrysy" (432), its deceptive "serymonys and popetly plays" (415), the singular truth of John's proto-Protestantism can be maintained only by impossibly asserting it as something plain and immediate, as something unfeigned; that is, it can be maintained only by repressing the fact of the play itself' (' "Holy Wordes" ', p. 272; cf. Walker, *Plays of Persuasion*, pp. 190–4). Kastan quotes from Barry Adams' edition of the play, but line numbers here are the same as for Happé's edition.

23 See further Edwin Miller, 'The Roman Rite'. Rainer Pineas, however, rightly points out that Miller's analysis overlooks the importance of the way the force of the attack 'is derived from the fact that it is the papal characters themselves who are made to parody their own ritual' ('The English Morality Play', p. 175, n.35).

24 John Gunstone (*The Liturgy of Penance*, ch.8) analyses the Latin rite for private penance as given in its commonest form in the *Rituale Romanum*. Despite slight variation according to diocese, the rite was established in this form by the sixteenth century.

25 This point has been demonstrated at some length by other critics. See e.g. Kendall, *The Drama of Dissent*, pp. 97–101; Blatt, *The Plays of John Bale*, pp. 201–8. Interestingly, both critics point to ways in which Bale's writing undercuts his own ideal of plain style: Kendall shows that Bale's

prose is 'not so much plain as it is crude and brutal ... blunt, coarse, and anatomical' (*The Drama of Dissent*, pp. 99–100), while Blatt demonstrates Bale's indebtedness to classical and biblical Latin, pointing out that he probably knew the Vulgate better than Tyndale's English bible (*The Plays of John Bale*, pp. 193–8).

5 THE VALUE OF LEARNING

1 Truth does not in fact hand the bible directly to Elizabeth, according to Holinshed's account. She gives it to the child who speaks the verse that interprets the pageant, and he in turn hands it to Sir John Parrat, who passes it on to the queen.

2 My attention was drawn to the Venetian ambassador's account by David Bergeron (*English Civic Pageantry*, p. 20), who also offers a full description and discussion of the 1559 pageant in chapter 1 of his book.

3 Richard Bauckham notes this passage as the only exception he can find to a general ignoring of Queen Elizabeth in early apocalyptic works. Elizabeth, though seen as 'a noble conqueror of antichrist and his wicked kingdom' (Thomas Becon's words in 1564), was never identified as fulfilling apocalyptic prophecy in any more significant way until after the defeat of the Armada in 1588 (*Tudor Apocalypse*, pp. 128–30).

4 Foxe began by publishing, in Strasbourg in 1554, Latin versions of the stories of a few fifteenth- and sixteenth-century religious martyrs, and followed this with an expanded version published in Basle in 1559, including accounts of Marian martyrs that had reached him in the intervening period. The English edition of 1563 was twice the size of the Basle publication (William Haller, *Foxe's Book of Martyrs*, p. 13).

5 J. W. Martin (*Religious Radicals*, p. 80), however, draws attention to some continuity in Catholic use of the vernacular up to the mid-sixteenth century, noting in particular the example of Richard Whitforde's immensely popular *Work for Householders* of 1530 (eight editions by 1537; cf. Christopher Haigh, *English Reformations*, pp. 25–8) and chapter 4, p. 76 above). Martin discusses in another essay (*Religious Radicals*, ch.5) the more unusual case of Miles Hogarde, a hosier and a Catholic, who wrote in English on religious subjects in the mid-sixteenth century. There is no doubt, as Martin argues, that Hogarde's position was anomalous within his church, which did not approve of uneducated laymen contributing to the discussion of theological matters, far less publishing their views.

6 The technique appropriates in reverse the strategy of the Lollard *Examination of Master William Thorpe*, which was well known to Foxe, as it had been to Bale and Tyndale. In this autobiographical Latin account of a Lollard trial, special focus is given to the vernacular when it is made to irrupt into the Latin narrative. This is discussed more fully by Ritchie Kendall, *The Drama of Dissent*, pp. 58–67.

7 The first quotation is taken from the Lollard text, *The Lantern of Light* (ed. L. M. Swinburn, p. 33) while the case of the Whitechapel bricklayer is cited in Patrick Collinson, *The Birthpangs of Protestant England*, p. 38.

8 For fuller discussion of Foxe's debt to Bale see Leslie Fairfield, *John Bale*, chs.5 and 6, Bauckham, *Tudor Apocalypse*, ch.4 and John Knott, *Discourses of Martyrdom*, pp. 46–60.

9 The book's life was one of continued renewal and centrality until almost the end of the seventeenth century: two more editions were published in 1583 and 1587, another in 1596 after Foxe's death, and four more up to 1684.

10 We must beware, however, of assuming from the title 'free grammar school', that this degree of education usually cost nothing and was available to all classes (see David Cressy, 'Educational Opportunities'). Though the expansion of grammar school education in the Tudor period did broaden the social spread of literacy to include more gentry and merchants, the link between literacy and social status continued to be more significant than any general increase in literacy throughout the Tudor period. Keith Wrightson concludes that 'Educational expansion had produced not a literate society, but a hierarchy of illiteracy which faithfully mirrored the hierarchy of status and wealth' (*English Society*, p. 190; cf. Cressy, *Literacy and the Social Order*). The struggle for education, like the struggle for access to an English bible, was still a class struggle.

11 Though William Lily, the grammarian, was the grandfather of John Lyly, the dramatist, mentioned below, I have followed G. K. Hunter's practice (*John Lyly*) of retaining the most familiar spelling of each.

12 William Malim's statement of his school's policy on dramatic performance is, T. H. Vail Motter argues, 'undoubtedly a summary of the policy of his predecessors in office as well as a statement of his own practice', and Motter quotes from it extensively (*The School Drama in England*, pp. 50–1). Audiences for academic drama in various institutions, however, were not necessarily entirely composed of the academic community. See further chapter 6 below, esp. pp. 150–2.

13 The phrase is Hunter's (*John Lyly*, p. 229). Hunter points out that the absence of any mention of court performance on the title page of *Mother Bombie* makes it unlikely that it was ever played at court. He also first makes the suggestion that the difference between *Mother Bombie* and Lyly's other plays may be thought about in terms of putting the 'pert pages' at the centre (pp. 229–31).

14 This is not, of course, how scenes focusing on teaching and learning Latin functioned in the public theatres, where only a limited sector of the audience could identify with the experience of learning grammar.

15 I have left these lines untranslated here in order to convey the obviously intentional effect for a non-Latinate audience. The play itself goes on to translate them in the next verse as follows:

Emongs thy carfull busines use sume time mirth and joye
That no bodilye worke thy wytts breke or noye.   (lines 13–14)

The precept suggests that this play intends to prioritise entertainment over didactic value, though the play ends with a warning against deceivers like Jack Juggler.

16 William Tydeman does not mention her possible activity as a translator, but a fragment of Seneca's *Hercules Oetaeus* is attributed to her.

17 More detailed defences of the academic drama were published by John Case (in Latin) in 1585 and by William Gager (in English). Gager's defence was part of a correspondence with the Puritan John Rainolds, who wrote attacking the drama; it was written in 1592 and published in 1599 (see further ch.6, p. 147 below).

18 References to this play, together with *Lusty Juventus* and *The Disobedient Child*, are taken from John S. Farmer's edition of *The Dramatic Writings of Richard Wever and Thomas Ingelend*. This edition has no line numbers, so references are given in the form of page number only.

19 'Juggling', a word used scornfully by Cranmer as a term for transubstantiation, may have been intended to stand for the difficult logic of Catholic doctrine, perceived as excluding the laity from the capacity to engage in doctrinal dispute (see further Marie Axton, ed., *Three Tudor Classical Interludes*, pp. 19–20). The epilogue hints that 'this triflyng enterlud … May sygnifye sum further meaning if it be well serched' and warns that 'the fashyon of the worlde now a dayes' is to multiply subtle ways of deluding 'symple innosaintes' (lines 998–1006). ('Juggling', however, was not used only by Protestants as a term of abuse: for a comparison with Catholic use see chapter 8, note 8 below.) The fact that the epilogue is in direct contradiction with the prologue's assurance that the play does not deal with serious matters can be read in contradictory ways: either the disavowal of serious intent serves to alert the audience to look for a message or the epilogue is a later addition to the play (see e.g. Bruce Smith, *Ancient Scripts*, pp. 148–9 and David Bevington, *Tudor Drama*, pp. 124–6).

20 *The Disobedient Child* is a version of Ravisius Textor's Latin play, *Pater, Filius et Uxor*, and the portrayal of youth in all three plays is indebted to the New Comedic tradition as well as to the biblical story of the prodigal son.

21 I have emended Farmer's text here following comparison with the early printed text reproduced in the Tudor Facsimile Texts series. Farmer prints 'doth' for 'both' in the second line.

22 'Hoddypeak' means 'fool' or 'simpleton', possibly with particular application to learned fools. The OED cites Latimer using the term in 1549 alongside 'doddy poll', which it glosses in similar terms, but the phrase was especially familiar as a term of abuse for learned pedants. Cf. Free Will's mockery of Perseverance in *Hick Scorner*, p. 52 above.

23 The first words of the primer Matins are taken from Psalm 50 (51 in the Authorised Version). The English primer edited by William Maskell (*Monumenta Ritualia*) translates the phrase as 'Lord, thou schalt opyne myn lippis'. I have again emended Farmer's inconsistent punctuation of this phrase, which is consistently printed without any punctuation at all in the early printed text.

24 See also T. W. Craik, *The Tudor Interlude*, Richard Southern, *The Staging of Plays Before Shakespeare* and Suzanne Westfall, *Patrons and Performance* for further discussion of potential audiences and performance locations for semi-professional and household troupes.

25 The three plays discussed earlier in the chapter also have prologues which pronounce on truths from outside the playworld, but they do not share the heavily Latinate discourse of Mercy and the Prologue to *The Longer thou Livest*.

26 This disruptive, topsy-turvy mode is characteristic of the Vice, with whom Moros thus aligns himself through this linguistic strategy. Cf. the stage direction in Thomas Lupton's *All for Money* (1559–77) which reads: 'Here the vyce shall turne the proclamation to some contrarie sence at everie time All For Money hath read it' (p. 147). Inversion is the Vice's typical response to the other speaker's discourse.

27 This is another jibe at the Catholic church, which attempted to claim superiority over the Protestant church by virtue of chronological priority – cf. p. 84 above.

28 OED does not suggest that 'testament' is normally used for any kind of book. Standing alone, it usually indicates the New Testament as distinct from the Old. Perhaps the play, like Foxe's *Book of Martyrs*, deliberately attempts to collapse the distinction between learning generally and specifically sacred learning. Foxe's stories, cited earlier in the chapter, of illiterate men and women both using the New Testament in order to learn to read and learning to read in order to read the New Testament suggest how inseparable for Protestants was education from education in the faith.

29 I am grateful to Richard Winton and colleagues in the Department of Classics at Nottingham University for discussion of the possible translations of this line.

6 SHAPING A RHETORIC

1 Walter J. Ong ('Latin Language Study') discusses the grammar school education of the Renaissance as a male rite of passage designed to initiate adolescent boys into a code of maleness via a language from which women are excluded. As Peter Womack has pointed out, however, Ong does not comment on the fact that his thesis neatly punctures the humanist claim to universality. Latin, accorded an ideologically central place in Renaissance culture, masquerades as

reason itself. 'What Ong's insight reveals, therefore, is that classical culture in this institutional context is a contradictory sign, on the one hand representing a universal humanism, but on the other constituting male difference' (*Ben Jonson*, p. 122).

2 The debate has been documented in great detail by R. F. Jones (*The Triumph of the English Language*, to whom the following account is indebted.

3 The term was used by Percival Wilburn in 1581 (Patrick Collinson, *The Elizabethan Puritan Movement*, p. 27).

4 See also, however, Margot Heinemann's warning against assuming too automatic a link between Puritanism and hostility to the theatre (*Puritanism and Theatre*, pp. 26–31).

5 Many critics remark on this change. Peter Burke notes its crucial and lasting significance for popular culture. It is, he argues, no mere episode, but rather the articulation of 'a major shift in religious mentality or sensibility' (*Popular Culture in Early Modern Europe*, p. 212).

6 On these gatherings see further e.g. Collinson, *The Elizabethan Puritan Movement*, especially Part Four, chs.2, 5 and 6.

7 For an account of this work see J. W. Binns, *Intellectual Culture*.

8 Despite Mulcaster's published enthusiasm for adopting English as the language of instruction in schools, he may well have used dramatic performance in the traditional way, to improve his boys' command of spoken Latin. His scholars performed at court as well as in the Merchant Taylors' Hall, and may, like the Eton boys, have been accustomed to perform in different languages as well as different locations.

9 This dating of *The Spanish Tragedy* is J. R. Mulryne's. There is no good reason to limit dating to the narrower range of 1585–9 suggested in Harbage's *Annals*.

10 Chapter 7 below is devoted to a discussion of the functioning of foreign vernaculars in English plays, but the focus there is on anti-alien feeling. The effect in *Orlando* considered here, together with the parallel instances that follow, belong more naturally to the context of this chapter, even though the fact that foreign vernaculars can be made to express madness is potentially linked with anti-alien feeling.

11 Quotation from *Antonio and Mellida* is taken from the Revels series edition by Reavley Gair.

12 Quotations are taken from Philip Edwards' edition.

13 Analogies with musical form are recurrent in criticism of the play, and appropriately so. Michael Hattaway (*Elizabethan Popular Theatre*) uses operatic terminology to illuminate potential performance effects, and Jonas Barish suggests that certain speeches 'perhaps, should be spoken like incantations' ('*The Spanish Tragedy*', p. 72). Barish also notes (p. 68) that two of these three names are in fact added by Kyd to the account of the underworld he borrows from Virgil.

14 The Latin speech incorporates stage directions at these points: first, in the statement that the peoples '*curvato poplite... / Succumbunt*' ('sink to

the ground on bended knee'); and second, in the line: '*Qui iacet in terra non habet unde cadat*' ('He who lies on the ground has no further to fall').

15 Hattaway also compares the Latin tags with Brecht's captions, in their capacity 'to turn image to emblem' (*Elizabethan Popular Theatre*, p. 109).

16 The phrase is Barish's ('*The Spanish Tragedy*', p. 69). Although Barish does not discuss the effects of Latin verse in this scene, he gives a full analysis of how the account of battle is formalised into symmetrical patterns by the rhetoric of the description. 'Turmoil and hubbub', as he says, 'are rendered with a certain pictorial sharpness of outline by the antithetic rhetoric, as in a tapestry, while the free play of detail helps keep the symmetries unobtrusive' (p. 70).

17 The phrases are J. R. Mulryne's (ed., *The Spanish Tragedy*, pp. xxvii, 69). Mulryne is defending the play against those who would condemn it for these qualities, but his terms of reference are apologetic, still trying to contain the play within the frame of that kind of judgement. Such defences are more damaging in their effects than straightforward attack. Barish's seminal essay ('*The Spanish Tragedy*') remains one of few attempts to assess the play in terms of the pleasures it offers rather than in terms of failed naturalism.

7 ENGLISH AND ALIEN

1 The St Bartholomew Massacre was widely perceived as 'the first step in a concerted catholic action against all protestant countries' (G. R. Elton, *England Under the Tudors*, p. 304). This kind of suspicion illustrates the tendency to collapse racial and religious differences together. Even English Catholics could be considered 'foreign' by virtue of their treasonous position with regard to the English Protestant state.

2 Although not relevant to the context of this play, it is equally the case that Germanic languages would be likely to be heard by an English audience unfamiliar with them as collapsing into one another, but distinctly different from Latin.

3 For further discussion of stage foreigners see e.g. Wilson Clough, 'The Broken English of Foreign Characters', G. K. Hunter, *Dramatic Identities*, ch.1, Marlene Santos, 'Theatre for Tudor England' and A. J. Hoenselaars, 'Broken Images', *Images of Englishmen* and 'Reconstructing Babel'. Santos notes that the figure of the Vice is often polyglot in earlier drama and often either a traveller and/or of foreign origin ('Theatre for Tudor England', pp. 217, 261, 361). Hunter and Hoenselaars take a curiously benevolent view of the presentation of foreigners in Elizabethan drama. Discussing *Englishmen for My Money* (considered here below), for example, Hunter argues that the foreignness of the suitors is a matter of 'local colour' rather than 'moral structure' (*Dramatic Identities*, p. 16), while Hoenselaars argues similarly that the broken English of the suitors has no negative implications, and serves only to increase comic effect (*Images*

of Englishmen, p. 56; cf. 'Reconstructing Babel', p. 473). In my view comedy and local effects cannot be separated from function in this way. The comedy is straightforwardly racist.

4 Santos ('Theatre for Tudor England') notes that the only good foreigner to emerge from a reading of English interludes is Wilson's Gerontus, who is a Turkish Jew (but not a 'Turk'; not only does this term function as a religious category in the play, but presumably an English audience also made a clear racial distinction between Jewish and Turkish).

5 'Scrupulous' in this period most commonly means 'meticulous in moral matters'; yet its coupling with 'fantastical' here in a context that clearly refers to stylistic rather than moral choice would seem to place it as an early example of the sense 'minutely exact or careful', which the OED records as first occurring in 1638. It clearly has negative force here, implying over-fastidiousness, precisianism (rather in the way that 'precise' is used with negative force against Puritans in this period).

6 Wilson Clough cites figures from census reports to demonstrate the increased numbers of foreigners in London between 1567 and 1580. Netherlanders remain the largest single group, while French numbers increase more dramatically than any other, due to Huguenot refugees ('The Broken English of Foreign Characters', p. 256). Susan Brigden (*London and the Reformation*, p. 136) estimates that there were five or six thousand aliens in London by the middle of the sixteenth century, though their tendency to cluster in ghettos made the number look more than it was. Ian Archer, citing Roger Finlay, confirms a total of about 5,000 for the later sixteenth century, a figure representing about 4–5 per cent of the total city population (*The Pursuit of Stability*, p. 132). Further information in this paragraph is indebted to Valerie Pearl, *London and the Outbreak of the Puritan Revolution* and 'Change and Stability'; Steve Rappaport, 'Social Structure and Mobility', and *Worlds Within Worlds*, pp. 42–60; and Ian Archer, *The Pursuit of Stability*, pp. 131–40. It should be noted that 'foreigners', in Elizabethan usage, are usually inhabitants of London who were born in England but are not free of the city (i.e. not part of the company structure), while the words 'stranger' or 'alien' are used to refer to immigrants from abroad. Though the terms are sometimes used interchangeably, the distinction between the two unfree sectors of the London population was important to contemporaries (Rappaport, *Worlds Within Worlds*, p. 42; cf. Archer, *The Pursuit of Stability*, pp. 131–2).

7 Puttenham's slipping in of a matter of national concern bears comparison with Thomas Wilson's strategy in *The Arte of Rhetorique*, as discussed by Andrew Hadfield (*Literature, Politics and National Identity*, ch.4). 'What seems peripheral – the example of England – ', Hadfield argues, 'is really the central concern of *The Arte of Rhetorique*' (p. 108).

8 This dating refers to the extant revision of the play. The *Annals* dates the original version to *c*.1590–3; and the play's most recent editors (Vittorio

Gabrieli and Giorgio Melchiori) concur with Scott McMillin (*The Elizabethan Theatre*) in dating the first composition to no later than 1593. The riots of 1592–3 (discussed further below in this chapter) increase the probability that the play should be dated within these specific and narrower parameters.

9 A contemporary account of a riot by apprentices at a play in Southwark on 11 June 1592 attributes it to the imprisonment without cause of a feltmaker's servant (G. B. Harrison, *An Elizabethan Journal*, p. 138, citing the *Remembrancia*). Scott McMillin argues for its association with anti-alien feeling (*The Elizabethan Theatre*, pp. 67–72).

10 Roger Manning explains that the term 'apprentices' was used loosely by contemporaries, and might include servants, vagrants and discharged soldiers and sailors as well as different classes of apprentices (*Village Revolts*, pp. 191–4).

11 I here follow W. W. Greg's dating, which seems to me more plausible than the very early dating (1561 to *c.*1563) of Harbage's *Annals*.

12 Wilson is not the first dramatist to make this point. William Wager makes the same accusation in *Enough is as Good as a Feast* (lines 985–8).

13 Though most of the liberties lay outside the walls, the largest alien settlements were located in the liberties of Blackfriars and St Martin le Grand, just inside the western end of the city wall (Rappaport, *Worlds Within Worlds*, pp. 42–3).

14 On the subject of riot versus stability in sixteenth- and seventeenth-century London, see further Robert Ashton, 'Popular Entertainment', Frank Foster, *The Politics of Stability*, K. J. Lindley, 'Riot Prevention and Control' and Valerie Pearl, 'Change and Stability' and 'Social Policy'.

15 Critics who discuss Elizabethan responses to black or coloured races include Emily Bartels (*Spectacles of Strangeness*), Elliot Tokson (*The Popular Image of the Black Man*) and Peter Hulme (*Colonial Encounters*). John Gillies' work on 'the new geography', *Shakespeare and the Geography of Difference*, is also relevant here.

16 I am conscious of crossing over the chronological borders of my own study here in order to compare the relative stages of awareness in the 1590s and the first decade of Jacobean rule.

17 As Andrew Gurr points out in his New Cambridge edition of the play, Holinshed mentions that sixteen hundred Irishmen fought with the English at the siege of Rouen after Agincourt and records a Scottish James in Henry's company after Agincourt, though he was not a captain but a king (James I, who had been in captivity in England from the age of 11 and had already fought for Henry on several occasions; see further Gurr, ed., *Henry V*, Appendix 2). Wales had been united with England during the reign of Henry VIII.

18 Fluellen, whose speech heading is given by name before and after this point, is called 'Welch' from Act III, scene ii, line 68 to the end of the scene, while the other two speech headings are 'Scot' and 'Irish'

throughout the scene. Neither the Scot nor the Irishman appears in the Quarto text.

19 Philip Edwards offers a rather different reading of these lines (*Threshold of a Nation*, pp. 75–6). I cannot agree, however, with his contention that 'the idea of "Britain" was one of the major enthusiasms of Englishmen, and some Welshmen and some Scotsmen, in Tudor and Stuart times' (p. 74). The resistance of the English parliament to King James' attempts to impose the title of Great Britain on the realm is sufficient evidence of English lack of enthusiasm.

20 After writing this chapter I was sent Lisa Jardine's *Reading Shakespeare Historically* for review and found that her introduction shares many of the concerns outlined here and also concentrates on the scenes with the French princess. Jardine makes two historical points in particular that seem to me to shed light on the issues of this chapter, both important for the play's anxieties around masculinity and national identity: first, that tensions around the contradiction between lineage and conquest would not have seemed strange 'to a public whose cultural memory included the strain of the marriage of Mary Tudor to Philip of Spain, and anxiety over the (unsuccessful) courtship of Elizabeth by the French Duke d'Anjou' (p. 10); and secondly, that Henry's claim to France rests in the play (and rested historically) 'precisely on the *impurity* of his blood' (p. 13). Jardine's account in this same essay of the importance of the 'indeterminacy' of texts, and how 'our own historical moment presses us to choose as the subject of our conversation [with texts] topics which have only now once again come into cultural view, after a period of occlusion' (p. 7) offers the best explanation for how this overlap between contemporary critics occurs, an overlap which Jardine also acknowledges in her own work (e.g. ch.2, n.172).

21 This passage from Philip Stubbes is quoted by Jean-Christophe Agnew (*Worlds Apart*), to whose fuller consideration of this issue my brief discussion is indebted.

22 S. F. Johnson ('*The Spanish Tragedy*', pp. 23–4) cites the reservations of Muriel Bradbrook and Philip Edwards, and Edwards cites the view of P. W. Biesterfeldt before him as parallel to his own view of how the playlet was staged (*The Spanish Tragedy*, ed., p. xxxvii).

23 Anecdotal reports of the 1982 Cottesloe revival at the National Theatre, London suggest that audiences then were similarly stunned by Hieronimo's play and deaf to the reasoned explanation he offers after it. Sheldon Zitner notes that only two reviewers mentioned that the play was performed in different languages, and that some of his own colleagues were 'oddly unable to remember whether the playlet had been translated into English' ('*The Spanish Tragedy*', p. 89). For further accounts of the effect of this moment in the 1982 production see Elizabeth Maslen, 'The Dynamics of Kyd's "Spanish Tragedy"' and Richard Proudfoot, 'Kyd's *Spanish Tragedy*'.

8 REBELS AND OUTCASTS

1 A. L. Beier (*Masterless Men*) and Roger Manning (*Village Revolts*) both discuss numbers and conclude that, though the estimates of contemporaries are 'nearly worthless' (Beier, *Masterless Men*, p. 14), there was a demonstrable and alarming growth in the number of vagrants. See also Ian Archer, *The Pursuit of Stability*, pp. 204–15, on the problems of using the available sources. Literary sources, as he points out, are influenced by literary tradition, which should lead historians to be suspicious of using them as documentary evidence.

2 'Cunning' men and women were popular healers, often charlatans, of course, and clearly overlapping with witches. It is well known, however, that accusations of witchcraft, as Reginald Scot points out, tend to be levelled at women of a certain type, and only much more rarely at men.

3 The quotation is taken from Herford and Simpson's edition of the Quarto of 1601, which is presumably closer to what was played in 1598 than Jonson's revision of the play for the Folio of 1616. All subsequent quotations from Jonson's plays are from Herford and Simpson's edition.

4 The occasion was a commission of inquiry set up to investigate allegations of heresy in the county of Dorset.

5 The very language used to express this recognition of eloquence as powerful and controlling conveys the deeply rooted nature of the link between speech and control. The Latin word *fascinum* (a magic charm) is cognate with *fascere* (to bind), while the ancients believed that *lingua* (tongue, language) derived from *ligare* (to bind) (Neil Rhodes, *The Power of Eloquence*, p. 7).

6 Edward Pechter, citing this story, describes the invocations as 'perhaps the dirtiest words imaginable in Marlowe's culture, and though they are uttered in the play ... not sanitized by that context' (*What Was Shakespeare*, p. 92).

7 This paragraph is indebted to Rupert Taylor (*The Political Prophecy*) and Sharon Jansen (*Political Protest*). See also Alistair Fox and John Guy, *Reassessing the Henrician Age*, ch.4, and Keith Thomas, *Religion and the Decline of Magic*, pp. 461–514.

8 The Jesuits are already noted by 1599 as 'too hardie aequivocators'. 'Equivocation', moreover, was already associated with religious difference. More accused Tyndale of 'juglinge, by equivocacion of thys worde church' (See OED, s.v. equivocation, equivocator).

9 This is the date assigned to the play by Stanley Wells and Gary Taylor (*William Shakespeare: A Textual Companion*). The *Riverside* chronology also dates the play to 1590–1.

10 Significant differences between the Quarto and Folio texts are noted where relevant.

11 The Simpcox story is not told by Hall, and Shakespeare could have found it in Grafton or Foxe. Holinshed's second edition ends by

referring the reader to Foxe for more detail on Duke Humphrey (Geoffrey Bullough, *Narrative and Dramatic Sources*, vol. III, p. 90; *Holinshed's Chronicles*, vol. III, p. 212).

12 The first English witchcraft statute was enacted in 1542 under Henry VIII, repealed in 1547, and not replaced until the act passed under Elizabeth in 1563. Prior to that witchcraft seems to have been treated as a branch of heresy, punishable by death after the statute *De heretico comburendo* of 1401 (see p. 14 above). On the subject of witchcraft legislation, see further Alan MacFarlane, *Witchcraft in Tudor and Stuart England*, ch.2.

13 The *Riverside* follows the Folio in printing 'Asmath', but this is almost certainly a misprint for 'Asnath'.

14 The *Riverside*, like the Folio, gives the speech-headings [George] Bevis and John Holland. Since these names are generally agreed to have been those of actors in the company, however, it seems inappropriate to use them as if they were characters' names. The point about these workmen is their anonymity. William Montgomery, editing the text for Wells and Taylor, calls them First and Second Rebel, but this is to pre-empt their discussion. I have simply labelled them First and Second Workman below.

15 Shakespeare conflated different historical sources, taking material from Hall's narrative of the Cade rebellion and weaving into it details mainly from either Holinshed's or Grafton's account of the 1381 Rising (Hall's chronicle does not cover this period). This scene is presumably expanded from Holinshed's remark that 'it was dangerous among them to be knowne for one that was lerned, and more dangerous, if any men [*sic*] were found with a penner and inkhorne at his side: for such seldome or never escaped from them with life' (*Hall's Chronicle*, vol. II, p. 746); and Holinshed was in turn following Walsingham (*Historia Anglicana*, vol. II, p. 308). Annabel Patterson's recent study of Holinshed's *Chronicles* mounts a persuasive argument in favour of Holinshed's 'populism' (*Reading Holinshed's Chronicles*, ch.8), though not everything she presents as Holinshed's additions originates with Holinshed (some of the material she rightly identifies as absent from Walsingham in Holinshed's description of the 1381 rising, for example, originates with Knighton). The 1381 rebellion became topical in 1590, when it formed part of a pageant in honour of the new Lord Mayor, John Allot, a fishmonger like William Walworth (the mayor of 1381 who had won honour by slaying the rebel Wat Tyler) (Geoffrey Bullough, *Narrative and Dramatic Sources*, vol. III, p. 91; the pageant is also reprinted by Bullough, pp. 133–8).

16 The detail concerning their fury against Latin grammar does not feature in Holinshed or Grafton.

17 No dialogue is recounted by Hall, who presents Lord Say's immediate execution as the result of Cade's anger towards his 'dilatorie ple' to be tried by his peers (*Hall's Chronicle*, p. 221).

Bibliography

EDITIONS OF PLAYS

Bale, John, The Complete Plays of, ed. Peter Happé (2 vols., Woodbridge: D. S. Brewer, 1985–6).

Bale, John, *King Johan,* ed. J. H. P. Pafford, MSR (1931).

King Johan, ed. Barry B. Adams (San Marino, California: Huntington Library, 1969).

Castle of Perseverance, The, see *Macro Plays, The,* ed. Mark Eccles.

Chester Mystery Cycle, The, ed. R. M. Lumiansky and David Mills, EETS, SS, 3 (1974).

Dekker, Thomas, The Dramatic Works of, ed. Fredson Bowers (4 vols., Cambridge: Cambridge University Press, 1953–61).

Disobedient Child, The, see *Wever and Ingelend.*

Edmund Ironside, MSR (1927).

Entertainments for Elizabeth I, see Wilson, Jean.

Four Elements, The, see *Rastell Plays, Three.*

Greene, Robert, The Plays and Poems of, ed. J. Churton Collins (2 vols., Oxford: Clarendon Press, 1905).

Haughton, William, *Englishmen for My Money,* MSR (1912).

Heywood, Thomas, The Dramatic Works of, ed. Richard Herne Shepherd (6 vols., London: John Pearson, 1874).

Hick Scorner, see *Tudor Interludes, Two.*

Ingelend, Thomas, see *Wever and Ingelend.*

Jack Juggler, see *Tudor Classical Interludes, Three.*

Jack Straw, The Life and Death of, MSR (1957).

Jonson, Ben, ed. C. H. Herford and Percy Simpson (12 vols., Oxford: Clarendon Press, 1925–52).

Jonson, Ben, *Epicoene,* ed. L. A. Beaurline (London: Edward Arnold, 1966).

Kyd, Thomas, *The Spanish Tragedy,* ed. Philip Edwards (London: Methuen, 1959).

The Spanish Tragedy, ed. J. R. Mulryne (London and Tonbridge: Ernest Benn, 1970).

Locrine, The Tragedy of, MSR (1908).

Lodge, Thomas, *The Wounds of Civil War*, MSR (1910).
Lupton, Thomas, *All For Money*, in *Three Centuries of Drama* (microfilm), ed. Henry W. Wells, *English 1500–1641*.
Lusty Juventus, see *Wever and Ingelend*.
Lyly, John, *Mother Bombie*, MSR (1939).
Macro Plays, The, ed. Mark Eccles, EETS, OS, 262 (1969).
Macro Plays, The, ed. David Bevington, Folger facsimiles, MS series 1 (New York: Johnson Reprint Corporation, 1972).
Magnificence, see *Morality Plays, Four*.
Mankind, see *Macro Plays, The*, ed. Mark Eccles.
Marlowe, Christopher, *The Complete Works of*, ed. Fredson Bowers, 2nd edn, (2 vols., Cambridge: Cambridge University Press, 1981).
Marston, John, *Antonio and Mellida*, ed. W. Reavley Gair (Manchester and New York: Manchester University Press, 1991).
Medieval Drama, ed. David Bevington (Boston, Mass.: Houghton Mifflin, 1975).
Morality Plays, Four, ed. Peter Happé (Harmondsworth: Penguin, 1979).
Morality Plays, Three Late Medieval, ed. G. A. Lester (London and New York: Ernest Benn, 1981).
More, Sir Thomas, see Munday, Anthony, and others, ed. Gabrieli and Melchiori.
Munday, Anthony, and others, *Sir John Oldcastle Part 1*, in *The Oldcastle Controversy*, ed. Peter Corbin and Douglas Sedge (Manchester and New York: Manchester University Press, 1991).
  Sir Thomas More, ed. Vittorio Gabrieli and Giorgio Melchiori (Manchester and New York: Manchester University Press, 1990).
Nice Wanton, see *Wever and Ingelend*.
N-Town Play, The, ed. Stephen Spector, 2 vols., EETS, SS, 11 (1991).
Oldcastle, Sir John, Part I, see Munday, Anthony, and others, ed. Corbin and Sedge.
Orlando Furioso, see *Greene, Robert, The Plays and Poems of*.
Peele, George, *Edward I*, MSR (1911).
Rastell Plays, Three, ed. Richard Axton (Cambridge and Totowa, NJ: D. S. Brewer, Rowman and Littlefield, 1979).
Select Collection of Old English Plays, A, ed. Robert Dodsley, 4th edn ed. W. Carew Hazlitt (15 vols., London: Reeves and Turner, 1874–6).
Shakespeare, The Riverside, ed. G. Blakemore Evans et al. (Boston: Houghton Mifflin, 1974).
Shakespeare, William: The Complete Works, ed. Stanley Wells and Gary Taylor (Oxford: Clarendon Press, 1988).
Shakespeare, William, *Henry V*, ed. Andrew Gurr (Cambridge: Cambridge University Press, 1992).
  Henry VI, Part Two, ed. Arthur Freeman in *Henry VI, Part One, Henry VI, Part Two, Henry VI, Part Three* (1963, reprinted New York and Markham, Ontario: Penguin Books Canada, 1989).

The First Part of the Contention: The First Quarto, facsimile reproduction (London: C. Praetorius, 1889).

Towneley Plays, The, ed. Martin Stevens and A. C. Cawley, 2 vols., EETS, SS, 13, 14 (1994).

Towneley Cycle, The: A Facsimile of Huntington MS HM 1, introd. A. C. Cawley and Martin Stevens (Leeds: University of Leeds School of English, 1976).

Tudor Classical Interludes, Three, ed. Marie Axton (Woodbridge and Totowa, NJ: Boydell and Brewer, Rowman and Littlefield, 1982).

Tudor Interludes, Two, ed. Ian Lancashire (Manchester and Baltimore: Manchester University Press and Johns Hopkins University Press, 1980).

Tudor Tragedies, Two, ed. William Tydeman (Harmondsworth: Penguin, 1992).

Wager, William, *The Longer Thou Livest and Enough Is As Good As a Feast*, ed. R. Mark Benbow (reprinted London: Edward Arnold, 1968).

Wakefield Cycle, see *Towneley Plays, The.*

Weakest Goeth to the Wall, The, ed. Jill L. Levenson (New York and London: Garland, 1980).

Wever, Richard and Thomas Ingelend, The Dramatic Writings of, ed. John S. Farmer (1905, reprinted Guildford: Charles W. Traylen, 1966).

Wilson, Jean, *Entertainments for Elizabeth I* (Woodbridge and Totowa, NJ: D. S. Brewer, Rowman and Littlefield, 1980).

Wilson, Robert, *The Pedlar's Prophecy*, MSR (1914).

Three Ladies of London, see *A Select Collection of Old English Plays*, vol. VI.

Three Lords and Three Ladies of London, see *A Select Collection of Old English Plays*, vol. VI.

Youth, see *Tudor Interludes, Two.*

SECONDARY AND NON-DRAMATIC WORKS

Adams, Barry B., see Bale, John, *King Johan.*

Aers, David, *Culture and History 1350–1600: Essays on English Communities, Identities and Writing* (Hemel Hempstead: Harvester Wheatsheaf, 1992).

Agnew, Jean-Christophe, (*Worlds Apart: The Market and the Theater in Anglo-American Thought 1550–1750* (Cambridge: Cambridge University Press, 1986).

Anglo, Sydney, 'An Early Tudor Programme for Plays and Other Demonstrations Against the Pope', *Journal of the Warburg and Courtauld Institutes* 20 (1957), pp. 176–9.

Spectacle, Pageantry, and Early Tudor Policy (Oxford: Clarendon Press, 1969).

Archer, Ian W., *The Pursuit of Stability: Social Relations in Elizabethan London* (Cambridge: Cambridge University Press, 1991).

Ardolino, Frank, '"Now Shall I See the Fall of Babylon": *The Spanish Tragedy*', *Shakespeare Yearbook* 1 (1990), pp. 93–115.

Ashley, Kathleen, 'Titivillus and the Battle of Words in *Mankind*', *Annuale Medievale* 16 (1975), pp. 128–50.

Ashton, Robert, 'Popular Entertainment and Social Control in Later Elizabethan and Early Stuart London', *London Journal* 9 (1983), pp. 3–19.

Aston, M. E., 'Lollardy and Sedition 1381–1431', *Past and Present* 17 (1960), pp. 1–44.

'Lollardy and the Reformation: Survival or Revival?', *History* 49 (1964), pp. 149–70.

Lollards and Reformers: Images and Literacy in Late Medieval Religion (London: Hambledon Press, 1984).

'Wyclif and the Vernacular', in Anne Hudson and Michael Wilks (eds.), *From Ockham to Wyclif, Studies in Church History*, Subsidia 5 (Oxford: Blackwell, 1987), pp. 281–330.

England's Iconoclasts, vol. 1 (Oxford: Clarendon Press, 1988).

Augustine, St, *On Christian Doctrine*, trans. D. W. Robertson Jr (Indianapolis and New York: Liberal Arts Press, 1958).

Axton, Marie, see *Tudor Classical Interludes, Three*.

Baker, Derek (ed.), *Medieval Women, Studies in Church History*, Subsidia 1 (Oxford: Blackwell, 1978).

Bakhtin, M. M., *The Dialogic Imagination*, ed. Michael Holquist, trans. Caryl Emerson and Michael Holquist (Austin: University of Texas Press, 1981).

Baldwin, T. W., *William Shakspere's Small Latine and Lesse Greeke* (2 vols., Urbana: University of Illinois Press, 1944).

Barish, Jonas A., '*The Spanish Tragedy*, or The Pleasures and Perils of Rhetoric', in John Russell Brown and Bernard Harris (eds.), *Elizabethan Theatre*, Stratford-upon-Avon Studies 9 (London: Edward Arnold, 1966), pp. 59–85.

The Antitheatrical Prejudice (Berkeley, Los Angeles and London: University of California Press, 1981).

Barney, Stephen A., 'The Plowshare of the Tongue: The Progress of a Symbol from the Bible to *Piers Plowman*', *Medieval Studies* 35 (1973), pp. 261–93.

Bartels, Emily C., *Spectacles of Strangeness: Imperialism, Alienation, and Marlowe* (Philadelphia: University of Pennsylvania Press, 1993).

Bauckham, Richard, *Tudor Apocalypse* (Abingdon: Sutton Courtenay Press, 1978).

Beadle, Richard, 'Plays and Playing at Thetford and Nearby 1498–1540', *Theatre Notebook* 32 (1978), pp. 4–11.

'Dramatic Records of Mettingham College, Suffolk, 1403–1527', *Theatre Notebook* 33 (1979), pp. 125–31.

'The Scribal Problem in the Macro Manuscript', *English Language Notes* 21 (1984), pp. 1–13.

Beckwith, Sarah, 'Problems of Authority in Late Medieval English Mysticism: Language, Agency, and Authority in *The Book of Margery Kempe*', *Exemplaria* 4 (1992), pp. 171–99.

Beier, A. L., *Masterless Men: The Vagrancy Problem in England 1560–1640* (London and New York: Methuen, 1985).

Belsey, Catherine, *The Subject of Tragedy* (London: Methuen, 1985).

Bergeron, David M., *English Civic Pageantry 1558–1642* (London: Edward Arnold, 1971).

Bevington, David, *From Mankind to Marlowe* (Cambridge, Mass.: Harvard University Press, 1962).

  Tudor Drama and Politics: A Critical Approach to Topical Meaning (Cambridge, Mass: Harvard University Press, 1968).

  see also *Macro Plays, The* and *Medieval Drama*.

Binns, J. W., 'Shakespeare's Latin Citations: The Editorial Problem', *Shakespeare Survey* 35 (1982), pp. 119–28.

  Intellectual Culture in Elizabethan and Jacobean England: the Latin Writings of the Age (Leeds: Francis Cairns, 1990).

Blake, N. F., *Non-Standard Language in English Literature* (London: André Deutsch, 1981).

Blatt, Thora Balslev, *The Plays of John Bale: A Study of Ideas, Technique and Style* (Copenhagen: G. E. C. Gad, 1968).

Boas, Frederick S., *University Drama in the Tudor Age* (1914, reprinted New York: Benjamin Bloom, 1966).

Bolton, Brenda M., '*Vitae Matrum*: A Further Aspect of the *Frauenfrage*', in Derek Baker (ed.), *Medieval Women*, pp. 253–73.

Bradbrook, M. C., *The School of Night* (Cambridge: Cambridge University Press, 1936).

Brakelond, Jocelin of, *Chronicle of the Abbey of Bury St Edmunds*, trans. and introd. Diana Greenway and Jane Sayers (Oxford and New York: Oxford University Press, 1989).

Brigden, Susan, *London and the Reformation* (Oxford: Clarendon Press, 1991).

Briscoe, Marianne G., 'Some Clerical Notions of Dramatic Decorum in Late Medieval England', *Comparative Drama* 19 (1985), pp. 1–13.

Britton, G. C., 'Language and Character in Some Late Medieval Plays', *Essays and Studies* 33 (1980), pp. 1–15.

Bruce, F. F., *History of the Bible in English*, 3rd edn (Guildford and London: Lutterworth Press, 1979).

Bullough, Geoffrey, *Narrative and Dramatic Sources of Shakespeare* (8 vols., London and New York: Routledge and Columbia University Press, 1957–75).

Burke, Peter, *Popular Culture in Early Modern Europe*, 2nd edn (Aldershot: Scolar Press, 1994).

Bynum, Caroline Walker, *Jesus as Mother: Studies in the Spirituality of the High Middle Ages* (Berkeley, Los Angeles and London: University of California Press, 1982).

Camille, Michael, *Image on the Edge: The Margins of Medieval Art* (London: Reaktion Books, 1992).

Capua, Raymond of, *The Life of St Catherine of Siena*, trans. George Lamb (London: Harvill Press, 1960).

Cawley, A. C. and Stevens, Martin, see *Towneley Cycle, The: A Facsimile of Huntington MS HM 1*.

Chambers, E. K., *The Medieval Stage* (2 vols., London: Oxford University Press, 1903).

The Elizabethan Stage (4 vols., Oxford: Clarendon Press, 1923).

Clanchy, M. T., *From Memory to Written Record: England 1066–1307*, 2nd edn (Oxford and Cambridge, Mass.: Blackwell, 1993).

Clare, Janet, '*Art Made Tongue-Tied by Authority*': *Elizabethan and Jacobean Censorship* (Manchester and New York: Manchester University Press, 1990).

Clopper, Lawrence M., '*Mankind* and Its Audience', *Comparative Drama* 8 (1974–5), pp. 347–55.

(ed.), *Records of Early English Drama: Chester* (Manchester: Manchester University Press, 1979) .

Clough, Wilson O., 'The Broken English of Foreign Characters of the Elizabethan Stage', *Philological Quarterly* 12 (1933), pp. 255–68.

Coleman, Janet, *English Literature in History 1350–1400: Medieval Readers and Writers* (London etc.: Hutchinson, 1981).

Colet, John, *Oratio Habita . . . ad Clerum in Convocatione* (London: 1511).

Collier, J. Payne, *The History of English Dramatic Poetry to the Time of Shakespeare* (3 vols., London: John Murray, 1831).

Collinson, Patrick, *The Elizabethan Puritan Movement* (Worcester and London: Ebenezer Baylis, 1967).

The Birthpangs of Protestant England: Religious and Cultural Change in the Sixteenth and Seventeenth Centuries (London and Basingstoke: Macmillan, 1988).

Conley, Carey, *The First English Translations of the Classics* (New Haven and London: Yale University Press and Oxford University Press, 1927).

Coogan, Mary Philippa, *An Interpretation of the Moral Play, Mankind* (Washington DC: Catholic University of America Press, 1947).

Craik, T. W., *The Tudor Interlude: Stage, Costume, and Acting* (Leicester: Leicester University Press, 1967).

see also *Revels, Hisory of Drama in English, The*.

Crashawe, W., *The Sermon Preached at the Crosse, Feb xiiii 1607* (London, 1608).

Cressy, David, 'Educational Opportunities in Tudor and Stuart England', *History of Education Quarterly* 16 (1976), pp. 307–13.

Literacy and the Social Order: Reading and Writing in Tudor and Stuart England (Cambridge: Cambridge University Press, 1980).

Cross, Claire, ' "Great Reasoners in Scripture": The Activities of Women Lollards 1380–1530', in Derek Baker (ed.), *Medieval Women*, pp. 359–80.

de Grazia, Margreta, 'Shakespeare's View of Language: An Historical Perspective', *Shakespeare Quarterly* 29 (1978), pp. 374–88.

'Babbling Will in *Shake-speares Sonnets* 127 to 154', *Spenser Studies* 1 (1980), pp. 121–34.

Deanesly, Margaret, *The Lollard Bible and Other Medieval Biblical Versions* (Cambridge: Cambridge University Press, 1920).

Dekker, Thomas, *The Wonderful Year, The Gull's Hornbook, Penny-Wise, Pound-Foolish, English Villainies Discovered by Lantern and Candlelight and Selected Writings*, ed. E. D. Pendry (London: Edward Arnold, 1967).

Denley, Marie, 'Elementary Teaching Techniques and Middle English Religious Didactic Writing', in Helen Phillips (ed.), *Langland, the Mystics and the Medieval Religious Tradition* (Cambridge: D. S. Brewer, 1990), pp. 223–41.

Dickens, A. G., *The English Reformation* (London: Batsford, 1964).

Dillon, Janette, *Geoffrey Chaucer* (London: Macmillan, 1993).

'*Mankind* and the Politics of "Englysch Laten', *Medievalia et Humanistica*, NS 20 (1993), pp. 41–64.

'The Making of Desire in *The Book of Margery Kempe*', *Leeds Studies in English* 26 (1995), pp. 113–44.

Dobson, R. B., *The Peasants' Revolt of 1381* (London: Macmillan, 1970).

Douglas, Mary, *Purity and Danger* (1966, reprinted London and New York: Routledge, 1984).

Duffy, Eamon, *The Stripping of the Altars: Traditional Religion in England c.1400–c.1580* (New Haven and London: Yale University Press, 1992).

Dunn, E. Catherine, 'The Literary Style of the Towneley Plays', *American Benedictine Review* 20 (1969), pp. 481–504.

'Voice Structure in the Liturgical Drama: Sepet Reconsidered', in Jerome Taylor and Alan H. Nelson (eds.), *Medieval English Drama: Essays Critical and Contextual* (Chicago and London: University of Chicago Press, 1972), pp. 44–63.

Dutton, Richard, *Mastering the Revels: The Regulation and Censorship of English Renaissance Drama* (London and Basingstoke: Macmillan, 1991).

Eccles, Mark, see *Macro Plays, The.*

Edgerton, William L., *Nicholas Udall* (New York: Twayne, 1965).

Edwards, Philip, *Threshold of a Nation: A Study in English and Irish Drama* (Cambridge: Cambridge University Press, 1979).

Eisenstein, Elizabeth L., *The Printing Press as an Agent of Change: Communications and Cultural Transformations in Early-Modern Europe* (2 vols., Cambridge: Cambridge University Press, 1979).

Elton, G. R., *England Under the Tudors*, 3rd edn (London and New York: Routledge, 1991).

English Historical Documents, ed. David C. Douglas (12 vols., London: Eyre and Spottiswoode, 1955–77).

English Metrical Homilies, ed. John Small (Edinburgh: William Paterson, 1862).

Erasmus, *Praise of Folly and Letter to Martin Dorp 1515*, trans. Betty Radice, introd. and notes by A. H. T. Levi (Harmondsworth: Penguin, 1971).

Fairfield, Leslie P., *John Bale: Mythmaker for the English Reformation* (West Lafayette, Ind.: Purdue University Press, 1976).

Farmer, John S., see *Wever, Richard and Thomas Ingelend, The Dramatic Writings of*.

Fasciculi Zizaniorum, ed. Walter Waddington Shirley, Rolls Series, 5 (1858).

Fletcher, Alan J., 'John Mirk and the Lollards', *Medium Aevum* 56 (1987), pp. 217–24.

'The N-Town Plays', in Richard Beadle (ed.), *The Cambridge Companion to Medieval Theatre* (Cambridge: Cambridge University Press, 1994), pp. 163–88.

Foster, Frank Freeman, *The Politics of Stability: A Portrait of the Rulers in Elizabethan London* (London: Royal Historical Society, 1977).

Fowler, David C., 'John Trevisa and the English Bible', *Modern Philology* 58 (1960), p. 81–98.

Fox, Alistair and Guy, John, *Reassessing the Henrician Age: Humanism, Politics and Reform 1500–1550* (Oxford: Basil Blackwell, 1986).

Foxe, John, The Acts and Monuments of (8 vols., reprinted New York: AMS Press, 1965).

Freeman, Arthur, 'Marlowe, Kyd, and the Dutch Church Libel', *ELR* 3 (1973), pp. 44–52.

see also Shakespeare, William, *Henry VI, Part Two*.

Gardiner, Harold C., *Mysteries' End* (New Haven: Yale University Press, 1946).

Gascoigne, Thomas, *Loci e Libro Veritatum*, ed. James E. Thorold Rogers (Oxford: Clarendon Press, 1881).

Gash, Anthony, 'Carnival against Lent: The Ambivalence of Medieval Drama', in David Aers (ed.), *Medieval Literature: Criticism, Ideology and History* (Brighton: Harvester, 1986).

Gibson, Gail McMurray, *The Theater of Devotion: East Anglian Drama and Society in the Late Middle Ages* (Chicago and London: University of Chicago Press, 1989).

Gifford, George, *A Dialogue concerning Witches and Witchcraftes*, introd. Beatrice White, Shakespeare Association Facsimiles, 1 (Oxford and London: Oxford University Press, 1931).

Gildersleeve, Virginia Crocheron, *Government Regulation of the Elizabethan Drama*, (1908, reprinted New York: Burt Franklin, 1961).

Gillespie, Vincent, 'Vernacular Books of Religion', in Jeremy Griffiths and Derek Pearsall (eds.), *Book Production and Publishing in Britain, 1375–1475* (Cambridge: Cambridge University Press, 1989), pp. 317–43.

Gillies, John, *Shakespeare and the Geography of Difference* (Cambridge: Cambridge University Press, 1994).

Gradon, Pamela, 'Langland and the Ideology of Dissent', *Proceedings of the British Academy* 66 (1981), pp. 179–205.

Green, V. H. H., *Bishop Reginald Pecock: A Study in Ecclesiastical History and Thought* (Cambridge: Cambridge University Press, 1945).

Greenslade, S. L., see *Tindale, William*.

Greg, W. W., *A Bibliography of the English Printed Drama to the Restoration* (4 vols., London: Bibliographical Society, 1939–59).

Gunstone, John, *The Liturgy of Penance* (London: The Faith Press, 1966).

Gurr, Andrew, *Playgoing in Shakespeare's London* (Cambridge: Cambridge University Press, 1987).

Hadfield, Andrew, *Literature, Politics and National Identity: Reformation to Renaissance* (Cambridge: Cambridge University Press, 1994).

Haigh, Christopher, *English Reformations: Religion, Politics and Society under the Tudors* (Oxford: Oxford University Press, 1993).

Hall's Chronicle, ed. Henry Ellis (London: J. Johnson et. al., 1809).

Haller, William, *Foxe's Book of Martyrs and the Elect Nation* (London: Jonathan Cape, 1963).

Hanna, Ralph, III, 'Sir Thomas Berkeley and his Patronage', *Speculum* 64 (1989), pp. 878–916.

Hanson, Elizabeth, 'Torture and Truth in Renaissance England', *Representations* 34 (1991), pp. 53–84.

Happé, Peter, see *Bale, John, The Complete Plays of* and *Morality Plays, Four*.

Harbage, Alfred (ed.), *Annals of English Drama 975–1700*, revised S. Schoenbaum and Sylvia Stoler Wagonheim, 3rd edn (London and New York: Routledge, 1989).

Harris, Jesse W., *John Bale: A Study in the Minor Literature of the Reformation* (Urbana: University of Illinois Press, 1940).

Harris, John Wesley, *Medieval Theatre in Context: An Introduction* (London and New York: Routledge, 1992).

Harrison, G. B., *An Elizabethan Journal: Being a Record of Those Things Most Talked Of During the Years 1591–1594* (London: Constable, 1928).

(ed.), *Willobie his Avisa* (1926, reprinted Edinburgh: Edinburgh University Press, 1966).

Harrison, William, *The Description of England*, ed. Georges Edelen (Ithaca, NY: Cornell University Press, 1968).

Harsnett, Samuel, *A Declaration of Egregious Popish Impostures* (London, 1603).

A Discovery of the Fraudulent Practises of John Darrell (London, n.d.).

Hattaway, Michael, *Elizabethan Popular Theatre* (London, Boston etc.: Routledge and Kegan Paul, 1982).

Heffernan, Thomas J., *Sacred Biography: Saints and their Biographers in the Middle Ages* (New York and Oxford: Oxford University Press, 1988).

Heinemann, Margot, *Puritanism and Theatre: Thomas Middleton and Opposition*

Drama under the Early Stuarts (Cambridge: Cambridge University Press, 1980).

Helgerson, Richard, *Forms of Nationhood: The Elizabethan Writing of England* (Chicago and London: University of Chicago Press, 1992).

Herman, Peter C., ' "O, 'tis a gallant king' ": Shakespeare's *Henry V* and the crisis of the 1590s', in Dale Hoak (ed.), *Tudor Political Culture* (Cambridge: Cambridge University Press, 1995), pp. 204–25.

Hirsh, John C., 'Author and Scribe in *The Book of Margery Kempe*', *Medium Aevum* 44 (1975), pp. 145–50.

Hoccleve, Selections From, ed. M. C. Seymour (Oxford: Clarendon Press, 1981).

Hoenselaars, A. J., 'Broken Images of Englishmen and Foreigners in English Renaissance Drama', *Germanisch-Romanische Monatsschrift*, NS 41 (1991), pp. 157–73.

Images of Englishmen and Foreigners in the Drama of Shakespeare and his Contemporaries: A Study of Stage Characters and National Identity in English Renaissance Drama 1558–1642 (Rutherford NJ, London and Toronto: Fairleigh Dickinson University Press, Associated University Presses, 1992).

'Reconstructing Babel in English Renaissance Drama: William Haughton's *Englishmen for My Money* and John Marston's *Antonio and Mellida*', *Neophilologus* 76 (1992), pp. 464–79.

Holinshed's Chronicles of England, Scotland and Ireland, ed. Henry Ellis (6 vols. London: J. Johnson et al., 1807–8).

Holloway, Julia Bolton, 'Crosses and Boxes: Latin and Vernacular', in Julia Bolton Holloway, Constance S. Wright and Joan Bechtold (eds.), *Equally in God's Image: Women in the Middle Ages* (New York etc.: Peter Lang, 1990), pp. 58–87.

Hudson, Anne, 'Old Author, New Work: The Sermons of MS Longleat 4', *Medium Aevum* 53 (1984), pp. 220–38.

Lollards and their Books (London and Ronceverte: Hambledon Press, 1985).

'Wyclif and the English Language', in Anthony Kenny (ed.), *Wyclif in His Times*, pp. 85–103.

The Premature Reformation: Wycliffite Texts and Lollard History (Oxford: Clarendon Press, 1988).

'*Laicus litteratus*: the Paradox of Lollardy', in Peter Biller and Anne Hudson (eds.), *Heresy and Literacy 1000–1530* (Cambridge: Cambridge University Press, 1988), pp. 222–36.

(ed.), *Selections from English Wycliffite Writings* (Cambridge: Cambridge University Press, 1978).

Hughes, Paul L. and Larkin, James F. (eds.), *Tudor Royal Proclamations* (3 vols., New Haven: Yale University Press, 1964–9).

Hulme, Peter, *Colonial Encounters: Europe and the Native Caribbean 1492–1797* (London: Methuen, 1986).

Hunter, G. K., *John Lyly: The Humanist as Courtier* (London: Routledge and Kegan Paul, 1962).
Dramatic Identities and Cultural Tradition: Studies in Shakespeare and his Contemporaries (Liverpool: Liverpool University Press, 1978).
Jager, Eric, *The Tempter's Voice: Language and the Fall in Medieval Literature* (Ithaca and London: Cornell University Press, 1993).
Jansen, Sharon L., *Political Protest and Prophecy under Henry VIII* (Woodbridge: Boydell Press, 1991).
Jardine, Lisa, *Reading Shakespeare Historically* (London and New York: Routledge, 1996).
Jennings, Margaret, 'Tutivillus: The Literary Career of the Recording Demon', *Studies in Philology* 74: 5 (1977), pp. 1–95.
Jocelin of Brakelond, see Brakelond, Jocelin of.
John Bale's Index of British and Other Writers, ed. Reginald Lane Poole and Mary Bateson (Woodbridge, Suffolk: D. S. Brewer, 1990).
Johnson, Lynn Staley, 'The Trope of the Scribe and the Question of Literary Authority in the Works of Julian of Norwich and Margery Kempe', *Speculum* 66 (1991), pp. 820–38.
Johnson, S. F., '*The Spanish Tragedy*, or Babylon Revisited', in Richard Hosley (ed.), *Essays on Shakespeare and Elizabethan Drama in Honor of Hardin Craig* (London: Routledge and Kegan Paul, 1963).
Johnston, Alexandra F. and Rogerson, Margaret, *Records of Early English Drama: York* (2 vols., Toronto, Buffalo and London: Manchester University Press, 1979).
Jones, R. F., *The Triumph of the English Language: A Survey of Opinions Concerning the Vernacular from the Introduction of Printing to the Restoration* (Oxford: Oxford University Press, 1953).
Judges, A. V., *The Elizabethan Underworld* (London: Routledge and Kegan Paul, 1930).
Justice, Steven, *Writing and Rebellion: England in 1381* (Berkeley, Los Angeles and London: University of California Press, 1994).
Kastan, David Scott, ' "Holy Wurdes" and "Slypper Wit": John Bale's *King Johan* and the Poetics of Propaganda', in Peter C. Herman (ed.), *Rethinking the Henrician Era: Essays on Early Tudor Texts and Contexts* (Urbana and Chicago: University of Illinois Press, 1994), pp. 267–82.
Keen, Maurice, 'Wyclif, the Bible, and Transubstantiation', in Anthony Kenny (ed.), *Wyclif in His Times*, pp. 1–16.
Kempe, The Book of Margery, ed. Sanford Brown Meech and Hope Emily Allen, vol. 1, EETS, OS, 212 (1940).
Kendall, Ritchie, D., *The Drama of Dissent: The Radical Poetics of Nonconformity, 1380–1590* (Chapel Hill and London: University of North Carolina Press, 1986).
Kenny, Anthony (ed.), *Wyclif in His Times* (Oxford: Clarendon Press, 1986).
Kirk, Elizabeth, 'Langland's Plowman and the Recreation of Fourteenth-

Century Religious Metaphor', *Yearbook of Langland Studies* 2 (1988), pp. 1–21.

Knighton, Henry, *Chronicon*, ed. J. R. Lumby (2 vols., Rolls Series, 92, 1889, 1895).

Knott, John R., *Discourses of Martyrdom in English Literature 1563–1694* (Cambridge: Cambridge University Press, 1993).

Kolve, V. A., *The Play Called Corpus Christi* (Stanford, California: Stanford University Press, 1966).

Kramer, Heinrich and Sprenger, James, *Malleus Maleficarum*, trans. Montague Summers (1928, reprinted New York: Dover, 1971).

Lambert, Malcolm, *Medieval Heresy: Popular Movements from the Gregorian Reform to the Reformation*, 2nd edn (Oxford and Cambridge, Mass.: Blackwell, 1992).

Laneham, Robert, *A Letter*, facsimile reprint (Menston: Scolar Press, 1968).

Langland, William, *Piers Plowman: The B Version*, ed. George Kane and E. Talbot Donaldson (London: University of London, Athlone Press, 1975).

Lanham, Richard A., *The Motives of Eloquence: Literary Rhetoric in the Renaissance* (New Haven and London: Yale University Press, 1976).

Lantern of Light, The, ed. L. M. Swinburn, EETS, OS, 151 (1917).

Larner, Christina, *Witchcraft and Religion* (Oxford: Basil Blackwell, 1984) .

Latimer, Hugh, Selected Sermons of, ed. Allan G. Chester (Charlottesville: University Press of Virginia, 1968).

Lawton, David, 'Voice, Authority, and Blasphemy in *The Book of Margery Kempe*', in Sandra J. McEntire (ed.), *Margery Kempe: a Book of Essays* (New York and London: Garland, 1992), pp. 93–115.

Leech, Clifford, see *Revels History of Drama in English, The*.

Lepow, Lauren, *Enacting the Sacrament: Counter-Lollardy in the Towneley Cycle* (Rutherford etc.: Fairleigh Dickinson University Press, Associated University Presses, 1990).

Lester, G. A., see *Morality Plays, Three Late Medieval*.

Letters and Papers, Foreign and Domestic, of the Reign of Henry VIII, ed. John S. Brewer, James Gairdner and Robert H. Brodie (21 vols., London: HMSO, 1826–1910).

Levack, Brian P., *The Witch-Hunt in Early Modern Europe* (Harlow: Longman, 1987).

Lever, J. W., *The Tragedy of State* (London: Methuen, 1971).

Levenson, Jill L., see *Weakest Goeth to the Wall, The*.

Lewalski, Barbara Kiefer, *Protestant Poetics and the Seventeenth-Century Religious Lyric* (Princeton, NJ: Princeton University Press, 1979).

Limon, Jerzy, *Gentlemen of a Company: English Players in Central and Eastern Europe 1590–1600* (Cambridge: Cambridge University Press, 1985).

Lindley, K. J., 'Riot Prevention and Control in Early Stuart London', *Transactions of the Royal Historical Society*, 5th series, 33 (1983), pp. 109–26.

Lochrie, Karma, *Margery Kempe and Translations of the Flesh* (Philadelphia: University of Pennsylvania Press, 1991).

Love, Nicholas, *Mirror of the Blessed Life of Jesus Christ*, ed. Michael G. Sargent (New York and London: Garland, 1992).

Lupton, J. H., *A Life of John Colet, D. D.*, 2nd edn (London: George Bell, 1909).

Lydgate, John, *The Pilgrimage of the Life of Man*, ed. F. J. Furnivall, EETS, ES, 77, 83, 92 (1889–1904).

Macfarlane, Alan, *Witchcraft in Tudor and Stuart England: A Regional and Comparative Study* (London: Routledge and Kegan Paul, 1970).

Manley, Lawrence, *Literature and Culture in Early Modern London* (Cambridge: Cambridge University Press, 1995).

Mann, David, *The Elizabethan Player: Contemporary Stage Representation* (London and New York: Routledge, 1991).

Manning, Roger B., *Village Revolts: Social Protest and Popular Disturbances in England, 1509–1640* (Oxford: Clarendon Press, 1988).

Martin, J. W., *Religious Radicals in Tudor England* (London and Ronceverte: Hambledon Press, 1989).

Maskell, William (ed.), *Monumenta Ritualia Ecclesiae Anglicanae* (3 vols., London: William Pickering, 1846–7).

Maslen, Elizabeth, 'The Dynamics of Kyd's "Spanish Tragedy"', *English* 32 (1983), pp. 111–25.

McMillin, Scott, *The Elizabethan Theatre and The Book of Sir Thomas More* (Ithaca and London: Cornell University Press, 1987).

Meredith, Peter, 'Scribes, Texts and Performance', in Paula Neuss (ed.), *Aspects of Early English Drama* (Woodbridge and Totowa, NJ: Boydell and Brewer and Barnes and Noble, 1983).

Miller, Edwin S., 'The Roman Rite in Bale's *King John*', *PMLA* 64 (1949), pp. 802–22.

Miola, Robert S., *Shakespeare and Classical Comedy: The Influence of Plautus and Terence* (Oxford: Clarendon Press, 1994).

Mirk's Festial, ed. Theodor Erbe, EETS, ES, 96 (1905).

Motter, T. H. Vail, *The School Drama in England* (London, New York and Toronto: Longmans, Green, 1929).

Mulcaster, Richard, *The First Part of the Elementarie*, facsimile reprint, (Menston: Scolar Press, 1970).

Mullaney, Steven, 'Lying Like Truth: Riddle, Representation and Treason in Renaissance England', *ELH* 47 (1980), pp. 32–47.

The Place of the Stage: License, Play, and Power in Renaissance England (Chicago: University of Chicago Press, 1988).

Mulryne, J. R., 'Nationality and Language in Thomas Kyd's *The Spanish Tragedy*', in M. T. Jones-Davies (ed.), *Langues et Nations au Temps de la Renaissance* (Paris: Klincksieck, 1991), pp. 67–91.

see also Kyd, Thomas.

Munday, Anthony, *The English Romayne Lyfe*, ed. G. B. Harrison (1925, reprint Edinburgh: Edinburgh University Press, 1966).

Neuss, Paula, 'Active and Idle Language: Dramatic Images in *Mankind*', in Neville Denny (ed.), *Medieval Drama*, Stratford-upon-Avon Studies 16 (London: Edward Arnold, 1973), pp. 41–67.

Nichols, John Gough (ed.), *Narratives of the Days of the Reformation* (London: Camden Society, 1859).

Ong, Walter J., 'Latin Language Study as a Renaissance Puberty Rite', *Studies in Philology* 56 (1959), pp. 103–24.

Orme, Nicholas, *English Schools in the Middle Ages* (London: Methuen, 1973).

Owst, G. R., *Preaching in Medieval England: An Introduction to Sermon Mss of the Period c.1350–1450* (Cambridge: Cambridge University Press, 1926).

Pafford, J. H. P., see Bale, John, *King Johan*.

Parker, Patricia, *Literary Fat Ladies: Rhetoric, Gender, Property* (London and New York: Methuen, 1987).

Patterson, Annabel, *Reading Holinshed's Chronicles* (Chicago and London: University of Chicago Press, 1994).

Patterson, Lee, ' "For the Wyves love of Bathe": Feminine Rhetoric and Poetic Resolution in the *Roman de la Rose* and the *Canterbury Tales*', *Speculum* 58 (1983), pp. 656–95.

Pearl, Valerie, *London and the Outbreak of the Puritan Revolution: City Government and National Politics, 1625–43*, corrected 1st edn of 1961 (Oxford: Oxford University Press, 1964).

'Change and Stability in Seventeenth-Century London', *London Journal* 5 (1979), pp. 3–34.

'Social Policy in Early Modern London', in Hugh Lloyd-Jones, Valerie Pearl and Blair Worden (eds.), *History and Imagination: Essays in Honour of H. R. Trevor-Roper* (London: Duckworth, 1981), pp. 115–31.

Pechter, Edward, *What Was Shakespeare: Renaissance Plays and Changing Critical Practice* (Ithaca and London: Cornell University Press, 1995).

Perkins, William, *A Discourse of the Damned Art of Witchcraft*, in *The Works of William Perkins*, ed. Ian Breward, Courtenay Library of Reformation Classics, 3 (Abingdon, Berks.: Sutton Courtenay Press, 1970).

Petroff, Elizabeth Alvilda, *Medieval Women's Visionary Literature* (New York and Oxford: Oxford University Press, 1986).

Pierce the Ploughmans Crede, ed. W.W. Skeat, EETS, OS, 30 (1867).

Pineas, Rainer, 'The English Morality Play as a Weapon of Religious Controversy', *Studies in English Literature 1500–1900*, 2 (1962), pp. 157–80.

Plato, *Cratylus*, trans. H. N. Fowler, Loeb Classical Library (Cambridge, Mass. and London: Harvard University Press, 1939).

Potter, Robert, *The English Morality Play: Origins, History and Influence of a Dramatic Tradition* (London and Boston: Routledge and Kegan Paul, 1975).

Prestwich, Michael, *English Politics in the Thirteenth Century* (Basingstoke and London: Macmillan, 1990).

Proudfoot, Richard, 'Kyd's *Spanish Tragedy*', *Critical Quarterly* 25 (1983), pp. 71–6.

Puttenham, George, *The Arte of English Poesie*, ed. Gladys Doidge Willcock and Alice Walker (Cambridge: Cambridge University Press, 1936).

Rappaport, Steve, 'Social Structure and Mobility in Sixteenth-Century London: Part I', *London Journal* 9 (1983), pp. 107–35.
  Worlds Within Worlds: Structures of Life in Sixteenth-Century London (Cambridge: Cambridge University Press, 1989).

Raymond of Capua, see Capua, Raymond of.

Records of Early English Drama (REED): York, see Johnston, Alexandra and Rogerson, Margaret; *Chester*, see Clopper, Lawrence, M.

Revels History of Drama in English, The, ed. T. W. Craik and Clifford Leech (8 vols., London and New York: Methuen, 1975–83).

Rhodes, Neil, *The Power of Eloquence and English Renaissance Literature* (Hemel Hempstead: Harvester Wheatsheaf, 1992).

Richardson, Malcolm, 'Henry V, the English Chancery, and Chancery English', *Speculum* 55 (1980), pp. 726–50.

Robbins, Rossell Hope (ed.), *Historical Poems of the Fourteenth amd Fifteenth Centuries* (New York: Columbia University Press, 1959).

Robertson, D. W., Jr., 'Who Were "The People"?' in Thomas J. Heffernan (ed.), *The Popular Literature of Medieval England*, Tennessee Studies in Literature, 28 (Knoxville: University of Tennessee Press, 1985), pp. 3–29.

Rosen, Barbara (ed.), *Witchcraft*, Stratford-upon-Avon Library, 6 (London: Edward Arnold, 1969).

Salter, Elizabeth, *Fourteenth-Century Poetry: Contexts and Readings* (Oxford: Clarendon Press, 1983).
  English and International: Studies in the Literature, Art and Patronage of Medieval England, ed. Derek Pearsall and Nicolette Zeeman (Cambridge: Cambridge University Press, 1988).

Santos, Marlene Soares dos, 'Theatre for Tudor England: An Investigation of the Ideas of Englishness and Foreignness in English Drama *c.*1485–1592', PhD dissertation, Shakespeare Institute: University of Birmingham (1980).

Sargent, Michael G., see Love, Nicholas, *Mirror of the Blessed Life of Jesus Christ*.

Scot, Reginald, *The Discoverie of Witchcraft*, introd. H. R. Williamson (London: Centaur Press, 1964).

Shepherd, Simon, *Marlowe and the Politics of the Elizabethan Theatre* (Brighton: Harvester, 1986).

Shute, John, *The Firste Parte of the Christian Instruction* (London: 1565).

Sidney, Philip, *An Apology for Poetry*, ed. Geoffrey Shepherd (1965, reprinted Manchester: Manchester University Press, 1973).

Sisam, Kenneth (ed.), *Fourteenth Century Verse and Prose* (Oxford: Clarendon Press, 1970).

Smart, Walter K., 'Some Notes on *Mankind*', *Modern Philology* 14 (1916–17), pp. 45–58, 101–313.

'*Mankind* and the Mumming Plays', *Modern Language Notes* 32 (1917), pp. 21–5.

Smith, Alan G. R., *The Emergence of a Nation State: The Commonwealth of England 1529–1660* (London and New York: Longman, 1984).

Smith, Bruce R., *Ancient Scripts and Modern Experience on the English Stage 1500–1700* (Princeton: Princeton University Press, 1988).

Smith, G. Gregory (ed.), *Elizabethan Critical Essays* (2 vols., Oxford: Oxford University Press, 1904).

Southern, Richard, *The Staging of Plays Before Shakespeare* (London: Faber and Faber, 1973).

Spinrad, Phoebe S., *The Summons of Death on the Medieval and Renaissance English Stage* (Columbus: Ohio State University Press, 1987).

Staines, David, 'The English Mystery Cycles', in Eckehard Simon (ed.), *The Theatre of Medieval Europe: New Research in Early Drama* (Cambridge: Cambridge University Press, 1991).

Stallybrass, Peter and White, Allon, *The Politics and Poetics of Transgression* (London: Methuen, 1986).

Statutes of the Realm, ed. A. Luders et al. (9 vols., London: 1810–24).

Stevens, Martin, 'Language as Theme in the Wakefield Plays', *Speculum* 52 (1977), pp. 100–17.

Four Middle English Mystery Cycles: Textual, Contextual and Critical Interpretations (Princeton: Princeton University Press, 1987).

Stubbes, Philip, *Anatomy of Abuses in England*, part II, ed. Frederick J. Furnivall, New Shakspere Society (London: N. Trübner, 1882).

Swanson, R. N., *Church and Society in Late Medieval England* (Oxford: Blackwell, 1989).

Tanner, J. R., *Tudor Constitutional Documents A.D.1485–1603 with an Historical Commentary* (Cambridge: Cambridge University Press, 1930).

Taylor, Rupert, *The Political Prophecy in England* (New York: Columbia University Press, 1911).

Thomas, Keith, *Religion and the Decline of Magic: Studies in Popular Beliefs in Sixteenth- and Seventeenth-Century England* (1971, reprinted Harmondsworth: Penguin, 1973).

Thomson, John A. F., *The Later Lollards 1414–1520* (Oxford: Oxford University Press, 1965).

Tindale, William, The Works of, ed. S. L. Greenslade, with an essay on Tindale and the English language by G. D. Bone (London and Glasgow: Blackie, 1938).

Tokson, Elliot H., *The Popular Image of the Black Man in English Drama, 1550–1688* (Boston: G. K. Hall, 1982).

Tretise of Miraclis Pleyinge, see Hudson, Anne (ed.), *Selections from English Wycliffite Writings*.

Trevisa, John, *Dialogue between a Lord and a Clerk*, in *A Book of Middle English*, ed. J. A. Burrow and Thorlac Turville-Petre (Oxford and Cambridge, Mass.: Blackwell, 1992).

Tribble, Evelyn B., *Margins and Marginality: The Printed Page in Early Modern England* (Charlottesville and London: University Press of Virginia, 1993).

Turville-Petre, Thorlac, 'The "Nation" in English Writings of the Early Fourteenth Century', in Nicholas Rogers (ed.), *England in the Fourteenth Century: Proceedings of the 1991 Harlaxton Symposium* (Stamford: Paul Watkins, 1993), pp. 128–39.

Tydeman, William, *The Theatre in the Middle Ages* (Cambridge: Cambridge University Press, 1978).

English Medieval Theatre 1400–1500 (London, Boston and Henley: Routledge and Kegan Paul, 1986).

see also *Tudor Tragedies, Two*.

Tyndale, William, see *Tindale, William*.

Ullmann, Walter, 'This Realm of England is an Empire', *Journal of Ecclesiastical History* 30 (1979), pp. 175–203.

von Nolcken, Christina, *'Piers Plowman*, the Wycliffites and *Pierce the Plowman's Creed'*, *Yearbook of Langland Studies* 2 (1988), pp. 71–102.

Waldron, Ronald, 'John Trevisa and the Use of English', *Proceedings of the British Academy* 74 (1988), pp. 171–202.

Walker, Greg, *Plays of Persuasion: Drama and Politics at the Court of Henry VIII* (Cambridge: Cambridge University Press, 1991).

Walsingham, Thomas, *Chronicon Angliae 1328–1388*, ed. E. M. Thompson, Rolls Series, 64 (1874).

Historia Anglicana, ed. H. T. Riley, 2 vols., Rolls Series, 28 (1863–4).

Weimann, Robert, *Shakespeare and the Popular Tradition in the Theater: Studies in the Social Dimension of Dramatic Form and Function*, ed. Robert Schwartz (Baltimore and London: Johns Hopkins University Press, 1978).

Authority and Representation in Early Modern Discourse, ed. David Hillman (Baltimore and London: Johns Hopkins University Press, 1996).

Wells, Stanley and Taylor, Gary, *William Shakespeare: A Textual Companion* (Oxford: Clarendon Press, 1987).

Wenzel, Siegfried, *Acedia in Medieval Thought and Literature*, 2nd edn (Chapel Hill: University of North Carolina Press, 1967).

Westfall, Suzanne R., *Patrons and Performance: Early Tudor Household Revels* (Oxford: Clarendon Press, 1990).

White, Allon, 'The Dismal Sacred Word: Academic Language and the Social Reproduction of Seriousness', *Literature/Teaching/Politics* 2 (1983), pp. 4–15.

White, Paul Whitfield, *Protestantism, Patronage and Playing in Tudor England* (Cambridge: Cambridge University Press, 1993) .

Wickham, Glynne, *Medieval Theatre*, 3rd edn (Cambridge: Cambridge University Press, 1987).

Willobie his Avisa, see Harrison, G. B.

Womack, Peter, *Ben Jonson* (Oxford: Blackwell, 1986).

'Imagining Communities: Theatres and the English Nation in the

Sixteenth Century', in David Aers (ed.), *Culture and History 1350–1600*, pp. 91–145.

Woolf, Rosemary, *The English Mystery Plays*, (1972, reprinted Berkeley and Los Angeles: University of California Press, 1980).

Wright, Robert, 'Community Theatre in Late Medieval East Anglia', *Theatre Notebook* 28 (1974), pp. 24–39.

Wrightson, Keith, *English Society 1580–1680* (London: Hutchinson, 1982).

Yates, Frances A., *The Occult Philosophy in the Elizabethan Age* (London: Routledge and Kegan Paul, 1979).

Zitner, Sheldon P., '*The Spanish Tragedy* and the Language of Performance', in A. L. Magnusson and C. E. McGee (eds.), *The Elizabethan Theatre* 9 (Port Credit: P. D. Meany, 1990), pp. 75–94.

Index

Printed in the United Kingdom
by Lightning Source UK Ltd.
132922UK00001B/26/A